Life to those Shadows

Life to those Shadows

Noël Burch

translated and edited by
Ben Brewster

University of California Press

Berkeley and Los Angeles

First published 1990 by the University of California Press

Library of Congress Catalog Card Number: 90-50406
ISBN 0-520-07143-3 (cl.)
ISBN 0-520-07144-1 (pbk.)

1 2 3 4 5 6 7 8 9

Contents

Introduction

This book was written for the most part between 1976 and 1981. It grew out of debates which, by at least 1965 in France and Italy and from around 1970 in Britain and the USA, had transformed the agenda of the history, æsthetics and sociology of the cinema. The remarkable results then achieved in two continents were made under the ægis of structuralism, dialectical and historical materialism, and, in Britain and the USA, left-wing feminism, and in consequence the advances made in this period have suffered a certain eclipse in the current 'post-modernist' reaction. In the present period of triumphant empiricism, anything suggesting, however weakly, systematisation or theorisation seems irredeemably 'old hat'. Similarly, anything amounting to a basic opposition to the values secreted by capitalism seems simply ridiculous.

Unfortunately all minds do not move at the same speed. I suffer from this affliction. I am a laggard, one who always catches the later train. At a time when everyone around me—including even my own students—was working on the first consistent materialist critique of the cinema comparable with Brecht's of traditional theatre, when attempts were being made to dismantle the underlying mechanisms of the cinema as the Russian and Czech 'Formalists' had dismantled those of the novel, when, for the first time since Vertov and Eisenstein, there were efforts to recreate a cinema which would be both committed and innovatory in its language—at this time, the author of these lines still propounded a 'musicalist' formalism close to the art-for-art's-sake positions of the turn of the century.[1] And I have to admit that, despite attempts at the time to bring myself up to date—vis-à-vis Japanese cinema: see Burch (1979)—this book was originally conceived more as a rejoinder to a very classical cinephile and pre-structuralist historiography of the cinema than as an advance along the line laid down in works by writers such as Christian

Metz and Jean-Louis Baudry with which I was only just becoming familiar.

But I should point out that the book was also conceived in the penumbra of a broad aspiration shared at the time by certain film-maker theorists (the most prestigious of whom were Godard and Straub), an aspiration to *practices breaking with current standards*, pointers as it were towards the political practices of the future Revolution. It is this aspiration, which, as the film-maker I am, I then shared, that explains why this book was intended above all as a critique of theoretical and historical discourses tending to naturalise the 'Hollywood' system of representation whose primary function seemed to have been to misinform and anæsthetise the masses of the people. Thus the first aim of this book was to lay down historical bases for contestatory practices.

To this end I turned to the cinema of the earliest years, the primitive cinema.[2] The point was to show that the 'language' of the cinema is in no way natural, *a fortiori* that it is not eternal, that it has a history and is a product of History. To do this it was necessary to go back to a period in which this 'language' did not yet really exist, in which, in particular, there was not as yet that institution of the cinema within which we all, spectators and film-makers, live, and 'which works to fill cinemas, not to empty them' (Metz 1982, p.7). But it was this Institution I wished to interrogate, or more precisely its characteristic mode of representation. For, and this is the main thesis of this book, I see the 1895-1929 period as one of the constitution of an Institutional Mode of Representation (hereinafter IMR) which, for fifty years, has been explicitly taught in film schools as the Language of Cinema, and which, whoever we are, we all internalise at an early age as a *reading competence* thanks to an exposure to films (in cinemas or on television) which is universal among the young in industrialised societies.

In addition, if this undertaking is still morally and socially justifiable, it finds that justification in the observation that millions of men and women who are taught to read *and to write* 'their letters', will never learn to do anything but *read* images and sounds, and can therefore only ever receive the discourse of images and sounds as 'natural'. It is to the *denaturalisation* of this experience that I wish to contribute here.

My insistence on substituting for the term 'language' that of 'mode of representation' does not derive from any belief that the set of symbolic systems at work in the cinema of the Institution is not, in the last analysis, 'semiotic' in nature. It is just that the object of the present essay is not that set of systems as a whole but rather the underlying conditions that make it possible, somewhat as monocular perspective makes possible the very complex iconographic codes of this or that school of Renaissance painting (though this parallel is very loose!). Furthermore, I am concerned to emphasise that, however universal, however fundamental this mode of representation, it is no more neutral than it is ahistorical—whereas the 'natural languages' are still, despite Bakhtin, conceived of as neutral—that it produces meanings in and of itself, and that the meanings it produces are not unrelated to the place and time in which it developed: the capitalist and imperialist West in the first quarter of the twentieth century.

Basically I have come to the same positions as the analyses once produced around the journals *Cinéthique* and *Tel Quel* which already denounced as a ruse the innocence tacitly conceded this notorious 'language', just as Vertov had done, in a more narrowly polemical way. But at the same time, I reject a certain leftist theology and the technological determinism that traces the 'original sin' of the cinema to the camera and its *one-eyed gaze*. Of course, I also reject that other, idealist theology which sees the original sin in the 'theatricality' of the beginnings and the progress of the 'language' as a series of 'technical' advances. Lastly, I refuse to see the system whose genealogy I wish to explore here, and *a fortiori* its products, the films, as *bad objects*. For it is clear that many films with no ambitions to 'deconstruct' the codes of institutional narrativity, let alone the foundations of the IMR, are nonetheless the bearers of a host of meanings other than those repeated over and over again by the IMR as such. *A fortiori* I cannot accept the modernist vision of the Institution as a bad object alienating our senses in some way, any more than I can accept the modernist fantasy of the primitive cinema as a kind of Prelapsarian Lost Paradise, the Fall being the result of that other bad object, 'narrativity' (others would say 'the language'), brought by Porter and Griffith as one brings the plague. By which I do not mean that the primitive cinema lacks masterpieces (I shall discuss some of them), but that it is absurd to overvalue them in comparison with those that have emerged from the Institution or its margins.

At any rate, my central concern now is the nature of the cinematic experience most widespread 'amongst us' (in the countries of the 'centre'), the cinematic experience that I partake of when I go to the pictures, *au cinoche,* to the movies, the cinematic experience that I share with millions of men and, to a certain extent, with millions of women, too. From now on I shall refer to exceptional works as, precisely, exceptional.

Certain chapters of this book have appeared in English and French magazines,[3] in versions often deviating from the texts presented here in crucial respects. The reason is that the present work evolved over a period of more than six years, and contains considerable changes in viewpoint from those of its earliest sketches—a process of revision I believe to be endless.

Finally, I wish to thank: Jorge Dana, who played an essential role in my earliest reflection on these matters and without whom this book would never have been undertaken; Ben Brewster, whose expert scholarship and scrupulous attention to detail spared me much embarrassment; Tom Gunning, who corrected a number of factual errors; and Michel Chion, whose re-working of the original French text brought to light a number of further errors and loose formulations.

NOTES

1 I am not surprised that *Theory of Film Practice* (Burch 1973) was very successful in the USA in a period of formalist modernism. That the intellectual climate in France should have evolved to the point that there was a demand for a reprint is all the more suggestive.
2 I am concerned to justify persisting in the use of this term, discredited in other disciplines because of its ethnocentric implications. This cinema really is primitive, in the sense that it is 'first' and 'original', but also in the sense that it is 'rough' and 'crude' in respect to all the norms that we have all (in all classes) come to accept in the industrialised countries.

3   The first chapter approximates Burch (1981a), i.e., 'Charles Baudelaire versus Doctor Frankenstein', *Afterimage* nos.8-9, Spring 1981, pp.4-21; the sixth Burch (1983), i.e., 'Passion, poursuite: la linéarisation', *Communications* no.38, 1983, pp.30-50; the eleventh Burch (1982), i.e., 'Narrative/Diegesis: Thresholds, Limits', *Screen* v 23 n 2, July-August 1982, pp.16-33. The third, fourth and fifth were the subject of a presentation at a seminar on primitive cinema held at Dartington in September 1980.

Charles Baudelaire versus Doctor Frankenstein

During the nineteenth century, in a series of fairly distinct and generally spectacular stages, the way was cleared for a major aspiration, for what can perhaps be seen as the carrier wave of the bourgeois ideology of representation. From Daguerre's Diorama to Edison's project of a Kinetophonograph, each of the technologies that positivist historiography sees as a series of advances converging on the Cinema, was intended by its technicians and perceived by its publicists as one more step towards the Recreation of Reality, towards the realisation of a perfect illusion of the perceptual world.

The reconstruction 'as if you were there' of famous natural disasters or architectural monuments in the Diorama (just like the art of Madame Tussaud, contemporaneous with it) is an (ideo)logical extension of the *trompe l'œil* scene painting at which Daguerre excelled, as was the invention of photography, to which his name, along with that of Niepce, remains attached. After this, each new achievement was perceived by the ruling ideology in the area as *supplying a deficiency:* thus, the presentation at the London Exhibition of 1851 of the *Stereoscope,* an apparatus for which there was immediately an extraordinary craze (250,000 sold in three months) was greeted in the following terms by a contemporary: '... photography, reinvigorated, perfected and crowned by the stereoscope, is so superior to its former self that the day will soon be here when all photographic pictures ... will come ... in pairs to reproduce in all their truth, in all its gentle or harsh beauty, immaterial and living nature' (Moigno 1852, pp.9-10; cit. Deslandes 1966, p.67). And Baudelaire, sworn enemy of the naturalistic ideology of representation, railed against 'these thousands of greedy eyes bent over the holes of the stereoscopes as if over peepholes to the infinite' (1965, p.153). Let me anticipate the results of my investigations and reflections: I believe it was this aspiration to three-dimensionality that was satisfied by the blossoming of the Institutional Mode of Representation from around 1910, and that the latter continues to satisfy it more than all the ephemeral re-appearances of red-and-green or polarising spectacles, raster screens, etc.

That other 'lineage' constituted by the succession of graphic animation devices, from Plateau's Phenakistiscope to Reynaud's Praxinoscope, had a similar reception, as, *a fortiori,* did all the attempts to link together, however imperfectly, these various strategies for the reconstitution of reality: 'The stereoscope gives the sensation of three-dimensionality to objects, the Phenakistiscope that of movement. The Stereofantascope or Bioscope, as its name implies, gives at one and the same time the sensations of three-dimensionality and of movement, or the sensation of life.'[1]

And of course, Edison's wish to link to his phonograph an apparatus capable of recording and reproducing pictures, fulfilling a dream of 'grand opera being given at the Metropolitan Opera House at New York ... with artists and musicians long since dead' (Edison 1895), is not just the ambition of an astute captain of industry; it is also the pursuit of the fantasy of a class become the fantasy of a culture: to extend the 'conquest of nature' by triumphing over death through an ersatz of Life itself.[2]

Later I shall examine some of the ways this genuine collective drive was delayed and sidetracked in the first decade of the cinema, before the constitution of the Institutional Mode of Representation whose genealogy it is my intention to trace. We shall see how that constitution occurred under the ægis of the reproduction in the field of the cinema of the theatrical, pictorial and literary modes of representation that had been prized by the bourgeoisies of Europe and the Americas for more than a century in 1915. And we will see how the series of advances towards the system of representation reigning by and large over the cinema today arrived to fill *deficiencies* that are in the last analysis analogous with those the bourgeois ideology of representation felt when confronted with the Daguerrotype or the Phenakistiscope.

But we shall also see that for a decade this ideology found it hard to master the cinema, and that, thanks to this 'failing' and the contradictions it gave rise to, something else developed, which I shall have to try to define when the time comes. For the moment, however, there is another factor to be examined, one which contributed directly to the invention of moving photographic pictures, but also helped to cause the important 'detour' made in an otherwise ineluctable historical movement; I must go back and examine the relations between scientific and technological research on the one hand, and what, following C.W. Ceram (1965), is usually called the 'archæology of the cinema' on the other.

****

Photography was invented just as painting, with Turner in particular, was 'changing spaces', as, in Francastel's words, it ceased to give the patron 'a view of a piece of land to dominate' (1977, p.170). This 'proprietary' dimension of the representation of space emerging in the quattrocento is unquestionably taken over by photography throughout the second half of the 'bourgeois century' in the portraits, still lives and genre pictures denounced by Baudelaire (1965, p.153), even if, as Francastel also emphasised, photography helped, through its impact on innovatory artists, in the gradual destruction of the system of representation inherited from the Renaissance.

But it is impossible to reduce the diachrony of this system, so tightly bound up with the rise of bourgeois power, to a mere symbolic and ideological instrumentalism. Panofsky (1953, pp.86-7) has demonstrated in Leonardo's anatomical experimentation the dialectical links beginning to be forged between artistic and scientific practices in Renaissance Italy, and, in the same study, suggested other such links in the centuries that followed:

> Anatomy as a science (and what applies to it applies to all the other 'descriptive' disciplines) was simply not possible without a method of preserving observations in graphic records complete and accurate in three dimensions. For, in the absence of such records, even the best observation was lost because it was not possible to check it against others and thus to test its correctness and, no less important, its general validity. It is no

exaggeration to say that in the history of modern science the invention of perspective, coupled with the nearly simultaneous emergence of the multiplying arts, marks the beginning of a first period; the invention of the telescope and the microscope that of a second; and the invention of photography that of a third. In the descriptive sciences illustration is not so much the elucidation of a statement as the statement itself.

Indeed, if the researches that culminated in the invention of photography corresponded in immediate awareness to an ideological drive, it is just as clear that this new technology objectively answered a need of the descriptive sciences of the period (botany, zoology, palæontology, astronomy, physiology). At the same time, it should not be forgotten that the economic expansion and accession to political power of the bourgeoisie were closely linked to advances in the sciences and in technology, and that hence by evoking the strictly scientific effects of some instrument or mode of representation we are by no means leaving the historical terrain of the relations of production. Here, therefore, no more than anywhere else, can one set scientific practices apart from ideological ones without the utmost care.

Turning for a moment to another current contributing to the prehistory of the cinema, i.e., the search for a pictorial but non-photographic illusion of movement, beginning with optical illusions like the Thaumatrope and culminating in a kind of dead-end with Reynaud's Praxinoscope, here too we can see a dialectical relationship between science and ideology.

The English scientists studying the persistence of vision who, around 1825, discovered the principle of the Thaumatrope—a disc the rapid rotation of which perceptually superimposed two images, one drawn on each of its sides—do not seem to have tried to locate their discovery in the movement towards naturalistic representation. For them it was nothing but an illusion and its designation as such was inseparable from the desired effect. In fact, the applications they suggested for it seem to have been primarily pedagogic, either directly, to teach about the phenomenon of persistence of vision, or symbolically, as a memory aid in teaching other things.[3]

The crucial studies of the great researcher Plateau, also

concerned with the persistence of vision (to the extent of losing his sight in attempts to gaze at the sun) suffered a similar downgrading. But in parallel with the process that made his Phenakistiscope an enormously fashionable toy, the latter did, unlike the Thaumatrope—and this suggests the existence of a historical threshold—come to find a place in the Frankensteinian ideology. The Austrian scientist Stampfer (1833, p.11; cit. Deslandes 1966, p.37), simultaneously perfecting a disc like the Phenakistiscope but without knowledge of Plateau's work, praised it in the following terms: 'It is clear that in this way it is possible to represent not only the different movements of a human being or animal, but also machines in motion or even longer lasting actions, theatrical scenes or pictures from life.'

Alongside a claim that prefigures the representational vocation of the cinema institution, this formulation contains an allusion to potential technical and scientific applications. But on the one hand, only an *analytic* description of animal or human movement (or that of machines) could be of interest to the science of the period, for which mere representation was *redundant*—as we shall see with Janssen, Marey and Londe—and on the other, the Phenakistiscope and its successors (the Zoetrope and the Praxinoscope) constituted a *regression* on the level of graphic representation (they essentially adopted the flat-tint engraving techniques of the *Images d'Epinal* or the caricatures in the illustrated press). That is why such inventions were abandoned to the children of the bourgeoisie as 'educational toys' (we shall see later the importance to be attached to the privileged connections between these children and certain modes of representation which, right through the nineteenth century, continued to deviate in these essential respects from those that engaged the serious attention of their parents).

Despite all the Stereofantascopes, Phasmatropes and Omniscopes whose ingenious inventors sought, like the alchemists of the middle ages, the Great Secret of the Representation of Life (notice the appeal to the very significant term Bioscope), the first technologically decisive steps were taken under more modest auspices. On the one hand there was a rather curious team formed by a Californian millionaire governer and race-horse breeder, and an English photographer fascinated by the photographic freezing of movement, who first joined forces to perfect training methods for a pedigree trotter—on the other a top French scientist who also had no interest in the representation of the movement of life but only in its analysis. I believe this detour via scientific and technical practices in which photography ceased to be a substitute for academic painting and became, as Baudelaire wished, 'the servant of the sciences' (1965, p.154), was to have a certain impact on the early cinema.

It is true that Muybridge's status seems somewhat ambiguous today, that there was much of the showman about him. But the use he made of his Zoogyroscope—derived from the Phenakistiscope and later rechristened the Zoopraxinoscope—to animate shots of a galloping horse at the end of the lectures he organised (notably in Parisian salons in 1881) was simply to 'prove the excellence of the method for the analysis of movement that he had perfected: the analysis was accurate because from it he was able to achieve a synthesis and reconstitute the real appearance of the subjects he was studying' (Deslandes 1966, p.101). For the first pictures obtained by Muybridge *were not believed.* That is perhaps one of the most symptomatic features of his experiment. Even Meissonier, the great equine painter, steeped in the codes of representation of academic painting thanks to which the West as a whole was persuaded of the phenomenal identity of a certain idealisation of the movement of the horse and Reality, refused for a time, we are told (Foster-Hahn 1973, p.91), to believe in the authenticity of the documents Muybridge had published. This was perhaps the first time that 'photography—the possibility of mechanically recording a picture in conditions more or less analogous to those of vision—revealed not the real character of traditional vision but, on the contrary, its systematic character' (Francastel 1977, p.44). Need I add that all those—and there seem to have been many of them in Paris—who found these pictures unrealistic also found them *ugly.* This sentiment was shared by Marey himself, moreover, who later made the following remark about Muybridge's pictures: 'Is it not that the ugly is only the unknown, and that the truth seen for the first time offends the eye?' (Marey 1895, p.183).[4] This first break between photography and the codes of representation of the 'naturalistic' painting of the nineteenth century made by Muybridge seems to me to be absolutely crucial, for, from a certain point of view, all the work of the 'Great Pioneers of the Cinema' was to consist of restoring to moving photography the 'beauty'—that of bourgeois painting, but also of bourgeois theatre and the novel—which Muybridge's innocent procedure had robbed it of. In a certain sense, of course, the act of passing these snapshots one after another to prove their *veracity* already resulted for the first spectators in London and Paris in their reintegration into the domain of Beauty. But if we are here closer than is generally realised to Lumière's founding procedure, we are also at the antipodes of the IMR. And it can even be said that a true history of the gestation of the latter must trace the itinerary from this flat, remote silhouette of a trotting horse, however 'real' its movement, to the carefully modelled shot of Al Jolson tossing off his famous sentence 'You ain't heard nothin' yet!'

Technologically speaking, Marey's efforts, deriving like Muybridge's from the Phenakistiscope (via Janssen's Photographic Revolver), lie in the direct line of the great Frankensteinian dream of the nineteenth century: the recreation of life, the symbolic triumph over death. But the man and his works were in some sense innoculated against the virus of representation by the ideology then suffusing his discipline. For Marey, and the physiology of his period, animals, and hence men, are machines: 'Living beings have been frequently and in every age compared to machines, but it is only in the present day that the bearing and the justice of the comparison are fully comprehensible' (1874, p.1). A vulgar and mechanistic materialism whose utility to the ruling classes in the era of wild capitalism is clear—Sadoul (1973, t.I, p.76) underlines the fact that the investigations into the graphic inscription of movement undertaken at the beginning of his career by the future inventor of the Chronophotographe[5] enabled him to find a 'way to subordinate man more closely to the machine, since his *odographe* is nothing but the first "spy in the cab", familiar to railwaymen and lorry drivers.'[6] It might be added that the other aspect of his earliest endeavours—the graphic analysis of animal and human movements—opened the way to Taylorism.

It was their mechanistic materialism that made Marey and Londe (at any rate until the international enthusiasm for the

Kinetoscope) ferocious opponents of the synthesis of movement. In 1899, Marey could still write about *moving photographs:* 'But after all, what they show, our eyes could have seen directly. They have added nothing to the power of our vision, subtracted nothing from our illusions. But the true character of a scientific method is to supply the inadequacies of our senses or to correct their errors. To do so chronophotography must therefore renounce the representation of the phenomena such as we see them.' And he concluded that 'only slow and fast motion are of any interest for scientific synthesis' (Marey 1899; cit. Sadoul 1973, t.I, p.100). Albert Londe, a photographer and, in 1891, the inventor of a twelve-lens camera designed for medical research, shared the same strict viewpoint: 'Leaving aside the curiosity aspect that enables us to reproduce various scenes, there is no doubt that seeing these series leaves us in exactly the same position as we are before the model itself' (1896, p.726; cit. Sadoul 1973, t.I, p.100). It is gratifying, but also instructive, to compare such declarations with those of Dziga Vertov—'we cannot improve the making of our own eyes, but we can endlessly perfect the camera' (1984, p.15)—or Jean Epstein—'a documentary shot describing in a few minutes twelve months in the life of a plant ... seems to free us of terrestrial, i.e., solar time, of the rhythm to which we seemed ineluctably bound' (1946, pp.49-50). But the comparison is only meaningful in the context of an analysis of the objectively real but highly complex links between a whole 'anti-illusionist' aspect of the cinema before Griffith and the global critique made by Vertov, Epstein, Dulac and others of the cinema usually said to have begun with Griffith.

Moreover, Marey, with his customary obstinacy in research, following his photographic rifle and before his film Chronophotographe—correctly regarded as the first moving picture camera—made a third invention running directly counter to linear, analogical representation. This was the plate Chronophotographe, which produced the first stroboscopic photographs, synchronic decompositions of movement on the surface of a single picture. This is perhaps the clearest material trace among all those that locate Marey outside the Frankensteinian tendency. Let me also cite the following blind spot, in the same sense: the system of arresting the film by friction he insisted on retaining and which precisely prevented him from obtaining from his second Chronophotographe projections able to produce the illusion of continuity, because the images jumped about so much: Marey, as he himself said, did not care.

It is true that in 1892-3, spurred on nonetheless, it seems, by the successes of Edison, he did try to perfect a machine 'to project the synthesis of movement in an effective way' (Marey 1898, p.24). But having run into difficulties in transforming an apparatus which was poorly adapted in principle to the task, he quickly abandoned this experiment in an undertaking he regarded as secondary.

****

So far, my reading of the history of the cinema is not basically in contradiction with the classic perspective. I have simply been concerned to bring out certain features I believe will make what follows clearer. However, my claim that Lumière's works—and at any rate the characteristic picture they gave rise to—reflect an attitude closer to that of Marey than to that of Daguerre may seem more surprising. For the Cinématographe Lumière was universally perceived as the culmination of the long quest for the 'absolute', for the secret of the duplication of life, a few milestones in which I have just singled out. But to hold such a view is to ignore precisely the fact that the efforts of Janssen, Marey, Muybridge and Londe are evidence of an ideological configuration quite different from the one inspiring the achievements of the Daguerres, Dubosqs and company: it is to ignore the detour through applied science of which the achievements of Lumière and his cameramen are simply, in the last analysis, a continuation: it is also to neglect the essential features distinguishing the early films of W.K.L. Dickson—closer to the Frankensteinian tradition, and to be discussed in the next chapter—from most of the films shot by Lumière and the cameramen he trained.

Only after several months of trial and error did Louis Lumière, supported by the apparatus of research and manufacture provided by the firm producing sensitive plates and films that he and his brother Auguste had made the most important in Europe, succeed where so many other more isolated and less well-endowed investigators had failed. The first subject to be shot on celluloid film by the new camera in 1895 was **Sortie d'usine** ('Employees Leaving the Lumière Factory'—the first version, not included in the Lumière catalogue). Its mode of shooting, a mode clearly inscribed in the image itself and needing no resort to intentionalism for its reading, seems very significant to me in relation to the contribution Louis Lumière was to make as a filmmaker to the cinema of the first ten years.

This first subject consists, like all the earliest films, of a single *view* (shot). It shows the workers, men and women, of the Lumière plant leaving work, and also the exit of the carriage of the owners. 'The camera was set up in a room on the ground floor of a building,' explains François Doublier, an assistant of the Lumières, so that the 'subjects' would not be 'distracted by the sight of the camera' (cit. Pinel 1974, p.415). The framing chosen is such that the figures occupy about half the height of the screen when they move towards the frame edge to leave the field of vision. Although a wall occupies half the picture, the sense of space and depth which was to strike all the early spectators of Lumière's films is already present in the contrast between this wall blocking the background to the left and the movement of the crowd emerging from the dark interior on the right, its perspective emphasised by a framing which brings out what seem to be the supports of the roof. Once the workers had begun to leave the camera was started, and cranking continued until there was no more film in the camera, i.e., for about a minute (55 feet at about 16 frames per second).

Thus, as well as this being a decisive experiment made with the prototype of this historical camera, it also represents an experiment in the observation of reality; as we would put it today, it was a matter of 'catching' an action, known in its overall lines beforehand, predictable within a few minutes, but random in all its details, which randomness was deliberately respected by concealing the camera.

It is all these characteristics, adopted in a large number of the films of the 'Lumière school', linked to the 'slice-of-life' content of so many of their views, that have led to Lumière acquiring the reputation of having been the 'first documentarist', the first champion of a 'direct' or 'actuality' cinema. And this is a perfectly justifiable standpoint.

But I should like to examine these same characteristics (and also some others) in the light not of conceptions and practices which often grew up much later, but in the perspective of that short period of the primitive cinema.

Thus, this subject's characteristics are a certain breadth of the field of vision and a certain height of the 'actors' in the frame, thanks to the distance between the camera and the people filmed and the focal length of the lens used, and also a rigorous frontality. Now, as we shall see, these features reappeared constantly in the years to come, they mark almost all films between 1900 and 1905, and then eventually came to be felt by the most self-aware pioneers of the IMR to be obstacles to be overcome.

But what is the source of the choices that presided over the shooting style found in this film as in so many others? First, undoubtedly, practices then dominant in still photography. Georges Sadoul (1964, p.51) has emphasised how much **Repas de bébé** ('Baby's Dinner') and many other scenes of Lumière family life preserved on film by Louis Lumière resemble the photographs of his own family he found in an attic. And it should not be forgotten that Louis Lumière, co-director of a firm which had practically created the amateur photography market in Europe by the release of his first invention, the famous 'Etiquette Bleue' plates, was himself a very experienced 'amateur' photographer. But here, and even more in the innumerable street scenes that were to predominate in the successive catalogues of the company, we are dealing with a mode of photographic representation popularised by the picture postcard. This is the 'urban landscape' made possible, like the experiments of Marey and Muybridge, only by the appearance on the market of high-speed emulsions (as opposed to rural landscapes, of course, which were already accessible to the collodion wet plate process, whose limitations also helped produce the frozen portraits and genre pictures of the 'first generation' of photographers). What transformations was this mode of photographic representation to undergo as a result of its contact with the Cinématographe, and, more generally, when it came to be inscribed in the first filmic practices? The moving urban landscape was to be characterised by a maximalisation of the 'polycentrism' of a picture already free of the centripetal rules of academic painting.[7] In other words, neither the street scenes nor the other general views that succeeded them spontaneously offer the reader's guide that would allow their complex content to be grasped and enumerated, especially at a single viewing. For, once the 'subject' has been designated—by its title in the Lumière catalogue—what is the content of a film like **Sortie d'usine**, like **Arrivée d'un train à La Ciotat** ('Arrival of a Train at La Ciotat'), or like **Place des Cordeliers (Lyon)**? Only an exhaustive listing of all that can be seen in the picture (which is what the first newspaper accounts tried to provide) can give an answer to this question, which could easily give rise for each of the Lumière films to a text at least as prolix as Raymond Roussel's *La Vue*. But it was a standard practice at the earliest projections (and especially at those provided at the four corners of the earth by the Lumière cameramen) to run the films several times in succession, and one should not, I think, reduce this practice to the mere desire of the new audiences for a repeat of the 'shock'; these images carry inscribed in them the need to be seen and reseen, it is inconceivable that an audience of the period, any more than one of today, could have reckoned that they had seen them definitively after seeing them once, in the way that today we can say we have seen the film on last week at our local cinema which we will not go to see again precisely because we have seen it (and *consumed* it). Here we are touching on one of the basic contradictions between the primitive cinema and the IMR, one to which I shall return.

But it would be narrow and reductive to treat the 'Lumière picture' as a mere avatar of the postcard. Not only did it become the model for thousands of 'documentary' films in the first ten years of the cinema, but certain of its features are also found in one whole aspect of French narrative film-making from Zecca and Alice Guy to Perret and Feuillade.

Taking into account certain subjective factors (the ideology, education and all the activities of Louis Lumière and his brother Auguste) as well as the objective factors described above, the production and influence of this model picture can be linked with the 'scientistic' tendency manifested by Muybridge, Marey, etc., a tendency which seems to have made all these great researchers of the end of the archæological period immune to the seductive dream of total representation, probably because that dream is, precisely, a *spiritualist* one.

But the Lumière brothers saw themselves throughout their lives as researchers, as scientists. Their researches were, of course, applied ones. Auguste devoted most of his life to medical research. As for Louis, I agree completely with Vincent Pinel's estimate that his real life's work was the colour photography process called Autochromie, on which he began work in 1891 but which he did not perfect until 1907. Moreover I regard it as highly revealing as to the attitude he took to his work, an attitude diametrically opposed to that of an Edison or a Demenÿ, that the first presentation of the Cinématographe outside the laboratory was given as an addendum to a lecture devoted in the main to the projection of colour transparencies:

Louis Lumière had come to give a lecture on the Photographic Industry, on the Company of which he was a director, and on the attempts to industrialise the Lippmann colour photography process to which a large part of his research work was devoted at the time. However, at the end of the lecture there followed an impromptu presentation of a 'projection Kinetoscope' as the proceedings describe it. The three Lumières, all present at the projection, were more surprised than anyone by the wave of enthusiasm that greeted the projection of a single film: **Sortie d'usine**. The success obtained by this short subject was, to their astonishment, greater than that of the fixed colour projections (Pinel 1974, p.411).

Moreover, a few weeks later, Louis again presented a film 'as an encore' to a colour demonstration, and once again was surprised by the reactions.

But it is above all Lumière's attitude to his subjects, the framing that generally allows ample space for the development of the action in all directions, that reveals a quasi-scientific attitude. The scene in fact seems to unfold before his camera rather like the behaviour of a micro-organism under the biologist's microscope or the movement of the stars at the end of the astronomer's telescope. Nor is it without interest that that first film, **Sortie d'usine**, was re-filmed five months later to test a technical improvement, in exactly the same conditions as the first time. Of course it was a shot within arm's reach, as it were, but the fact that it was reproduced as precisely as possible seems to me to confirm my thesis about Louis's attitude to his work.

Of course, all the films conforming to this type were not shot with a concealed camera. In **Arrivée des congressistes à Neuville-sur-Saône** ('Disembarcation of Photography Congress Delegates at Neuville-sur-Saône'), the conferencees unselfconsciously take their hats off to the camera, and, looking at the various versions of **Arrivée d'un train à La Ciotat**, it seems possible that Lumière asked his wife to take a different path for each 'take'. But these films and all the other 'documentary tableaux' that share in the constitution of the Lumière model seem to me to derive in the end from the same procedure: to choose a framing as likely as possible to 'catch' a moment of reality, then to film it without any attempt to control it or to centre the action.[8] In this respect, moreover, I can only formally deny the thesis proposed by Georges Sadoul and other historians following him, that with **Arrivée d'un train à La Ciotat** Louis Lumière prefigured classical editing. This thesis, based on an analysis of frame stills—always a dangerous procedure if films are to be treated as a socio-phenomenal reality, which implies the end-result of cinematic projection—is of a piece with the overall approach of linear historiography, which attaches great importance to 'first times'. In fact, the result is to conceal the specificity of a procedure in which chance plays so large a part that it could not but produce such a succession of 'shot scales', but for which the way such successions demand to be read had nothing to do with what was to form the basis for the 'editing codes' (the stills so conveniently stationary in a book go by very quickly during projection).

Towards the end of his life, Louis Lumière confided in Georges Sadoul: 'My endeavours were endeavours of technological research. I never did what they call "direction" (*mise-en-scène*). And I can't see myself in a modern studio' (Sadoul 1964, p.107). '"In the cinema, the age of technicians is over, this is the age of theatre." On another occasion,' says Sadoul, 'I used the word "direction" in talking about his films and he raised his eyebrows.

It was clear that he holds that direction is not appropriate in a film' (ibid., p.100).

These declarations are, of course, perfectly compatible with the ideology and practice of 'documentary', which Lumière has been said to have initiated. Nevertheless I believe, as Vincent Pinel acutely suggests (1974, p.420), that one should speak rather of a practice and an ideology closer to those of amateur film-making (as it developed after the appearance on the market around 1900 of sub-standard-gauge cameras and films) than to those of, say, the GPO Film Unit. No doubt Lumière did make a number of technological contributions to the promotion of the Frankensteinian dream, not only in his invention of the Cinématographe but also in an improvised attempt at 'direct synchronisation' (at the Lyon Photographic Congress), in the giant screen of the 1900 Exposition, and in a three-dimensional cinematic process presented at the Cannes Festival in 1935. But in all we know of him, throughout his life he never fell victim to the lyrical dream of analogical representation, the mythology of victory over death. He and his brother belonged by their education to the same rationalist tradition as Marey and Londe, and it was this tradition that so decisively overdetermined films that were to exert a real hegemony over production and consumption internationally for a number of years, helping to point the latter into a path that was soon to seem a side track. The next chapter offers a very convincing proof of this in that strange phenomenon, 'Hale's Tours', which demonstrates so clearly that Lumière's 'hyper-realism' was *problematic*.

Of course, the Cinématographe was nevertheless recruited at the outset and in the footsteps of the Diorama and the Stereoscope in the service of the Frankensteinian ideology, whatever may have been the private feelings of its inventor or the objective characteristics of the figuration it established. A famous article printed in *Le Radical,* one of the two minor papers that announced the historic première in the Salon Indien (the established press failed to note the occasion) is highly suggestive: 'Whatever the scene thus taken, and however large the number of individuals thus surprised in their everyday activities, you see them again natural size, in colour [sic], with perspective, distant skies, houses, with a perfect illusion of real life.... Speech has already been collected and reproduced, now life is collected and reproduced. For example, it will be possible to see one's loved ones active long after they have passed away' (cit. Bessy & Lo Duca 1948, p.47). And it is noteworthy that the only other article on the matter that came out that December 30th 1895 (in *La Poste*) ends on the same mortuary note: 'When these cameras are made available to the public, when everyone can photograph their dear ones, no longer in a motionless form but in their movements, their activity, their familar gestures, with words on their lips, death will have ceased to be absolute' (cit. ibid., pp. 47-8).

Thus form, movement, colour (added because *it goes with the others,* even if this was to anticipate by a number of years),[9] all, for these bourgeois journalists, come together to fulfill the supreme fantasy: the suppression of death.[10]

NOTES

1 Dubosq, addition to patent no.13,609, November 12th 1852; cit. Deslandes (1966), p.73.

2 'Only in the sixteenth century did this modern pattern of death become the norm. In the Counter Reformation and the funereal and obsessive games of the Baroque, but especially in Protestantism which, by individualising each conscience before God and decathecting collective ceremonies, hastened the process of the individual fear of death. It too was to give rise to the mighty modern undertaking to exorcise it: the ethic of accumulation and material production, the sanctification by investment, labour and profit usually called the "spirit of capitalism" (Max Weber: *The Protestant Ethic*)—that machine of salvation from which intra-worldly ascesis has gradually withdrawn, giving way to worldly and productive accumulation without changing the purpose: protection against death.... Death has become a "right-wing", individual and tragic notion, "reactionary" in regard to movements of revolt and social revolution' (Baudrillard 1976, pp. 273-4).

3 'It has occurred to me that this amusing toy might be made instrumental in impressing classical subjects upon the memory of young persons .... Why can we not ... thus represent the Metamorphoses of Ovid; or what say you ... to converting the fleet of Æneas into sea-nymphs ...?' (Paris 1827, pp.11-12; cit. Deslandes 1966, p.29). This is the spirit in which the Thaumatrope became a fashionable toy, associations of this kind becoming the basis for 'comic quatrains, puns and political allusions' (Deslandes 1966, p.28).

4   He went on as follows: 'These positions, as revealed by Muybridge, at first appeared unnatural, and the painters who first dared to imitate them astonished rather than charmed the public.' The painters in question were Meissonier and, of course, Degas.

5   Muybridge's inspiration in the realisation of his first camera system.

6   Marey was aware and proud of the possible applications of his work. In *Movement* (1895), he explains that his analyses will enable soldiers to carry heavier gear longer distances.

7   Certain very acentric urban landscapes painted by Manet or Degas may probably be regarded as a kind of reaction from photography onto the most advanced painting of the period.

8   I am not here referring to **Repas de bébé** (and the other Lumière films deriving from it) or **Arroseur et arrosé** (properly **Le Jardinier et le petit espiègle**, 'The Gardener, the Bad Boy and the Hose' or 'Watering the Gardener') and other comic sketches. The latter, of course, open onto different horizons.

9   As we can see here—and will see again with Gorky (p.23 below)—colour has a place in the Frankensteinian dream. To this extent Lumière contributed to that dream, following Ducos du Hauron and others, with his Autochromie process. However, non-photographic colour was to appear very quickly in the cinema, without a decisive step being thereby taken towards institutional presence. In fact colour has never, even in our own day, provided more than an *extra reality* in the IMR.

10 In a famous article (Bazin 1967), André Bazin traces this 'mummy complex' back to the ancient Egyptians, regarding it as a kind of universal drive. As such it serves as a legitimation for his own attachment to bourgeois illusionism.

Life to Those Shadows

Last night I was in the Kingdom of Shadows. If you only knew how strange it is to be there. It is a world without sound, without colour. Everything there—the earth, the trees, the people, the water and the air—is dipped in monotonous grey. Grey rays of sun across the grey sky, grey eyes in grey faces, and the leaves of the trees are ashen grey. It is no life but its shadow, it is not motion but its soundless spectre.... And all this in a strange silence where no rumble of wheels is heard, no sound of footsteps or of speech. Nothing. Not a single note of the intricate symphony that always accompanies the movements of people.

The commentator so appalled by the *unnatural character* of the Cinématographe Lumière, discovered in a 'dubious' variety show in Nizhny Novgorod in 1896, is none other than that great apostle of literary naturalism, Maxim Gorky (1960, p.407). I think this is a key quotation. It contains a clear and complete expression of the requirements of the naturalistic ideology of representation then dominant among almost all the members of the European intelligentsia, major and minor:[1] a mode of expression with any claims to realism had to be endowed with colour, sound and speech, three dimensions, *spatial extension* ('All this moves, teems with life and, upon approaching the edge of the screen, vanishes somewhere beyond it').

So, if the scientist tradition descending from Muybridge and Marey and strong in **Sortie d'usine** and the subjects more or less directly deriving from it, together with forms of representation with a long history and still alive among the masses of the people, helped to direct the early cinema along paths which seem hardly compatible with naturalistic 'presence', the latter gradually tended to impose itself on moving pictures nonetheless. The conflict, lasting more than fifteen years, that stemmed from the objective resistance moving pictures put up, by reason of these circumstances of their birth, to this 'hegemonic will', was to produce in particular the labile, ambivalent character of a whole section of primitive cinema as compared with the monovalent stability of the IMR.

****

It is no accident that one of the only films in that first Lumière programme that found 'grace' in the eyes of the author of *The Lower Depths*—afflicted it is clear, with a quite neurotic attachment to naturalism—was **Repas de bébé**, probably the first film to catch faces 'from life' in and for themselves, on a scale allowing a close reading of those *constantly evolving fields of signs*. Gorky did not, of course, criticise **Sortie d'usine** for the anonymity of the workers in it; confronted there with a crowd of workers, with the masses, he tacitly conceded the legitimacy of this lack of priority of the notion of the individual (as embodied in the close-up). Already here are two poles of a problematic that was to undergo interesting developments in the USSR (the strike sequence in **Mat'**—'Mother'—for example). But it is clear that, in the absence of the Word, the remoteness of faces and bodies from the camera and the acentric image it implies were felt by all those who shunned picture shows once the novelty effect had worn off to be the crucial defect of the more characteristic films of this first period. This makes it all the more important to bring out everything in the early cinema that already reflects an 'awareness' of this defect and an attempt to redress it. For example, contrary to a highly tenacious myth, the medium close-up and even the true close-up are found in the very earliest stages of the cinema, in Europe and in the USA. They rapidly became an established presence in the first decade, so that it can be stated, with no wish to cultivate paradox, that the development of institutional editing among the Americans, the Danes, and so on, was to *reduce* the proportion of medium close-ups and close-ups in the cinema, and that for a number of years.

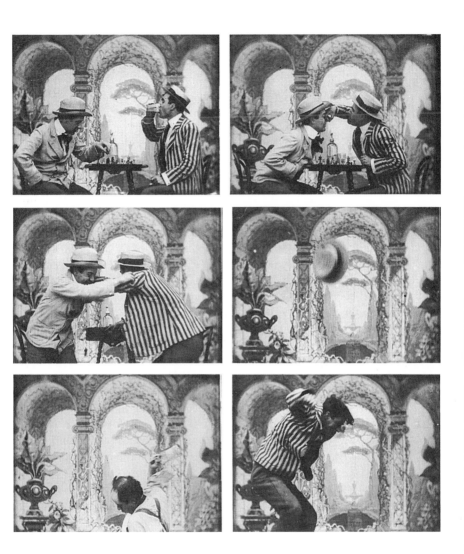

Fig. 1: **A Chess Dispute** (R.W. Paul, 1903). One of many primitive 'gag-films' shot in close-up or medium-close-up (here we have a rare use of off-screen space for added comic effect).

It is emblematic of the contradictions of the early cinema that it was an assistant of Marey, the inveterate enemy of analogical representation, who first introduced the Frankensteinian complex into the cinema:

> How many people would be happy if they could only see once again the features of someone now dead. The future will see the replacement of motionless photographs, frozen in their frames, with animated portraits that can be brought to life at the turn of a handle. Physiognomic expressions will be preserved as voices are by the phonograph. It will even be possible to combine the latter with the Phonoscope to complete the illusion.... We will do more than analyse, we will *bring back to life* (Demenÿ 1892, p.315; cit. Sadoul 1973, t.I, pp.169-70).

At the beginning of his career, the physiologist Georges Demenÿ added to the list of kinetic analyses produced by his patron Marey, extending it into the highly premonitory domain of an analysis of speech. To do this he himself posed for the Chronophotographe—*in close-up*, of course—articulating sentences with a great cinematic future: 'Je vous aime' (I love you) and 'Vive la France!' (Long Live France!). However, deaf mutes asked to read the single frames so obtained found it extremely difficult to do so, facing, in fact, the same problem horse lovers had with Muybridge's instantaneous pictures. Thus, it was in the name of scientific instrumentality (the idea was to enable deaf mutes to learn to lip-read) that Demenÿ followed in the footsteps of Muybridge and proceeded to transgress the 'taboo' pronounced by his patron against the synthesis of movement (there seems to be some connection between this transgression and the estrangement between the two men), perfecting his Phonoscope, first in a peepshow form, then a projecting one. This projector was a device to reproduce views taken by the Chronophotographe, and it was a great success at an 1892 exhibition of photography in the Champ de Mars, where it ran continuously.

This first inscription of the *gestures of speech* in moving pictures was portentous in two respects. On the one hand it foreshadowed a whole art of *mimed speech*, coeval with the Institution

and a dimension of many of its masterpieces. On the other, however, it led directly to the first talking cinema, that of the period
before 1910.

It is no accident that Demenÿ was one of the very first *to give
the cinema a soul*:[2] he had a real vocation for ideology. At first he
was so blinded by his fantasy of the living portrait—the Phonoscope was to become part of bourgeois domestic furnishings, like
the photo album, it was to be a kind of altar on which the small
shareholder could celebrate a Catholic version of the cult of
ancestors—that he took no interest in the idea of a show for a
large audience, which perhaps seemed more vulgar to him, until a
meeting with Léon Gaumont. But the apparatus he proposed to
Gaumont, in 1895, was the Phonophone, a combination of the
Phonograph and the projection Phonoscope, *intended to work in
synchrony*. And although in the first instance the Gaumont
engineers worked on a cinematography-and-projection system
deriving from the Phono*scope*, it was this meeting between Gaumont and Demenÿ that was to result in the Gaumont Chronophone in 1900, the system with which Alice Guy was to shoot
more than 100 singing or talking subjects between 1900 and 1907
(see Guy 1976, pp.188-92).

As is well known, the very first attempt at a talking cinema can
be attributed to an initiative of the 'father of the Phonograph',
Edison, himself. But unlike Demenÿ in this respect, the famous
inventor conceived the talking (or rather singing) cinema as a
mass spectacle—and what a mass spectacle!—from the outset: 'I
believe that in coming years by my work and that of Dickson,
Muybridge, Marey and others ... grand opera can be given at the
Metropolitan Opera House at New York without any material
change from the original, and with artists and musicians long
since dead' (Edison 1895).

It now seems established beyond dispute that Thomas Alva
Edison only played a marginal part in the invention of the
cinema (see Hendricks 1961). At most he can be regarded as the
source of a number of fruitful ideas, especially that of the per-
forated celluloid strip, which probably still has a considerable
future. Nonetheless, the part played by the laboratory he ran at
West Orange (in conjunction with his role as founder-mentor of a
huge electrical trust) and for which worked his assistant W.K.L.

Dickson, the 'inventor' of the Kinetoscope, justifies a consideration of Edison the man and his ideas as a portrait of the 'powers'
presiding over the birth of the cinema in the USA. Moreover,
the earliest endeavours at West Orange have a certain *symptomatic homogeneity*, which can be summed up precisely in
Edison's lyrico-theatrical dream. This vision embodies, in the
guise of the mere calculation of an astute businessman, an extension of the Wagnerian fantasy, of the ideology of the *Gesamtkun-
stwerk*, according to which more than one artist via equivalent
forms (Skryabin, but also Kandinsky) thought to 'aim simultaneously for unity and multiplicity, *to offer an equivalent to what
nature does*, to endow the work of art with a fourth, cosmic,
dimension' (Schneider 1963, p.63).

This association of naturalism and a certain petty-bourgeois
metaphysics is a perfect evocation of Edison's character. In him
we can locate the point at which the bourgeois fantasy par excellence, so well expressed in Demenÿ's living portraits, of the this-
worldly non-finitude of the subject, of the materialist victory over
death, is, as it were, sublimated in that of total representation, in
which spectators overstep the narrow limits of their lives in a
communion with 'artists and musicians long since dead', *projecting themselves into the latter's survival.*

For Edison, the project of moving photographs arose to supply
a *defect inherent in the phonograph*. The simultaneous reproduction of the visible and the audible was the aim of all the experiments conducted under his ægis by Dickson up to 1895, when a
Kinetophonograph was made available to the public, only one
year after the opening of the first Kinetoscope parlour in New
York. However, this apparatus, which did not even aspire to a
rigorous synchronisation, was never satisfactory, and only forty-
five models were manufactured, whereas the Kinetoscope was
already spreading around the globe in thousands. This technological failure has been attributed to Edison's lack of subsequent
interest in the perfecting of an invention whose original paternity
he nevertheless boasted: at any rate, there is no doubt that he
always regarded the Kinetoscope as an experimental passing stage
in a series of researches whose ultimate aim remained the reproduction of life, the projection in a vast auditorium of pictures
and sounds capable of constituting an analogue of reality.

Despite all their technological failures and blind spots (the fetishisation of electricity that encumbered Dickson with an enormous camera, the inability to solve the problem of film travel in projection), the Edison-Dickson duo do have an essential place in the establishment of the institutional vision. For, on the one hand, it was at West Orange that the first synchronised cinema was in fact realised, in 1913, and it was in the Edison studio that the first systematic experiments in editing in the United States were made, by Edwin S. Porter. But, above all, it was Edison and Dickson who built the first real studio, the Black Maria, a prefiguration of the soundproof stages of the 1930's; it was in the Black Maria that **The Kiss** was filmed for the *New York World* in 1896, introducing the iconography of bourgeois theatre into moving pictures for the first time, and also inaugurating the erotic vocation of the close view;[3] it was they who, when filming at greater distance, felt the need for a black backdrop that would centre the pictures destined for the 'peepholes' of the Kinetoscopes,[4] by contrast with the Lumière model; finally, it was they who decided to christen the projector they obtained in a rather unscrupulous way from its inventor Armat (see Sadoul 1973, t.I, pp.305-12) the Vitascope—'vision of life'—in emblematic opposition to the Cinématographe—'writing in movement'—the name chosen by Louis Lumière.

And there is a further striking confirmation of the place Edison occupied in the *tableau raisonné* of the early cinema, a place poles apart from that of Marey: almost exactly as the latter published the description of his Sphymographe, an instrument to record the slightest quiver of the 'animal mechanism' in a scrupulous graphism, Edison was perfecting an astonishing analogue of that animal mechanism known as Woman, a mechanical analogue moved by phonographs (a brilliant inversion of the set-up Marey had proposed).

Of course, this prodigy only occurred in a famous novel, Villiers de l'Isle-Adam's *L'Eve future* of 1880. But allow me to linger over this fable, in which the great writer embroiders around the already legendary figure of Edison a series of quasi-mystical variations on a reactionary ideology of the relations between the sexes, for it is of the greatest interest for an understanding of the Institution to come.

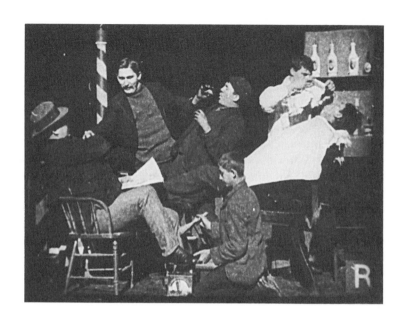

Fig. 2: It was no doubt as much his awareness of the difficulty of reading complex images through the peep-hole of the Kinetoscope as it was an urge to imitate the photographer's studio that led W.K.L. Dickson to shoot scenes like **Barber Shop** (1894) against a black backdrop.

All histories of the cinema do, indeed, allow space for this novel, regarded as prophetic insofar as in an aside in one chapter Villiers (in 1879 apparently) *deduces* from his hero's most famous invention—the Phonograph—the invention that was to make him even more famous—the cinema.[5] But in these evocations of this curious book, it does not seem to have been noticed that its main content, a specifically phallocentric variant of the Frankenstein complex, constitutes a marvellously apt metaphor for the imaginary operations of the future Institution.

When Edison, in order to prevent his former benefactor, the English dandy Lord Ewald, from committing suicide, succeeds in replacing his mistress Alicia, a woman of perfect beauty but with a 'vile' soul, with the *andréïde* Hadaly, a woman who is artificial but just as beautiful and who *perfectly reflects man's desire*, Ewald is at first horrified. But eventually he gives in to the arguments of the *andréïde*, who has become the double of the other whose 'spirit contradicts her body'. Hadaly whispers:

Who am I? A being of dreams ... who is half awake in your thoughts—and whose salutary shadow you can banish by one of those clear arguments which will leave you in my place only emptiness and painful boredom, the fruit of their supposed correctness. Oh, do not wake from me, do not banish me, on a pretext that treacherous reason, only capable of destruction, is already whispering quietly in your ear.... Who am I, you ask. My existence here below, *for you at least*, depends only on your free decision. Attribute existence to me, affirm to yourself that I exist, strengthen me from your own self, and suddenly I shall be, in your eyes, fully alive, animated with the degree of reality that your creative Good Will has inspired in me (Villiers 1977, p.337).

Can one help but recall the role of the female body offered as food for male fantasy by early film-makers? More generally, can one help but compare Hadaly's objurgations with Christian Metz's magisterial description (1982, pp.133-4) of the mode of existence of the spectator-subject in the cinema Institution:

In the filmic state as in the daydream, perceptual transference stops before its conclusion, true illusion is wanting, the imaginary remains felt as such; just as the spectator knows that he is watching a film, the daydream knows that it is a daydream.... Film viewing, like daydreaming, is rooted in contemplation and not in action. Both suppose a temporary, largely voluntary, change in economy by which the subject suspends his object cathexes or at least renounces opening a real outlet for them.

Add the fact that, among her 'wholly animal' perfections, Miss Alicia counts an admirable singing voice, and one can say that, in his recreation of the Edison legend, Villiers anticipated many of the aspects of the ideology characteristic of the socio-historical space in which the non-fictional Father of the Phonograph moved.[6] However, by making Edison the champion of his own critique of the bourgeois era in the name of a lost aristocratic paradise, Villiers (ironically, presumably) was historically astray. For Edison, the astute businessman, was certainly a man of his time who, while awaiting filmed opera, had no hesitation in allowing his associates to focus the Kinetograph on disreputable (and illegal) boxing matches, in order to profit from the first box-office successes known to moving pictures.[7] For Dickson and the other men who collaborated in productions for the Kinetoscope (in this case, the Latham brothers) quickly found subjects that answered to the tastes of the social strata that frequented the locations where their slot machines could be profitably installed: penny arcades in the USA, market fairs and funfairs in Great Britain and Europe. The success of the Kinetoscope was partly due to this show-business sense. But it was also due to the extraordinary novelty it represented, and all the histories emphasise that in the end this success was the same as that of a whole series of scientific marvels (X-rays, the Phonograph, etc.) to which the masses only had access as fairground phenomena but which as such were supposed to give the deprived an optimistic vision of the future of industrial society.

The failure of the firm's productions from 1896 on in comparison with those of the Lumière company is probably to be attributed to the powerful magic exerted by the 'scenics' that the latter revealed to the world which continued to work throughout the primitive period (see p.51 below). Dickson did transport the cumbersome Kinetograph out of the Black Maria (in 1894), but always, it seems, in order to shoot in a manner close to the 'centripetal' images against a black background taken in the studio. And the attempts to imitate the Lumière films after their eruption into the American market continued to suffer from the weight of the equipment and an already 'outdated' conception of mise-enscène. In fact this first failure of Edison in competition with French films is in certain respects comparable with that of the Film d'Art in France in 1908-1910. In either case it was a matter of an attempt to fulfill a wish while the conceptual, if not the material means were still lacking. Today it is clear that Edison, Dickson and their various collaborators in certain respects anticipated what was to become the IMR. But given their inability to create an analogue 'à la Hadaly', and especially to invent at one go a system able to solicit, to sustain a 'willing illusion' equivalent to that intended by Villiers's Edison, *but also by the real Edison*, their black backgrounds are merely a remote prefiguration of the falling-off lighting that came into being around 1915. On the other hand, the picture of Dickson playing the violin by an enormous Phonograph horn produces an intolerable contradiction in the context of these aspirations to the faithful reproduction of Life. Contradictions of the same kind recur throughout the primitive period, to which all the work of Dickson/Edison belongs.

The Lumière picture, on the contrary, even when not showing the features of a baby 'as if under a microscope' or adumbrating narrative closure as in **Arroseur et arrosé**, does *live* in its own way. It is non-linear, non-centred, impossible to grasp on first viewing, true, but it provides, as it were, a sense of closeness to reality, precisely insofar as the latter itself is non-centred, unclosed, non-linear, ungraspable on first viewing. This is no longer (not yet) a question of the construction of the real in the manner of naturalism, but of a picture which, while not an analogue of reality, is nonetheless the singular result of an encounter between the cine camera and 'raw reality'. The attraction these films still exert on us lies here. However, I have no intention of assigning Edison to an (unsuccessful attempt at) bourgeois *representationalism*, Lumière to popular (or scientistic) *presentationalism*. The pleasure Lumière himself and his spectators yesterday and today obtained and obtain from his films does indeed emanate from an *analogical effect* (produced by photography whatever one's intentions), but from one which is non-linear and acentric, which does not locate the spectator subject at the centre of an imaginary space; that is why I believe the pleasure—and also the knowledge—he produced is of quite another kind from the pleasure of the Institution to come.

And yet.

It can also be argued that these Lumière films and the practices deriving from them are at the root of what can be isolated as the *documentary ideology*, an ideology still, of course, very much alive today, but one which at the time took a particularly acute form we should look into.

****

Its sudden changes made the scenery rushing rapidly past almost a series of coloured pictures .... The lens dived down to the Villefranche harbour, picking up en route the grey masses of the battleships, constantly cut off by the series of telegraph poles or the darkness of tunnels.

This description of his shooting of a train trip as if the train itself were a film—a shooting carried out shortly after he left the Lumière company, in which he had been one of the first and the most talented cameramen—is by Félix Mesguich (1933, pp.27-8). I shall return to him, because we owe to him a true credo of the documentary ideology. But first we should get better acquainted with another important character in early cinema, one closely linked to the gradual strengthening within primitive cinema itself of a more dynamic, more conquering, more *proprietary* conception of representation: I mean the railway.

The first appearance of a train in the history of moving

pictures seems certainly to be Lumière's famous **Arrivée d'un train à La Ciotat** of 1895. Today there are at least two versions of this film, which at any rate testifies to the constant concern of the first real film-maker to improve the quality of the effect produced by his moving photographs. But his privileging of the shot in this way, and the fact that his cameramen produced remake after remake all over the world (Alexandria, Jaffa, Melbourne, Tokyo, etc.), stem not only from the symbolic place of the train in the spectacle of industrial progress it was felt apposite to offer to the masses, but also from the extraordinary effect of *depth* produced by a framing that makes the train arrive towards the spectator. This being so, it is not surprising that the shot was reproduced hundreds of times by the cameramen of all the producing countries for years, in fiction films, too, nor that it was with a re-edition of this same shot that Louis Lumière himself was to demonstrate his three-dimensional film process to the Paris Académie des Sciences forty years later. And the railway, with its direct, penetrating movement, an impressive image of the 'conquest of new spaces', both pictorial and geographic, by industrial power, was to mark the history of the cinema in spectacular ways, from **The Great Train Robbery** to **Das Stahltier**, via **La Roue, The Iron Horse, Turksib** and **La Bête humaine**.

But at that time the railway was only just entering its golden age, it had only recently become *the* modern means of transport, it had just granted 'Mr. and Mrs. Everyman' the new possibility of following in the footsteps of the great explorers of earlier centuries (the Orient Express began in 1883, the Trans-Caspian line opened in 1893). Of course, to go and stroll in Samarkhand or Istanbul cost money: the myth of the globe trotter first took root among the bourgeoisie, but the cinema helped to extend it as a fantasy through other strata. This was the principal task undertaken by the Lumière cameramen, traversing the globe, hands on their brass cranks. The films they brought back, long described as 'scenics', were such as to satisfy the new thirst for remote places and to sustain the colonial enterprise. But for those who could aspire to a real acquaintance with the streets trodden by a Loti or a Larbaud, these films long continued to exhibit the defects Gorky saw in the earliest Lumière subjects. For, whether produced by Pathé, Urban, Warwick, Edison or Biograph, the

Lumière model seems to have remained in force for at least a decade.[8]

However, nine years after the shooting of **Arrivée d'un train à La Ciotat**, eight years after Promio first (perhaps) introduced the 'tracking shot' in a 'scenic', filmed from a gondola on the Grand Canal in Venice, the USA, the country with the most spectacular growth of the railways,[9] was the birthplace of a curious enterprise combining cinema and railway train, with the avowed aim of overcoming the 'alienating' obstacles so well described by Gorky. A new credibility, a new presence was to be given to the Lumière tableau.

Visitors to the 1904 Saint Louis Universal Exhibition, as they tried the first ice-cream cones and hot dogs, attended the first public demonstrations of Lee DeForest's system of wireless telegraphy and sampled the sound cinema of the German pioneer Oskar Messter, were also introduced to a first version of Hale's Tours.

If this curious attraction was indeed exhibited at Saint Louis as its inventor, a certain William Keefe, envisaged, it consisted of a railway carriage with one side missing travelling in a circular tunnel whose wall formed an endless screen. Pictures shot from a moving train were to have been projected onto this screen.

> The purpose of this entertainment device was to provide the passengers with a fairly faithful representation of the scenes which they would see if they were to take a real train ride through scenic areas of the world, incorporating motion pictures which were to have been photographed from a real moving train. The illusion of the ride was to be heightened by the use of an unevenly laid track which would cause the car to sway and vibrate, thus suggesting a high rate of speed. Some sort of wind-producing machine was to be used within the tunnel to produce a rush of air throughout the length of the car. Presumably, a variety of appropriate sounds would also have been produced—the rush and roar of the steam engine, a whistle, the clanks and groans of the car, and so forth (Fielding 1973, p.17).

In the months that followed, the formula became less

spectacular but more manageable, but the *illusion of travelling* remained central to the undertaking: in the next stage the real journey was reduced to going to and from the ticket sales point and a stationary carriage in which the projections took place and to which the shuttle coach was attached. Finally, the formula according to which Hale's Tours were known throughout the world for seven prosperous years only used a single stationary 'carriage'. This

> provided a number of seats for its passengers, suitably inclined upwards towards the rear to provide good sight lines. Through the open front, the audience viewed a motion picture which had been photographed from the cowcatcher of a moving train, and which was thrown onto a slightly inclined screen from a motion-picture projector situated in a gallery above and slightly behind the car. The size of the screen, the distance of the screen from the car, and the distance of the projector from the screen were intended to provide an image which covered the entire field of vision of the car's occupants and which was 'life size' (ibid., p.18).

George C. Hale, who had purchased the idea from Keefe to exploit it in partnership with a magistrate named Gifford, had been fire chief in Kansas City and had made himself famous by organising ultra-realistic demonstrations of modern fire-fighting techniques at international conferences in Europe in 1893 and 1900 (we will see later the considerable importance of the still novel institution of the professional fireman in the iconography of early cinema in Britain and the USA). It seems likely that his sense of a spectacle 'as if you were there' derives from these antecedents, which recall Belasco, but also Daguerre.

Hale introduced his Tours towards the end of the primitive period, of course, and the problem they were supposed to overcome—the spectator's 'exclusion' from the classic primitive picture—had already received the beginnings of solutions from Smith, Williamson, Porter, etc., while the decisive advances of a Griffith and a Blackton which would make them obsolete were already close at hand. But what is relevant to us here is the fact that all the extraordinary devices (decor, sound effects, swaying)

Fig. 3: Billy Bitzer shooting a film for the Hales Tours type of presentation.

by means of which hundreds of locations (five hundred in the USA alone by 1905) enabled the poor to 'believe' in an impossible railway journey, provide a naively analogical prefiguration of what the IMR was to achieve perfectly fifteen years later at the imaginary level. For, as we shall see, the *transport*, the penetration of the spectator into the visual (and eventually aural) diegetic space is the main gesture around which the Institution itself revolves.

These showplaces of Hale's were the first permanent projection sites in the USA. And these spectators who called to pedestrians to get out of the way when subjects shot from a tramway were projected for them were already in another world than those who, ten years earlier, had jumped up in terror at the filmed arrival of a train in a station: the former are masters of the situation, they are ready to *go through the peephole*.

Of course, this move had already been made here and there by quite other methods: closer shots, sometimes even track-ins, invited spectators across the threshold; the first contiguity matches and alternating editing adumbrated the process of centring and envelopment. Hale's Tours soon became pointless and they disappeared for ever around 1911. But their enormous success over a number of years proves the strong psycho-social pressure exerted in favour of a mode of representation quite different from the one deriving from **Sortie d'usine** and the other scenics of Lumière and his cameramen. Moreover, it was 'Lumière space' that Hale's trains 'violated', allowing the spectator-subject of 1906 to break-and-enter, as it were.[10]

In addition to Hale's Tours, I should also say something about a whole series of projects, mostly abortive, whose aim, however, was identical with that of the American attraction: to produce the projection of moving pictures as an environment. The methods adopted were both grandiose and inconsistent: the aim was literally to surround the spectator with a single continuous picture reproducing, in theory at least, the conditions of real vision. The only one of these projects that seems to have been realised[11] was the Cinéorama of the French engineer Grimoin-Sanson, actually presented to the public in 1900 at the Paris Exposition Universelle. The Cinéorama is said to have given complete satisfaction for three shows, but then the fire service, worried by the large amounts of heat released, banned further presentations (the catastrophe of the Charity Bazaar was still fresh in everyone's memories, cf. p.48 below).

The principle of the Cinéorama was simple: in taking the pictures, ten cameras were arranged in a circle and operated in strict synchronisation thanks to a mechanical link; in projection, ten projectors similarly arranged in the middle of a more or less spherical auditorium replayed the ten films so made for each 'tableau'. For the show, scenes were shot in five European cities and in the Sahara desert, plus two taken from the gondola of a balloon which took off and then landed in the Place de la Concorde, pictures which were to open and close the show. To see this show, whose pictures were also coloured, the spectators boarded the gondola of a 'balloon' (vector of the imaginary voyage, like the train for Hale); the projection apparatus was located in a cabin beneath their feet. The effect, it seems, was gripping. The historians speak of it as the first experiment in total cinema. A significant phrase, which relates to Edison's dream of a total illusion, a dream that was to be realised, indeed, but by quite different means.

For my part, I see the Cinéorama as the site of an exemplary contradiction. In its attempt to secure the absolute presence of moving pictures, it placed the spectator 'in front of' an even more acentric tableau than the Lumière one. If a street scene shot in Moscow or Tokyo by Mesguich or Promio required (and often obtained) several viewings before it was 'exhausted', the tableaux of the Cinéorama show must have beggared description! Although what is achieved here seems to be the almost literal absorption of the spectator by pro-filmic space and time, it is also a total rejection of any linearisation of iconic signifiers, of any centring of the picture. And as we shall see below (pp.143ff.), the ultimate goal sought by Grimoin-Sanson and his emulators, the insertion of the spectator-subject in an imaginary space-time, in fact demanded that linearisation, that centring, as its *conditio sine qua non*. With the Cinéorama, on the contrary, we are closer to the audio-visual 'environments' of modernism, which deploy a quite different kind of perception from the one the IMR was to derive from the bourgeois theatre, the bourgeois novel and bourgeois painting.

As for colour, much more in evidence throughout the silent period than we usually realise today—thanks especially to the astonishing Pathé-Color system—we shall see later (pp.171ff. below) that although it did contribute to the films of Méliès, Zecca and others the supplement of reality already demanded by Gorky, as well as a certain linearisation/centring (differentiation of characters), it also produced other effects with the opposite tendency, notably a certain emphasis on the picture as decorated surface.

In fact, during this first decade, the 'drive' to supply the three defects stressed by Gorky—colour, sound, spatial extension, and, more generally, presence—often led to fundamental deviations from naturalism; one step backwards followed two steps forward, a phenomenon that was often to be repeated, as we shall see, and that each time we encounter it will help us understand the nature of the nascent system of representation.

NOTES

1   And not restricted to any particular socio-political ideology, for it is defended and illustrated by the Goncourts as much as it is by Zola or Gorky.

2   A phrase used about all the handymen and engineers, from the Englishman Will Barker to the American Lee DeForest, who 'made moving pictures talk'.

3   Intriguingly, the first true close-up in the cinema, **Fred Ott's Sneeze** (1894), was the result of a 'commission' from a journalist who wanted to see the Kinetoscope reproduce the picture of a *pretty girl* sneezing.

4   See Sadoul (1973), t.I, p.256, for an account of this phenomenon that attributes it solely to the smallness of the Kinetoscope picture.

5   The fact that Edison/Dickson themselves derived the one from the other is confirmed by their rather derisory attempt at the beginning of their researches to animate photographs by gluing them around a cylinder of the type used in the Phonograph.

6   A novel writen by Jules Verne a decade later (*Castle in the Carpathians*, 1893) has an astoundingly similar theme: a man shuts himself up in a lonely castle in order, night after night, to 'project' for himself the perfect simulacrum of a loved woman singer who had died young but whose image and voice he had managed to capture with a marvellous machine while she was still alive.

7   And it is an early sign of the social division that was to characterise the first two decades of cinema in the USA that Edison's very bourgeois hypocrisy led him, it seems, even to perjure himself, claiming that he had not attended the

re-enactments of the Corbett-Courtney and Leonard-Cushing fights (see Hendricks 1966, pp.89-97 & 108).

8 As early as 1896 a rudimentary form of 'syntagmatisation' does appear with the issue of series of tableaux (military views filmed on the occasion of the Tsar's official visit to France).

9 More than half the world's milage in 1895.

10 Assuming that all the films shown in this way were shot from moving vehicles, which is by no means certain.

11 Other famous projects were the American Chase's Cyclorama of 1894 and the French Cinématorama of 1896, both abortive.

The Wrong Side of the Tracks

All the historians who have discussed the cinema of the 1896-1914 period concur in recognising a very pronounced national specificity in the production of each of the three Western countries which between them more or less shared out the world market: France and Britain in the first period, France and America later. But the divergencies between these national cinemas —and also the Italian and Danish cinemas which soon came to the fore—seem to be perceived as self-explanatory cultural facts. Similarly, if there is broad agreement that during the first decade the cinema was the 'poor man's theatre', that it drew its audiences almost entirely from the lower classes (craftsmen and workers) of the urban centres, that too tends to be regarded as self-explanatory, as if it had nothing to do with the historical context.

At any rate, national differences, even in the content of films, have not hitherto received sufficient analysis in the light of the different class configurations of these societies. Finally, no attempt has been made to this day to analyse the connections between the development of the modes of representation ('the rise of cinematic language') and the development of the relations between different social classes and the cinema in the three countries taken one by one.

This chapter and the two following do not pretend to fill this gap completely; to do so I believe one would have to embark on an absolutely immense field of research (especially in those other countries for which the beginnings of the cinema seem less well documented—Sweden, Denmark, Germany, Russia). But I hope to be able to adumbrate certain avenues of investigation and to put forward some hypotheses, my aim being to give a certain social profile to phenomena that I shall examine elsewhere on the level of representation *sensu stricto.*

The country for which it can be said that the cinema and its audience were most massively and durably popular is France—particularly in the rather special sense of the French word *'populaire'*.

When the cinema began, class relations in France presented a quite specific picture, one contrasting strikingly with the situation in the two great English-speaking countries. In France the 1789 Revolution had been an essential stage in the struggle of the bourgeoisie against the feudal aristocracy, but it was by no means the final one. Several further serious confrontations (1830, 1848, 1858) and the disastrous adventure against Prussia were required before that bourgeoisie was firmly in the saddle. Nevertheless, twenty-five years after the Commune feudal ideology was still very much alive, particularly in the countryside, thanks to the confluence of the pressure of the Church and a remnant of feudal allegiance to the *château*. As a result, despite the horror of the Commune, despite the gulf opened up by the *Semaine Sanglante*, the bourgeoisie still, in certain respects, stood in serious need of the working class as a socio-political force (the force it had relied on already in 1830 and 1848)—notably in the fight for secular education, one of the basic issues at stake in the struggle against the monarchist party and the Church. The Radical Party, with its hectic republicanism and waggish populism, fulfilled this function perfectly. Thus, if *economic and political struggle* at this period revolved around the confrontation between a bourgeois-peasant alliance on the one hand and the proletariat on the other, the ideological struggle was more complex. To take one symptom: in Britain the campaign for temperance had been seen since the middle of the century by the 'ruling bloc' (the business bourgeoisie and the aristocracy) as contributing both to the needs of production and to the maintenance of public order (Chartist rioters often stoked the fires of their courage in a public house). Led in the main by the churches, the campaign can be seen as a real mass movement, and one of its ultimate results was the present English licensing hours, the restricted daytime opening of public houses and off-licenses. In France, by contrast, although a temperance movement did get off the ground, nearly fifty years later than its British equivalent (and on a much smaller scale), at the very same moment (1880), 'a law made it possible to open or move a drinking shop simply by making a declaration at the town hall. This was an essential step: *the tavern, that republican counter-church*, was no longer subject to the arbitrary functioning of administrative authorisation' (Mayeur & Rébérioux 1984, p.82—my italics).[1] This is a first indication that, even before the cinema appeared, the struggle for the control and use of popular leisure in France was not the same as in Britain.

For, in France, the structural development of industrial production had been quite different from that in Britain. Recent research (see Cottereau n.d.) has shown that the survival in France of dispersed production (craft workshops and outwork) at a time when the factory and its great concentrations of workers was becoming the norm in Britain is not simply a matter of backwardness. Rather, capitalist development in France took a different route. And although French working-class resistance only acquired major workers' organisations thirty years after the creation in Britain of the great trade unions, that resistance—apparently, at least, more 'anarchic', more individualistic—did force the employers to maintain more flexible (because more modest) structures of hiring and firing and labour discipline, making certain concessions to workers' control (over production norms, working conditions, etc.). Anarcho-syndicalism, the main strategy of the French working class until the First World War, was closely tied to this 'extended' nineteenth century, when a trade union in France was simply the gathering of a group of workers around a strike, and mass resistance consisted of a multiplicity of individual resistances. It was this anarchistic spirit that those who made films in France sought to please, massively until around 1908, then more selectively and indirectly by reference to a certain vulgar-but-acceptable literature through the 1920's and up to the present.[2]

Just what were the factors that helped keep the 'comfortable classes' (including for a long time even white-collar workers, minor civil servants and small peasants) away from the cinema and, correspondingly, drew to it particularly the manual workers of the cities and their families?

At least four kinds of immediate causes can be distinguished here: technological causes, economic causes, ideological causes and 'biological' causes. But, as we shall see, each of these categories comprises its own contradictions and maintains complex relations with the others, making this a rather clumsy taxonomy. For example, one factor that seems at first sight to be a technological one, the obligatory brevity of the earliest films, immediately turns out to have ideological and economic components, too.

In the earliest years, the level of development of certain technologies (particularly that of the manufacture of celluloid) made it objectively impossible to shoot for longer than a few tens of seconds at a time. Of course, as we shall see (pp.143f. below), in France and the USA in two very special genres—boxing matches and passion films—relatively long films were successfully made early on by attaching autonomous tableaux end to end. But the technology of direction—for direction really is a technology, and even in the primitive period a system of direction had to be developed—did not yet allow the establishment of a 'major narrative form' of any generalisability. In film programming the result for more than fifteen years was a sort of pot-pourri, a grouping of more or less 'varied' subjects, close, indeed, to the disjointed, open, relaxed forms liked by popular audiences (the circus, the music hall, the *caf'conc'*, the funfair) but only prized, among the bourgeoisie, by a very restricted intellectual elite (principally, in fact, the habitués of artistic cabarets like Le Chat Noir).

This disjunctive and heteroclite character of the cinema show—overdetermined by the contexts (the *caf'conc'*, the fairground, etc.) in which films were in the main projected—was to be socially determinant in France and in other countries, too. In France, the petty and middle bourgeoisie were drawn particularly to the homogeneous 'major forms' of vaudeville, boulevard theatre and naturalistic theatre, which allowed a limitless establishment and extension of the theatrical illusion. Thus it is clear that this 'technological cause' was in direct communication with the *ideological instance*.

No doubt the average French journalist was hardly equipped to formulate as explicitly as Gorky his class's reservations about the lack of realism of the Cinématographe. Nevertheless, the discourse that soon came to dominate the press concerned with it took it upon itself, much more explicitly in France than in other countries, to deny the cinema any possibility of access either to the continent of 'Reality' or to that of 'Art'. This discrepancy corresponds, of course, to the distance between the Russian bourgeois intelligentsia, progressive and proto-revolutionary, and the conservative, æstheticising Parisian intelligentsia. But the difference is, in this respect, not a pertinent one: the *defect* denounced is the same in both cases: the cinema 'is the best form of diversion for the mob. But it is not and cannot be an art.... It lacks the word, and that is no small matter!' (*Le Cinéma*, June 7th 1912). 'There are three great moments to the theatre: speech, three dimensions, staging. The Cinematograph, by contrast, is much less well endowed: it lacks speech and three dimensions, it only has staging' (ibid., April 10th 1912).

In France, even in a trade paper, presumably expected to favour the industry's interests, the absence of speech and three dimensions was the invariable motive for unfavourable comparisons with theatrical spectacle, only available to middle-class audiences, whose spokesmen these journalists were. I shall return to the point.

Another series of 'bourgeois-repellent' factors were of a 'biological' nature, or more strictly 'bio-ideological'. It now seems that the notorious fire at the Charity Bazaar which roasted dozens of choice specimens of the Parisian *beau monde* in 1897 did not slow down the growth of fairground cinema in France (as Georges Sadoul has been criticised for implying—see Deslandes & Richard 1968, p.164). But it is still reasonable to think that this disaster did for a time help differentiate the cinema audience and that Terry Ramsaye—out of fashion as a historian, although it should be remembered that he *lived through* the period—was not simply accepting an *a posteriori* myth when, in 1926, he wrote that, as a result of this fire, 'prejudicial feeling arose to impair seriously the status of the screen in the mind of the upper classes and their followers' (1926, p.356). Given that he is echoing an American viewpoint, one may imagine that it was even stronger in French minds at the turn of the century.

Indeed, the fear of fires caused by film projection was amply justified: most projection points in this period used nitrate film and acetylene or coal-gas lamps, an explosive combination if ever there was one. But at the same time, this fear was felt most particularly in those social strata for whom physical danger was not part of the normal conditions of the sale of their labour power. It was quite a different matter for the manual worker, *a fortiori* in a period of unrestrained capitalism in which industrial accidents, due in particular to fatigue (a twelve-hour day was still the norm), were even commoner than they are now. As well as the sense of risk in going to the cinema, there was the physical discomfort—also perfectly real—felt in looking at these jumpy, flickering pictures. The veteran American cameraman Fred Balshofer, who, in 1904, was working for a slide manufacturer, recalls in his memoirs that when he suggested to the latter that he might start making cinema films he was told: 'Make moving pictures? Why those flickering things hurt your eyes. They're just a passing fancy' (Balshofer & Miller 1967, p.3). Moreover, it is surely of some interest that the notorious Massachussets law forbidding movie houses from projecting pictures for more than two minutes at a time, with at least a five-minute pause 'to rest the eyes' between each projection, was only adopted in 1908, precisely at a time when the desire to bring the middle class into the movie house was beginning to gain ground.[3]

But danger *and* discomfort are the everyday lot of the manual labourer, be it the steeplejack, perched all day on his knees on a steep slope exposed to rain, sun and the risk of deadly falls, or factory workers (male and female), their ears filled with a constant din, their nostrils and lungs corroded by nauseous fumes and vapours, their fingers, their limbs, their life itself constantly at the mercy of a break in a cable or the overturning of a skip. Compared with these things, the cinema, with its smoke, its poor ventilation, its uncomfortable seats and the poorly policed atmosphere that was long the norm at every projection point, still seemed a haven of relaxation. But the discomforts of the venue, added to the fear of fire and eyestrain, helped put off a more squeamish middle-class audience.

Another, and perhaps more important reason for this affinity of the cinema with the popular strata, was economic. The low level of production, in numbers of films for four or five years, and in their lengths for at least fifteen, made it inconceivable for more than a decade (and not in France alone) that films could be profitably exhibited in a network of fixed cinemas, unless such a network were a very dense one from the outset. It was inevitable, at least in France (in the USA more diversified solutions were to be found), that recourse was had to already existing infrastructures, in particular to itinerant outlets, making it possible for each film to reach a sufficiently large audience to ensure a certain profitability. Most important was the network of fairs held regularly in every French city and town, but there was also the music hall and the *caf'conc'*. Hence the close cohabitation throughout the primitive period—which was to last in France until the First World War in certain respects—of the nascent cinema and the distractions of the lower classes of the cities, towns and even villages (although it seems established that in France fairground cinemas were rather unsuccessful among the rural population).[4]

This, therefore, was the set of conditions, already assembled at the beginning of the century, that was to give rise to production practices and a discourse about the cinema that simply reinforced and emphasised its *confinement to a popular ghetto*.

The French trade press reveals a clear class viewpoint: 'The cinematograph offers working people, after their daily toil, for a few *sous*, sometimes even in their local café, the illusions they crave in the most unexpected forms. It responds to ... the need ... [of] people with little leisure time who wish for violent nervous stimulation rather than intellectual exercise' (*Ciné-Journal* no. 67, 1908). For *Le Cinéma*, whose general attitude was very elitist, the cinema was, of course, 'the best form of diversion for the mob'. But as such it owed it to itself to remain as naive and 'direct' as possible. In a supposedly near future in which the cinema was to 'move towards science, geography, zoology, ethnography and reporting' (read: for bourgeois delectation and proletarian edification) 'only trick subjects, slapstick comedies interpreted by acrobats, and good old melodramas will survive. But audiences will quickly weary of cinematic adaptations which only give a very imperfect rendition of the literary works on which they are based.' This comment is directed against the Film d'Art and its aim to attract a middle-class audience, a tendency this paper did not encourage. 'It might be possible to create scenes for a specialised audience and attempt to make them artistic.... But the endeavour would be time-consuming, expensive and would only please a minority. What the producer wants, however, is quickly made films he can place in a large number of outlets.... The cinema just is what it is, with all its faults' (August 7th 1912).

This conservative Malthusianism and complacent elitism signify on the one hand: 'Don't rock the boat: we are dealing with a new opium of the people, which is also a source of profit' (mainly, it should be said, in the export market); and, on the other: 'Their cinema is good enough for them, so why should we, who have *our* theatre ...?' Five years after this article was published, Parisian high society was to discover **The Cheat** and the new American cinema, in which the incompatibility of cinema and bourgeois theatre was on its way to a resolution. But the attitude expressed here in the two main trade papers of the pre-War period proved durable, for the debate as to whether cinema could be an Art continued to fascinate the Parisian intelligentsia until the late 1920's. And this attitude probably goes a long way towards explaining why certain primitive and populist features persist in French films up to the First World War. In the USA, as we shall see, quite the contrary attitude was shared by ideologists, exhibitors and producers, and helped rapidly promote the embourgeoisement of film content and the installation of the IMR.

But this class viewpoint could also be expressed in less cynical, more idealistic guises.

In the memoirs written around 1930 which are one of the most fascinating sources on this period, Félix Mesguich (1933, pp.37-8) puts the 'credo' of the middle-class 'non audience' as follows:

If the views [I brought back] from London seem to me to justify the favour with which they were received at the Folies-Bergère, I fail to understand the widespread craze for a whole set of new creations [presented] at the same time. These pseudo-magical stories infuriated me. The audience's applause must, I suppose, be attributed to their surprise effect, and the fact that their extravagance was amusing. They no longer showed acrobatics, merely trickwork.[5]

In one film,

the dancer began his act on the floor, then climbed up a wall and carried on his movements upside down, with his feet on the ceiling, until he fell back to earth. Faced with such wretched stuff, I was more than ever convinced that something better than these improbable and childish fantasies was needed. Did not nature and the world still contain beautiful pictures for reproduction and revival? .... To my mind, the Lumière brothers had correctly established [the cinema's] true domain. The novel and the theatre suffice for the study of the human heart. The cinema is scenery, the dynamism of life, nature and its phenomena, crowds and their movements. Everything realised in movement falls to its part. Its lens, like the spectator's eye, is open on the world.

This states more or less the double position adopted initially by all the reasonably cultivated bourgeoisie of France and elsewhere. The analogical deficiencies, compared with the theatre, were, of course, aggravated by the *infantile* content of early films, and it is not, all in all, very hard to understand this antipathy of the respectable and those dependent on them to 'composed views'.

But how are we to explain the craze for 'actuality' cinema, for the 'scenic', typical of the 'enlightened' bourgeoisie *all over the then industrialised world?* For more than fifteen years in France, it is no exaggeration to claim that those middle-class spectators who did go to the cinema—and constituted only a tiny minority of the French audience—though they may have been exposed to other genres because of the mixed nature of the programmes, only went for a variety of forms of actualities. Two houses opened in 1906 on the Grands Boulevards in Paris. One of these, the Kinéma-Théâtre-Gab-Ka, centred its publicity on 'the ever novel attractions of actuality', while the other, the most luxurious cinema of the day, the Omnia-Pathé, displayed a poster 'representing an auditorium packed with old men, one looking like Monsieur Fallières. On the screen, an explorer presented his open umbrella to a lion. The caption, in capital letters, read "I tremble not"' (Fescourt 1959, p.29). An astute emblem, combining an evocation of the tastes of the comfortably-off—and masculine (see below)—audiences the cinema was trying to attract (at the Omnia seat prices were one, two and even three francs—see

Sadoul 1973, t.II, p.370),[6] tastes tending precisely toward travel films or films about exploration, and a concern to reassure social strata still deterred by trembling and flicker.[7]

But why this real fetishisation of the filmed document, which persisted in every country in its claim that 'the only real future' for the cinematograph lay in the class-room? *Le Cinéma*, launched in 1911, for several months gave twice as much space to reviews of new documentary and educational films as opposed to entertainment films. This proportion was eventually reversed in the Spring of 1912, probably in order to conform more to the realities of a profession which this journal had, after all, to recognise in order to survive. But even when not carried to such prescriptive extremes, the ideology was very widespread in the trade press.

Of course, there is the cult of reality, of nature, inherent in the analogistic ideology already discussed. But is that all?

One of the keys to a finer understanding of this phenomenon lies in the needs of the new French imperialism and the evolution of the relations between 'public opinion' and the colonial question since 1890: 'It is difficult today to imagine the vehemence and the extraordinary passion which characterised the arguments for and against colonisation in the 1880's' (Mayeur & Rébérioux 1984, pp.98-9). But from 1890 on, 'public opinion on colonisation was changing. Colonisation no longer aroused the hostility it had ten years earlier. The creation of the colonial army avoided the necessity of sending conscripts on overseas campaigns.' Indeed, no effort had been spared: 'The geographical societies were developing strongly; the Exhibition of 1889 gave much space to the colonies; exotic subjects were becoming more and more popular in literature' (ibid., p.172).

There is no doubt that the nascent cinema was to play its part in this propaganda concert and its aim: the banalisation of the scandal of colonisation (not only in France, either, since US imperialism soon took on new vigour with the war against Spain and Britain was endeavouring to consolidate its hold in Southern Africa). As early as 1896-7, the views of Algeria and Tunisia brought back by the Lumière cameramen are perfect examples of the vocation celebrated by the publicist F. Laurent fifteen years later in the following terms:

One indisputable advantage of the geographical film is that it helps link the colonies to the mother country. It shows us all the outlets offered to French enterprise by our vast overseas possessions.... It shows the mighty endeavours of our engineers over there, and reminds us of the Frenchmen sacrificing themselves to an ideal without even hoping for a little encouragement from a mother country so often ungrateful because it is ignorant. The cinema will be the best emigration agency of the future (*Le Cinéma*, May 24th 1912).

This directly propagandist activity of the scenic has a counterpart in the rubric 'military views' (more than seventy films in the Lumière catalogue of 1897) and the countless ceremonies of the Republic (and their monarchical equivalents abroad—the fascination the doings of royalty still exercise over the French petty-bourgeois mind is well known). Also in the Lumière catalogues for 1896-8: **Fêtes Franco-Russes** ('The Tsar's Visit to France', seven films); **Fêtes du jubilé de la reine d'Angleterre 1897** ('Queen Victoria's Diamond Jubilee Celebrations, 1897', nine films); **Voyage de M. le Président de la République en Russie** ('The French President's Visit to Russia', fourteen films); the same **en Vendée** ('The French President's Visit to the Vendée', nineteen films).

More generally, the pictures of distant places which very quickly became the speciality of the Lumière company and for several years ensured the success of its distribution activities harmonise wonderfully with the 'globe-trotter' fantasies of the medium and petty bourgeoisie, nourished by the tales of a Loti or a Barrès and by the new means of transport (see p.34 above).

As for poorer audiences, more than thirty years before paid leave they knew they had no chance of ever going to Japan, or even the Côte d'Azur. They could dream of it, of course, but were these films such as to stimulate their dreams, these series of culturally coded pictures, whether or no accompanied by a more or less learned lecture? And in fact, although popular audiences were familiar with this kind of film, which they saw in small cinemas with mixed programmes, the impression given by the trade press around 1908-11 (what would it have been in the great days of the Maison Lumière, before 1905?) is that they gave these films a fairly cool reception: 'Actualities and travel films have an important place in the programmes of the more elegant cinematographic theatres; our only cause for regret is that all audiences have not yet acquired the same taste for them' (*Ciné-Journal*, June 21st 1909). Deslandes and Richard (1968, pp.156-9) emphasise that there is no break between fairground 'actualities' (dioramas, waxworks) and those offered to the same audiences in the same social space by the cinematograph. But the abandonment of production by Lumière just as fairground exhibition was at its apogee, and the difficulties Mesguich experienced in finding employment in the only kind of production that he thought worthy of interest (he had to emigrate to Britain) are a fair indication that 'composed views' eventually supplanted 'scenics' in the tastes of popular audiences. It is true that spectacular actualities (e.g., the well documented events surrounding the struggle with the Bonnot gang) still pleased the masses in the fairgrounds in 1912, and it seems possible, or even probable, that, from the outset, there were two types of 'actualities', corresponding once again to a certain class division.

One last question: how did middle-class audiences, to the extent that they shared Gorky's criticisms, react to a picturisation that hardly changed until at least 1908? An anecdote from 1907, reported by Mesguich (1933, p.149), just back from a trip to Morocco, is perhaps significant:

> In a boulevard cinema I had the satisfaction of attending a representation of the events I had just witnessed.... The riflemen's bayonet charge was warmly applauded, but I also heard some comments:
>
> **A lady**—Superb, those Algerian sharpshooters, what style!
>
> **A gentleman**—I should have liked a closer view of the Chaouïas' faces.
>
> **The lady, without animosity**—Really the cameraman might have taken a few more risks.

Mesguich, like the middle-class spectators he overheard, took this problematic of 'a closer view' as a matter of simple physical courage, but the exchange is nevertheless the expression of a certain dissatisfaction at pictures of a 'brute reality' not yet enlivened either by editing with its closer shots or by synchronised sound. And yet the rather arid signs scattered over the screen did *speak* to these middle-class spectators, and with great eloquence. It was *their* war that they applauded, or else *their* army on manœuvres, or again the figure of *their* President of the Republic. As for some exotic landscape, it represented (perhaps) the location of their next holidays. In other words, the *proprietary dimension* of the cinematic image, already clearly recognised by the boulevard strollers in the first films of Louis Lumière (see pp.20f. above), was recaptured by most of the scenics. What could be more edifying for the 'uncultured masses' than the sight of these pictures portraying a reality stamped with the seal of possession in this way? Once again we have the fantasy of a cinema of the future entirely devoted to 'science, geography, zoology, ethnography and reporting'. However, the notion of the cinema as 'raising the level of the masses' was never, in France, to be translated into the reality it became in Britain and especially the USA. In fact—and perhaps this is what best defines the specificity of France in this field, the documentary ideology being shared by all these elites—the trade as a whole (producer-distributors, or, as they called themselves, 'publishers'—*éditeurs*—exhibitors and publicists) seems to have been *satisfied with a de facto situation* which disturbed neither their cultural privileges nor their economic interests. Indeed, in 1908, Pathé Frères, which produced the majority of French films up to the First World War, only realised 8 per cent of its enormous turnover in the French market. In 1912, the figure was still only 10 per cent. (See *Le Cinéma*, May 17th 1912.) At a time when the immigrant petty bourgeois who presided over the destinies of exhibition in America had long ago set out to conquer a *mass audience* (as opposed to a popular one), a 'respectable' audience, a conquest which was eventually to lead to the US domination of the world market, France remained content in the main to produce films characterised by a populism which, however strong and lively it may have been, remained in a rut. And these films, which in fact only reached a small minority of the French, soon threatened to lose their international audience, since everywhere this was gradually being embourgeoisified, and the Americans, the Danes and the Italians were already offering something different.

This lack of ambition can of course be explained in part by the traditional conservatism of French capitalism and by middle-class snobbery.[8] But I believe one of its sources is also the conviction that the populist cinema that had grown up in France, abounding in themes very close to the preoccupations and fantasies of a popular audience, borrowing its forms and its content from arts dear to the people, and, anyway, making back many times its costs on international sales alone (as it did until the War), had more advantages than disadvantages. There was no urgency to embourgeoisify the acknowledged source of amusement of a proletariat which was at the same time the most feared in Europe (for its revolutionary tradition) and one of the most exploited (throughout the period labour law lagged far behind that in Britain and Germany).

It should not, however, be concluded from this that no efforts were made in France to extend the cinema audience into the middle strata. On the one hand, as noted above, a few more comfortable houses had been established in Paris and in the provinces, and from 1910-12 these began to multiply. In production, mention must be made of the *séries d'art*, launched in 1908 by **L'Assassinat du duc de Guise**, the first film of the firm called Les Films d'Art, recently set up with the express aim of 'improving the quality' of French cinema. It was soon joined by the Société Cinématographique des Artistes et des Gens de Lettres (SCAGL), an outgrowth of Pathé, with Albert Capellani as its artistic director, and then by the Série d'Art made by Feuillade at Gaumont. For a few individuals had realised, especially after the brief recession of 1907 (more sharply felt in the USA, however, where its lessons were also better learnt), that an audience made up almost exclusively of the poor was a vulnerable one, that its loyalty was at the mercy of the economic cycle, and finally that its small size and low income did not provide a wide enough basis for an eventual expansion of the industry, in the face of the increasing strength after 1910 of international competition. On the other hand, despite a renewal of the comic tradition at Gaumont, the beginnings of a cinema of crime and adventure serials with the **Nick Carter** series (Jasset's first success with another new firm,

Fig. 4: **L'Assassinat du duc de Guise** (Le Bargy & Calmette, 1908).

Eclair), the notorious 'crisis of the subject' began to be felt: at Méliès, at Pathé, films began to repeat themselves. Of course, as we shall see, this was not just a crisis of the subject. It was also and above all a crisis of 'language'.

The *séries d'art*, with their Great Actors and Actresses and their Serious Subjects, survived in France until the War, but could hardly be considered a success overall. The audiences they were primarily intended for ignored them, just as they continued to ignore the cinema. The popular audiences of the fairgrounds and the cinemas of the lower-class districts that began to open in 1908 may have found them more congenial, especially when their 'Art' was tempered with a bit of 'good old melodrama', as was the case with a series like **Mimi Pinson** (1909-10) or a superproduction like **Les Misérables** (1912), produced respectively by Pathé and the SCAGL studio. But these firms, 'unlike Film d'Art, ... looked in the first place to a popular audience' (Sadoul 1973, t.I, p.48). Or rather, one should say, they had come so to look, given the coldness of the middle-class audience. Moreover, **Les Misérables** held the trump card of a large budget and production values way above those of most of the art films. But even this film could not boast more than what Georges Sadoul called 'a skimpy, mean budget. The production cost of **Les Misérables** (ten francs per metre of negative) was lower than that of Méliès's old *féeries*. This miserly policy blocked any progress with the new formula' (ibid., p.52).[9] This is one reason why these films remained so deeply attached to the primitive tableau with its painted backdrop, a relatively cheap formula. And it also suggests that this was not the most lucrative sector of French production. At any rate, it does not seem that the art series often received the moral support their promoters might legitimately have counted on from the publicists. We have already seen the opinions of the columnist of *Le Cinéma*, and if his counterpart in the *Ciné-Journal* felt he had to salute in the art film 'a new dignity for the cinema, hitherto held back by its mediocre ambitions,' he concluded nonetheless that he preferred 'real views, life as it flourishes all over the world, which the cinema should seek out everywhere.' And in the prestigious daily *Le Temps*, the theatrical critics Claretie and Brisson constantly stressed how the pictures of the Film d'Art and its successors suffered from their lack of the voice: 'The cinema is not in competition with the theatre, it creates a nostalgia for it,' claimed Brisson in 1912, and he spoke of 'these over-rapid, over-feverish, sometimes over-crowded, over-compact pictures.'

These reactions shed light on the basic contradiction of the art film, the fact that it insisted on reproducing in the cinema the grand gestures of bourgeois theatre, but did so by means of a *primitive mode of representation* (cf. pp.186ff.), one absolutely incapable of achieving this *translation* to the two-dimensional screen. It seems that it was not until the appearance in France of **The Cheat** and the American middle-class cinema, produced by an industry that had made gigantic strides between 1910 and 1915, that French publicists were able to find on the screen the novelistic or theatrical presence that was in fact what they wished for, that a Delluc, a Vuillermoz or an Epstein could become the enthusiastic defenders of this new American cinema, precisely in the name of bourgeois art.[10]

Also dating from before the War, one technological velleity, more a fantasy than an innovation, with the sole raison d'être of making the cinema more attractive to the middle class, offers a clue to the persistence of the aversion it still felt for the darkened picture houses ... precisely because they were dark. Around 1909 there is much discussion in the trade press of a projection system called, rather enigmatically, 'dactylographic'. This was a technique for making the screen image sufficiently bright to allow films to be projected without lowering the house lights. The editors of the *Ciné-Journal* saw the following advantages in this process: 'The show is not so tiring to the eyes as it is in the dark, and if it is boring one need only unfold one's newspaper and one can read' (January 21st 1909). A few months later, the same journal claimed that the new technique would spare the spectator 'the discomfort attendant on a long stay in the dark' and facilitate the evacuation of the auditorium in the event of a fire.[11] This project was, of course, never carried to completion, precisely because it is antinomic to the project of the *motionless voyage*, of the imaginary presence which is the raison d'être of a mode of representation already in gestation in the USA and elsewhere.

The suggestion that a constantly lit auditorium would allow one to 'unfold one's newspaper if the show is boring' is also interesting. Inscribed in it is the contempt the middle-class spectator felt for films still enjoyed by the masses. In this connection it is interesting to evoke one of the arguments put forward against the introduction, around 1912, of long films, which began to become an issue throughout the world thanks to the efforts of the Danes and the Italians, but also of French film-makers like Jasset and Capellani. In *Le Cinéma*, E.L. Fouquet pleaded for the maintenance of 'the variety of the shows .... Only in this way can one please all the different audiences' (March 29th 1912). In the contemporary context, this means, on the one hand, that popular audiences would never be able to follow the long films likely to be appreciated by 'cultivated' spectators, and, on the other, that the few members of the middle class who frequented popular projection sites were only there for the actualities interspersed in the programme, and that long films aimed at the masses would inevitably drive them away. The moral, as usual: things are all right as they are. This discourse undoubtedly contributed largely to a decade and more of 'backwardness' for French cinema, but it has to be recognised that it did not prevent the development of the tastes of the audience, or at any rate of exhibitors and distributors.[12]

Figures presented by Sadoul (1973, t.III, p.25) show that in 1913 the French popular audience substantially deserted French films, preferring, to judge by the number of films presented in Paris—I have no direct audience figures—the Italian blockbusters and above all the many often innovatory films from the USA. Many factors might·explain this phenomenon, including purely commercial and economic ones. As Sadoul suggests, the fading inspiration and thematic and stylistic repetitiveness into which the mighty Pathé machine had sunk, had at last sapped the complicity established in the first decade between French films and French audiences. But the fact that an urban popular audience with social, ethical and ideological reference points generally quite remote from those of the American cinema, which, in particular, often idealised the values of rural society, should nevertheless prefer that cinema to that of its own country, also tells us a great deal about the extraordinary, and ultimately libidinal, gratificatory power of the IMR in gestation in the USA, independently of manifest content.

We should now turn back to the heyday of that French populist cinema, to look more closely at its contents, and at its role in social control.

In his preface to the *Théâtre Complet* of Pixérécourt, the first codifier in France of the popular melodrama, Charles Nodier wrote: 'The pulpits were empty, only disquieting speeches were to be heard from the tribunes, the theory of material interests had displaced the notion of any other destination.... Where were men to draw lessons ... if not from melodrama?' (1841, pp.viii-ix; cit. Ubersfeld 1972, p.672).

The melodrama is undoubtedly the first great invention by the ideologists of the bourgeoisie to divert to its advantage—and profit—the leisure demands of a lower-class population, any inactivity of which they found disturbing: 'The melodrama is a hybrid: aimed at a popular audience, it partakes of the parade, the theatre, the fairground in its reliance on music and dance, of bourgeois drama in its sentimentalism; but its peculiar and novel character lies in the representation of violent actions and thrilling vicissitudes. It is a kind of "Western", a spectacle the bourgeoisie supplies to the people to satisfy and channel its supposedly violent instincts' (Ubersfeld 1972, p.669).

As for cinema, it emerged in a period when the secularisation of the mass of the French people had gone further than under the Restoration,[13] when the socio-political context was such that ideological control had to take new forms. If the melodramatic plot reappears as such in some films of this early period, it was not to be the privileged mode of intervention in the French primitive cinema,[14] but it may be that the hybrid character of the programmes and especially the 'cathartic' function of the dominant genres (comics, trick films), which had the same direct grip on the popular unconscious as the melodrama, represent an extension of its role.

I lack the ability—and the means—to undertake here the study it deserves of the extraordinary symbolism that surfaces so insolently in the *féeries* and trick films, and in the strange pre-1906 burlesques that we often find more disturbing than funny.

THE WRONG SIDE OF THE TRACKS 61

We need an inventory of the erotic and scatological motifs implicitly or explicitly present in almost all these films, an analysis of
the regressive and hysterico-aggressive structures that inform
them, and a definition of the infantilism (in the clinical sense) in
which they are steeped. This would probably make it even clearer
why middle-class audiences should have felt so ill at ease at this
flaunting of everything bourgeois propriety repressed at the turn
of the century. And why, on the other hand, popular strata
among whom a 'Rabelaisian' tradition still flourished and who
had never aspired to puritan respectability in the English manner
should have felt so much at ease with it.

In addition, at the level of manifest content—all I am going to
try to deal with here—it is obvious that a middle-class audience
just was not at home with a great many of these films. For,
unlike traditional melodrama, in which a 'popular form' was
yoked to an ideological schema clearly functioning as a 'vehicle
for the political mythology of the liberal bourgeoisie' (Ubersfeld
1972, p.674),[15] many of the films of this early period—and not
just comic films—reflect in a confused and contradictory way the
everyday experience and even the profound aspirations of working people. In other words, we are dealing with an approach
which is demagogic rather than edifying.

In his excellent study of the nickelodeon, which I shall return
to below (p.120), Russell Merritt criticises those historians and
publicists who have claimed, vis-à-vis American primitive cinema,
that immigrants and indigenous proletarians were 'reflected' in
the films they saw (the films they were, for a time, the only people to see). On the basis of a survey of the trade press in 1907
and 1908, he has established that, of 1,056 American-produced
films offered to exhibitors, a grand total of eight dealt with immigrants or the poor. Seven others produced by Pathé and Gaumont which found favour with American distributors can be
added to this modest total (1976, p.72 n.18).

To suggest the contrast that was possible between American
and French cinemas at this time, I can offer the following evidence: 292 French films produced between 1900 and 1909 (the
majority by Méliès and Pathé) which seem to constitute, at least
for the 1900-06 period, the surviving corpus of fiction films
currently listed by the Archives which are members of FIAF,

were viewed at Brighton in June 1978. They can be broken down as follows: 93 films reveal an explicit populism, insofar as either the urban lower classes are treated sympathetically in them (64) or they express popular prejudices and animosities (against the bourgeoisie, the peasantry, the police, etc.) (29), whereas 117 are *féeries* or trick films demonstrating in one way or another a profound affinity with the fairground, the circus, the music hall, etc. Thus a total of 223 films demonstrating a real complicity with the 'popular mind'. On the other hand, only 13 films address an edifying discourse to that same audience (of a melodramatic type: **Les Victimes de l'alcoolisme**—'Alcohol and its Victims'—and **La Probité recompensée**—'Honest Peggy'), and only five are religious. Only eleven can be regarded as addressed to members of the middle classes (but the figures exclude all scenics). By contrast, the number of films addressed explicitly to men[16] is impressive: 32 films of male voyeurism or with some other titillating feature.[17]

Let us now look more closely at the content of these populist films.

On the one hand, not forgetting my earlier point about the café, 'that republican counter-church', films in which wine appears in a sympathetic light as 'the worker's friend' seem to have been at least as numerous as temperance films. A subject like **La Fête à Joséphine** (1905) could not, I believe, have been produced anywhere but in France. A simple but quite charming film, in which a not very well-off man buys an enormous pot plant for his 'Joséphine's name day', then, on the way home, after repeated stops in cafés, accumulates both libations and friends. Finally the whole gang, drunk and happy, arrive home in a hired coach, where Joséphine chases them away with a broom .... This is much closer to the 'drinking stories' illustrated by caricatures in *L'Assiette au beurre* (or simply swapped at the bar) than to temperance propaganda. A Pathé film of 1906, **Je vais chercher du pain** ('I'll Fetch the Bread'), unfolds a very similar tale.

Temperance even became an object of ridicule, along with bourgeois morals: in **Drunkard Against His Will**, an abstaining bourgeois—who takes complacent pride in his abstinence as compared with his 'normally' indulging family—leaves home, presumably for the office. As a result of a minor accident which leaves him stunned, he almost unknowingly allows a group of sympathetic proletarians to administer him a glass of liquor as a stimulant; the resultant drunkenness causes a new accident, he has to swallow a new 'stimulant', once again administered by solicitous passers-by, and so on, until he is carried back home in a piteous state to suffer the taunts of his family.

The makers of these films—Zecca, then Heuzé, Nonguet and others at Pathé, Alice Guy at Gaumont—whatever their social origins (see pp.72f. below), quickly discovered a specially rich comic vein in class antagonisms. They appealed to the complicity of their normal audiences by mocking the real or supposed traits attributed to other social classes. Let me cite the admirable film preserved in the National Film Archive, London, as **Brown's Duel** (1906?), in which a *type* drawn from this stock of stereotypes— the irascible and repressive bourgeois paterfamilias—becomes, by a simple process of accumulation, the motor of an enormous hysterico-repetitive farce: having cut himself shaving, he begins by beating up the members of his own family; leaving home, he lashes out with his cane at passers-by, hits his own employees, and thrashes waiters and other customers in a café, until finally he is appropriately punished in a comic knockabout duel with another bourgeois; he is then brought back home in a terrible state but still in a furious temper.

I might also mention **Pauvre frac** ('Poor tailcoat'), in which a top-hatted bourgeois has his new tailcoat soiled, torn and finally stolen in the course of a series of entanglements he himself is hardly aware of but of which proletarians are always complicit witnesses along with the audience. Moreover, the film does not end with a picture of the bourgeois, who disappears from it, but with a group of tramps and thieves throwing the remains of the tailcoat into a river: 'We wouldn't be seen dead in that!' (the spirit of Richepin hovers over many of these films).

Another social category for which the lower classes of the towns have a traditional distrust: the peasantry.[18] Although it is a chase film, Zecca's **L'Incendiaire** ('The Incendiary', 1905) is not really a comic, and anyway rural subjects, uncommon as such, are more rarely comics than urban ones; the country is the location for stark tragedy. Here a tramp carelessly falls asleep under a haystack with his pipe in his mouth. Enraged by the costly fire that results, a mob of peasants chase the poor tramp over hill and dale, catch him, and hang him from a tree! Cut down at the last minute by a migrant working woman, he is taken to the migrants' camp and given shelter and care there. The film thus openly sides against the traditional rural community and with outlaws and marginals, to whom the urban lower classes felt much closer. Such anti-peasant prejudice appears again and again in the history of the populist cinema. Take **Jalousie et folie** ('Jealousy and Madness', 1906), a drama astonishing in its realism and its pessimism, in which a peasant, crazed by jealousy, dies a madman, shot by the police. Or some of the episodes of Feuillade's famous series *La Vie telle qu'elle est* ('Life as it really is', 1911-12), with their explicit titles: **Les Vipères** ('Village Gossip'—literally 'The Vipers'), **Un drame au pays basque** ('Tragedy in the Basque Country'), **Le Roi Léar du village** ('A Village King Lear'—based on Zola's *La Terre*; cinema was moving closer to naturalism proper). Such films are evidence of the close symbiosis between the cinema of the fairground period and the mentality of the urban proletariat, but also of the small number of peasants in the audience and the resultant lack of concern to spare their feelings.[19]

Of course, the political limitations of this urban populism emerge clearly once it touches on the realities of the class struggle. In evocations of distant events such as the Russian Revolution of 1905 it was still possible to be 'on the people's side'. In Zecca's fine film **La Révolution en Russie** ('Revolution in Russia', often known as 'Battleship Potemkin') there is no doubt that the audience is expected to sympathise with the oppressed and rebellious masses. The same is true of his **Le Nihiliste** ('Socialism and Nihilism', 1906). But **La Grève** ('The Strike'), again by Zecca (1903), with its action taking place much closer to home, also has a quite different class content, as George Sadoul's enumeration of the scenes that make it up shows: 1) The manager refuses to arbitrate. 2) The murder of the manager by the strikers. 3) The arrest of the trade-union secretary. 4) The return to work. 5) The future: the union of Capital and Labour (1973, t.II, p.311).

As for **La Grève des bonnes** ('The Maids' Strike', Pathé, 1906), it seems to amalgamate suffragette demonstrations and strikes of women workers, and rather heavy-handedly ridicules both.

However, at the end of the film the strikers' brutal arrest by policemen is more in accord with many of the spectators' experience (strikes were on the increase in France from 1905) and the burlesque fraternisation of strikers and soldiers in one of the sequences is an evocation of real aspirations.

In 1909, just as the class-collaboration projects proposed by Aristide Briand were in the public eye, a Gaumont film offers a highly appropriate discourse, combining populism with paternalism. **Un Drame à l'usine** ('Tragedy in the Factory') shows a foreman sacked for cruelty who re-establishes himself in the eyes of his subordinates and his bosses by saving a group of workers trapped by a fire.

The Commune itself, co-opted by 'Radical Socialism' since the turn of the century, made a few timid appearances on the screen. In **Sur la barricade** ('On the Barricade'), one of the last films made by Alice Guy at Gaumont (1907), the camera stands resolutely on the side of the insurgents. However, it is very much against his will that the young hero of the story is caught on the 'wrong side' by the Versaillais, and the final pardon torn from them by his mother on her knees is accompanied by a clear lesson: 'Better not get involved in such things.'

Generally speaking, contemporary politics in the narrow sense is what is most strikingly absent from this cinema. One can, of course, cite Méliès's very fine film on **L'Affaire Dreyfus** ('The Dreyfus Case') and another film on the same subject made that same year, 1899, by Pathé. But there seems to be no trace on the screen of the bitter struggle between Republican and Catholic forces which resulted in 1905 in a definitive separation of Church and State. It was just possible to evoke the great strikes that shook the country from 1906 on, in a style dear to anarchism (strikes as festivals), but the opposition between republicans and clericals probably divided the popular audience too sharply to receive similar treatment.

It is hardly surprising that it was an anarchist type of revolt, and especially 'individual recuperation' or scrounging, that were most sympathetically treated in this period of flourishing anarcho-syndicalism. It even seems justifiable to call it a *dominant feature*, one which was always present and reached its apotheosis, in the era of the Bonnot Gang, in the Feuillade of **Fantômas** and

Les Vampires. In comic films of this type, pride of place is given, not to the victim of the crime, the policeman or the customs officer, but to the thief, the poacher or the smuggler. For example, the wonderful **Dévaliseurs nocturnes** ('Burglary by Night', 1904), with its burglars walking the rooftops as black silhouettes like the shadow puppets of Le Chat Noir and escaping the policeman on his own bicycle, or the famous **Les Chiens contrebandiers** ('Dogs Used as Smugglers', 1906), an epoch-making film not only in the astonishing activities of its team of trained dogs, outwitting the customs officers again and again in a long chase through the Pyrenées, but also in the very advanced editing[20] with which this chase is represented. Also worth noting is a curious Pathé film of uncertain date, **The Dog and His Various Merits**, half fiction, half documentary, that gives equal status to the dogs of a huntsman, a baker, a shepherd and—a poacher!

The poverty of the lower classes and their life style, although they are legibly inscribed in the pictures of very many French films of this period, are rarely central to their plots. That is why **Il ne faut pas d'enfants** ('No Children!', 1906), the general tone of which would rather link it to the 'down with the rich' series, is something of an exception: a large family have been evicted and are looking for lodgings, but they meet repeated refusals from landlords who will not accept children. The comedy of the film derives from their efforts to smuggle their children into a flat owned by a particularly surly couple. But notwithstanding that it is a comic film, when the plot is discovered, the whole family are forcibly dumped on the street without further ado. No last-minute change of heart on the part of the landlords, no sentimental sympathy sweetens the final scene, which is presented, on the contrary, as an amusing but bitter reconfirmation of the realities of class oppression: the family pick up their overladen cart and set off again.

Another Pathé film with a noteworthy inscription of class differences and of special interest in this respect to the social historian is **The Clumsy Photographer** (1906). It retails the adventures of a photographer who tries to take snapshots of various people he meets while walking round the streets of Paris. On each occasion his attempt fails and ends in a minor gag-catastrophe at his expense. But what is most striking about this film is its social

Fig. 5: **Dévaliseurs nocturnes** (Pathé, 1904).

bias: when our hero wishes to photograph a bourgeois, the latter attacks him—and this attack constitutes the shot's gag. On the contrary, whenever he tries to photograph a small craftsman or a group of workers, the latter are delighted, comb their hair, pose to their best advantage ... and it has to be the photographer himself who produces the gag by some false move (e.g., he falls off a roof while trying to photograph a group of steeplejacks). There are two sides to the clumsiness of this petty-bourgeois artisan: facing lower-class people who are perfectly at their ease, he cannot control his own body; facing members of the bourgeoisie, he does the unforgivable, in ignorance of the fact that they *claim ownership of their own images*. Given that this is still a time when the cinematic image does not yet legally belong to anyone, belongs, in fact, to the poor, and that the latter certainly do not assume any right to their own images, knowing that all they possess is their labour power, the semantic richness of the film is clear (see Edelman 1979).

The small trades of Paris that appear one by one in this film are often the *tacit subject* of films of this period. Given the still largely artisanal character of Parisian economic activity, it can be said that with these films we are dealing with a cinema growing out of the everyday lives of its most immediate audiences. But of course, these films were also directed at a provincial audience, and even more at an international one. Some chase films or itinerary films (e.g., **Pauvre frac**, described above) offer, alongside the manifest plot—generally a series of gags as a set of variations on a theme—a secondary plot, a kind of 'guided tour' of the monuments of Paris.[21]

I have referred in the main to comic films, films whose comedy is, no doubt, still cruder than that of the great comic school of the USA in the next decade, less inventive than the great French school of 1908-15 (Cohl, Durand, etc.), but still offers—another *dominant* feature—an extraordinarily down to earth *cult of pleasure*, popular in the fullest sense, and inevitably offensive to the repressed bourgeois sensibility of the turn of the century. How much that occasional spectator must have regretted not being able to unfold his newspaper in the face of the animal pleasure created by a film like **Madame a des envies** ('Madame's Cravings'), in which a wonderfully sprightly pregnant woman falls on

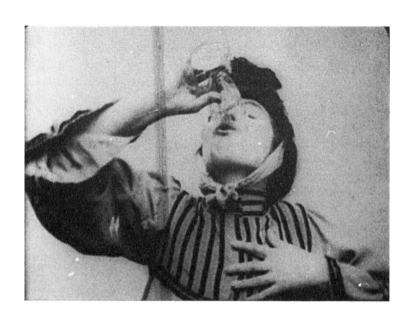

Fig. 6: **Madame a des envies** (Gaumont, 1907).

everything eatable, drinkable or suckable, including the pipe of a passer-by, which makes her so sick she vomits up her baby in the middle of a cabbage patch. Middle-class reactions to **Les Effets du melon** ('The Effects of a Melon'—presumably over-ripe, it causes a bottleneck at the lavatory door),[22] or **Erreur de porte** ('The Wrong Door'—a country bumpkin mistakes a telephone box for a lavatory and the telephone itself for the pan ....) are anyone's guess.

But genres other than the comics were recruited to this overriding populism. Some trick films, even, convey very explicitly the fantasies of the exploited worker: **Rêve d'un marmiton** ('A Scullion's Dream') and a film preserved in Wiesbaden under the title **The Dreams** (1906) present manual workers (servants, assistant cooks, boots, gardeners) who see in their dreams their daily tasks being carried out without effort as if by magic, thanks to the techniques of frame-by-frame animation.

Finally, after 1903, Pathé and its film-makers Zecca and Lucien Nonguet introduced a genre that does not appear again until the rise of television, a kind of semi-documentary, which I shall discuss later in relation to the place it occupies in what I call the Primitive Mode of Representation (see pp.186ff. below), but which is of interest to us here insofar as these films depict, sometimes with a 'gripping' realism, the life and/or work of the poor. The effect of authenticity here is due partly to remarkable sets (sometimes incorporating parts of the Pathé buildings at Vincennes) in which the artist, Lorant-Heilbronn, seems to have invented the 'poetic realism' of a Meerson, a Trauner or a Wakhevitch thirty years in advance. It is also, paradoxically, due to the introduction of fictional acting codes in a practically plot-free context, which confers upon these films an unusual 'spareness'. The introduction of actuality shots in a composed-view context, on the contrary, while contributing a kind of label of reality to some films, also affects their unity, bringing them closer to what, to the modern eye, almost looks like avant-gardism.

Among the most striking of these films is **Au pays noir** ('Tragedy in a Coal Mine', Nonguet 1905). The argument of this film is austere, but its pictures are sumptuous, stripped of all sentimentality and rich in social observation. In the first tableau, the younger son sets off for the mine, accompanying his elder brother and his father for the first time. But we also see that the grandfather is suffering from 'black lung'. The pan across an enormous painted backcloth accompanying the workers to the pit-head is very moving, the pathos of this passage to a workplace that the film shows to be highly dangerous being conveyed in a thoroughly modern litotes (cf. p.170 below). The tragedy of the 'fire damp explosion' may display a certain amount of overacting, but it is visually sharp and austere, while the dénouement is unsparing: the dead are dead, and can only be mourned.

In the same series, **Au bagne** ('Scenes of Convict Life', Nonguet?, 1905) describes a convict's life with an even more exemplary sobriety, and finally forces the spectator to sympathise *with the convict*, so visibly inhumane is the regime to which he is subjected. This is moreover the sentiment called for by the description in the Pathé catalogue, whose author banks on popular complicity: 'Spectators will delight in being able to spot a series of types of the social rebel, figures who, despite the dreadful repression to which they are subjected by the law, never give up, even unto death.' In fact, helped by 'primitive distance', the film is far more impassive. We see 'The Office' (the convicts arrive in the prison), 'The Fettering' (in the prison forge, the convicts' irons are welded on and they are then branded), 'Hard Labour', 'The Scourging', 'The Revolt', 'The Dungeon. The Escape' (several tableaux, including real exteriors), 'The Arrest' (also real exteriors), 'The Execution' and, finally, 'The Immersion' (again a real exterior showing very prosaically, but very movingly, the sinking of the body into the sea at the end of a long quay). These are the intertitles of the series of tableaux constituting this fine film, whose style and imagery recall those of the covers of *Le Petit Parisien*, but whose class content is appreciably more nuanced than that journal's, thanks especially to an astonishing de-dramatisation.[23]

This populist complicity is, of course, quite mixed in its makers' intentions: it is the product of opportunism, commercial unscrupulousness, a presumably barely conscious political calculation. But it is also true that of those making films in France in the early days many were of modest origins themselves. Ferdinand Zecca was the son of a theatre concierge and himself a *caf'conc'* stage manager, while Georges Hatot, who directed composed views for Lumière before moving to Pathé and then becoming one of the founders of the Eclair company, 'was a crook; he was eventually tried for his involvement in the Stavisky affair'. As for Louis Gasnier, future director of **The Perils of Pauline**, 'he was once the head of the *claque* at the Théâtre Saint Martin' (Diamant Berger 1977, pp.14-15).

It is true that Méliès came from a good family, but he had for years been a specialist in a type of show attracting above all children and their nurses. The objective complicity of the lower classes and the children of the middle class is an important reality in the early decades of the cinema. Henri Fescourt, who was 30 in 1910, explains in his memoirs (1959, p.47) that at this time

I walked past the Omnia-Pathés, the Gab-Kas, the other film theatres on the boulevards or in the suburbs, and even the Gaumont-Palace, without stepping inside.... Why is it, I may be asked, that neither you nor your friends ever saw a film worthy of the name? There are connoisseurs, René Clair or Jean Renoir, say, who can remember curious and comic films of the period. There is a simple explanation. These film-makers were little more than children at this time. As such they belonged to the cinema-going public. My generation preceded theirs and these entertainments had no attraction for us.

Indeed—Sartre, too, testifies to this in *Les Mots* (1964, p. 81)— although the respectable bourgeois would hardly venture into a cinema before 1910, he might well send his children there (with their nurses, mothers, grandmothers, etc.), since in its childishness the cinema was 'good enough for them'.

****

I think this picture of a French cinema seemingly quite content in the popular 'ghetto', a contentment actively supported by critics and publicists, of a cinema not just rejected by the middle class but making no effort to attract it, this picture sheds a lot of light on the persistence of certain primitive features in French films, on what is usually called their 'backwardness' with respect to American ones. The entrance into the cinema of petty-bourgeois film-makers with intellectual pretensions such as Feuillade, Jasset and Perret did not make any fundamental difference, at least not until about 1912. However innovatory they may have been, however beautiful the system of staging in depth that was their major contribution to the 'language' of the cinema, their films continued to observe the basic features of the primitive cinema (frontality, distance, centrifugality, autarchy of the tableaux) which I shall analyse in detail below. It is true that Perret, especially in **L'Enfant de Paris** ('In the Clutch of the Apaches') and **Le Roman d'un mousse** ('The Curse of Greed')—both of 1913—introduced linked series of shots, especially in a few exterior sequences, a few years later than the Danes and the Americans. But his interiors remain highly 'theatrical', just like almost all Feuillade's work until **Les Vampires**. Sadoul has admirably demonstrated how Méliès persisted in his system until he finally ceased production in 1912; yet Méliès does not seem to be a unique case of incomprehensible obstinacy but simply a rather extreme case of the historico-ideological situation which informed the whole French cinema until the World War, and left profound traces until the arrival of the talkies and beyond: see, for example, the enormous number of mismatched eyelines in Duvivier's **La Belle équipe** (1936!), when similar lapses were inconceivable in a comparably budgeted American film of the period.

Why then should one be surprised that it was not until the arrival in France of **The Cheat** and other advanced American films that the bourgeois intelligentsia began at last to take an interest in the cinema? Until then the French cinema practically failed to address it, and not only where content was concerned. For the same reasons, why should we be surprised that, despite the 'lessons' of American films on French screens for more than a decade, so many French films of the 1920's still show quite remarkable archaic aspects. **Le Miracle des loups**, made in 1924 by Raymond Bernard as his fourth feature film in five years, is still in many respects more like a pre-War film (the problem of the 360-degree spatialisation of the sets, in particular, is completely unsolved). Just like Epstein in a few scenes in **La Chute de la Maison Usher** and L'Herbier in a key scene in **L'Argent** (two masterpieces of 1928), his reverse shots still ignore the rules of screen direction.[24]

On the other hand, the American lesson was assimilated very quickly and with astonishing mastery by Antoine, Feyder, and especially Gance, whose **La Dixième symphonie** (1918), directly inspired by **The Cheat**, is in the forefront of world 'progress' as far as classical editing is concerned. The fact that his 1927 masterpiece, **Napoléon**, is located to some extent within the primitive space-time he grew up on seems more a matter of a kind of deliberate step backwards in the style of **Caligari**.

Nor had the arrival on the scene of a second generation of directors—Feuillade, Perret, Jasset—altered in any fundamental way the specifically French character of a cinema which nonetheless thrived mainly on its foreign market until the First World War. Charles Pathé, returning from the USA in 1918, delivered an ultimatum to his fellow professionals: the French industry must become Americanised or disappear. During the 1920's, however, with the gradual development of a national audience, this cultural specificity was maintained through a policy of popular quality productions—signed Jacques Feyder, Jacques de Baroncelli, Léon Poirier, Raymond Bernard and many others— no doubt to the detriment of the industry's capacity to conquer foreign markets ... and most notably that of the United States. This phenomenon can still be observed today

But all these questions of 'French backwardness', of the development of the audience in France—is it true, as some claim, that middle-class audiences only entered the cinema en masse when the latter began to speak, like *their theatre?*—remain to be studied on more solid foundations. My hope is that I have at least raised these highly complex problems.

NOTES

1   In the Catholic magazine *Le Fascinateur* (1904, p.134), there is a reference to the fact that the Church was explicitly responding to this dangerous rival in its use of projections, first of lantern-slides, later of moving pictures.

2   A contemporary film-maker like Paul Vecchiali subscribes to a populism deriving presumably from such novels as those of André Lhote, but also linked directly with that of Jacques Feyder (**Crainquebille, Visages d'enfants**). The latter, by contrast, is merely the literary echo (via Anatole France in particular) of the less mediated populism of someone like Zecca.

3   And only a year before the technology to suppress flicker began to be widely installed.

4   Our main debt of gratitude to Jacques Deslandes and Jacques Richard is for their admirable documentation of this cohabitation, their demonstration that 'the cinema was an extension by new technical devices of the traditional genres of fairground attraction' (1968, p.162).

5   Mesguich was so obsessed by authenticity and repelled by trick effects that thirty years later he shamefully 'confessed' to the few minor tricks he had had to use at the time, as if this was a real blot on his escutcheon.

6   Jean Mitry (1967, pp.145-6) is right to stress the fact that the working class were unable to go to permanent cinemas until 1911 not only because of the high seat prices, but also because of their working hours and conditions, which certain overdue reforms relieved somewhat after that date. But in doing so he seems to me to underestimate the links forged between the working class and the cinema by the fairgound—which he claims was only visited by what he calls '*le populaire*' once a year and then in small numbers, given the small capacity of the booths. This is to forget that the programmes presented by the fairground booths were often changed during their longer stopovers, which in a big town could be several weeks, and that there were many stopover points in the Paris suburbs. It is to forget the increasing size of the booths. Above all it is to forget that, while it was only in 1905 that permanent cinemas began to proliferate, in that same year Pathé sold at least 240,000 metres of film (2,700 copies at an average length of 88 metres) on the French market alone, still essentially a fairground market. Admission prices in fairgrounds varied from ten to forty centimes; it is known that by 1899 the typical working-class household in the Paris region spent from twenty to twenty-five per cent of its income in the *caf'conc'*; so it is by no means impossible that where cinema, too, is concerned, the demand for leisure could have over-ridden the effects of exploitation, which had by no means worsened in 1905. Finally, '*le populaire*' should not be restricted to the industrial worker in the modern sense, since most French 'industry' still took the form of small workshops. And in the large towns, the category also includes artisans and other modest groups (the messenger boys, saleswomen and dispatch staff of the large stores, for example). All in all, it seems very difficult to deny the existence of privileged connections between the popular audience and the cinema. Of course, Mitry's book was written several years before the appearance of Deslandes and Richard's key work, but his underestimation of the fairground cinema and privileging of the permanent theatre even before its presence was economically or socially determinant seem to result from ideological considerations: 'real cinema is seen in cinemas'. As for the claim that workers could not have found satisfaction in the edifying banalities of the production of the period, it

testifies to an ignorance, understandable enough in 1967, of the films of the first decade, in which, precisely, edifying cinema is the exception (see below).

7   The elimination of flicker only became more or less universal around 1909 when the existing stock of projectors had been replaced and the multi-bladed shutter—already commercially available several years previously—had become the norm.

8   *Ciné-Journal* complained on December 10th 1908 that, out of contempt for the cinema, the diplomatic corps had refused to encourage the implantation of French distribution in Turkey and other countries.

9   André Antoine joined SCAGL in 1913 to work on Capellani's **Quatre-Vingt-Treize** (from Victor Hugo). Perhaps it is for this reason that this splendid film—which was released in 1921 but would certainly not have seemed dated at that time—inaugurates the history of a French 'commercial' cinema that refuses to look down on its popular audience (by contrast with Louis Feuillade's well-known cynicism, for example). Its acting, the authenticity and beauty of its many location scenes and above all the intellectual, psychological and political qualities of a script that does full justice to Hugo's portrayal of the French Revolution's two 'extremisms' (Chouans and Jacobins), make this film at least the equal of **The Birth of a Nation**, a work in every way comparable to it and produced in the same year.

10 The Surrealists, of course, stand out in contrast; they had a high estimation of Feuillade's films, for example, from the end of the War, whereas Delluc, while conceding him the status of a peerless technician, 'never forgave Feuillade for devoting [his technique] to "the serial abomination"' (Lacassin 1964, p.83).

11 There are, of course, traces of similar projects in the USA at about the same time, where they strongly suggest a conservatism that still failed to comprehend what Griffith and others were up to. But the rationalisation is significant, for here it was implied that a fully-lit auditorium would be safer for unaccompanied women—the objects of an important campaign in the USA, see pp.122ff. below—and provide a guarantee against pickpockets!

12 When did the 'middle strata' start going to the cinema en masse in France, as they did in the USA, for example (from around 1913-15, it seems)? Witnesses such as Abel Gance, Marcel L'Herbier and Henri Langlois have always claimed that it was only after the introduction of sound. Emmanuelle Toulet (personal communication) has, however, traced more than 400 projection points in Paris in 1914 and disputes the claim that France was especially slow in extending the cinema audience socially ... as Charles Pathé maintained in a contribution to a public debate on cinema versus theatre in *L'Excelsior* (1913).

13 British churches (particularly the Methodists) were the first to discover the usefulness of projected pictures in the joint struggle against the secularisation and the alcoholism of the working classes, but the French Catholic Church eventually followed suit. The analyses it proposed when it came to try to convert its 'lantern soldiers' to the cinematograph are evidence of precocious insight. The following passage is drawn from *Le Fascinateur* of 1904: 'In the evenings, on our main boulevards, traffic is halted by a stupid throng of gawpers who stand around for hours, their feet in the mud, their noses in the

air, their eyes turned upward, jostled, trampled, indifferent to their own con- cerns and to how ridiculous they look, hypnotised by the magical screen set up on top of a five-storey building and resplendent with some wretched figures or advertisements. Before these luminous apparitions the crowd is in ecstasy, and Parisians take on the air of illuminati. We should not be surprised at this naive passion. It is so natural to mankind!' As is well known, relations between the cinema and the church, via the parochial *circuits de patronage*, have a long history in France.

14 Cinema melodrama developed later, particularly in Perret's films; a genre of complex plots, it required the feature-length format.

15 It consists, Ubersfeld writes, of 'a hatred of "tyrants", a contempt for the aristocracy (the villain is very often a *ci-devant* or a priest), and a hatred for monks and convents, all things that might satisfy a very superficial liberal demagogy.'

16 In an important study, 'The Lady Vanishes' (Fischer 1979), Lucy Fischer, an American scholar, has coincidentally singled out another patriarchal feature of the early French cinema, the frequency with which, in films by Méliès, Zecca, Velle, et al., a masculine magician displays a woman's body and then makes it disappear. However, I cannot accept her argument that a series of Pathé films in which a conjuring 'giantess' manipulates minute men represents an inversion of the masculine discourse; I see it rather as simply an extension of the iconography of misogynist terror well established in nineteenth-century French graphic art (cf. Félicien Rops, etc.).

17 I have not had time to examine the Pathé catalogues with their thousands of titles. These percentages could and should be made more precise, but I doubt very much that such an examination would substantially upset them.

18 A distrust whose causes are both political—the reaction against urban revolu- tionary movements has always come from the countryside (1848, 1870, etc.)—and socio-individual—those workers who were ex-peasants had gen- erally been forced to leave the villages and did not look with kindliness on the peasant milieu.

19 Bernard Eisenschitz has drawn to my attention the spectacular reversal of this cinematic representation of rural France in the cinema after the First World War. The countryside then became the mythical site of a France unsullied by the holocaust, and it was idealised in a whole series of often admirable films which constitute a kind of bucolic school, from Feuillade's **Vendémiaire** (1918) to Epstein's **Finis Terræ** (1929).

20 It is interesting to note that in the cinema of the first decade certain films have astonishingly advanced continuity figures (alternating editing in **The Cripple and the Cyclists**, **Dévaliseurs nocturnes** and **Les Chiens contrebandiers**). But the context I am trying to circumscribe here prevented these things from being taken further in France, and in the end they had to be re-learnt there from the USA.

21 E.g., **The Trusting Cabman**, who drives his cab round the tourist sites of Paris while his wife deceives him with the man he thinks he is driving. This is a genre aimed at the provinces, but even more at the foreign market.

22 So popular there was a shot-for-shot remake.
23 Of course, a lecturer could give it a quite different inflection, and must have done in many cases, but probably not in all.
24 According to Alberto Cavalcanti (in an interview made for the television series **Cinéastes de notre temps** but never broadcast), the script-girl, matching's traffic policeman, only appeared on French stages around 1927. It remains to be ascertained how long it took for this function to become generalised.

Those Gentlemen of
the Lantern and the Parade

As early as 1903—if one compares the frequent experiments in cinematic 'language' of Porter with the pure pictorialism of Zecca—France lagged behind the USA in the development of the IMR. Britain, on the other hand, had from the beginning been spectacularly ahead of all other producing countries. This lead, however, had no immediate follow-up, and remained no more than a kind of prototype.

But before proceeding further, one point must be made clear: while it is true that this comparative description of the development of cinema in various countries no doubt tends to enlist a bit too frequently the metaphor of the race, this is not necessarily how the 'competitors' actually saw things at the time. And as to whether all were hastening towards the same *telos* ....

On a general historical scale, this initial lead can be seen to be linked in the last analysis to that of Great Britain itself over all the other capitalist countries. Moreover, the relative exhaustion of British industrial dynamism, undermined towards the end of the nineteenth century by the suffocating rise of finance capital (due, it seems—see Hobsbawm 1968—precisely to that lead), was to play an important part in the (relative) bankruptcy of British film production after 1906, when only a move from artisanal to industrial production could have protected it from French and soon American competition.

Adumbrated as early as the Revolution of 1688, the great historical compromise between the rising bourgeoisie and the landed aristocracy that is surely the constitutive feature of British history was consummated in the middle of the nineteenth century after a career *without major confrontations*—neither Peterloo, nor the struggles with the Chartists are the equivalent of 1848 or the Commune. There followed the installation of a dyarchy ... working in harness so as to assure themselves of control of the country. Furthermore, those who had set up this two-headed system had been clever enough to try to integrate the third element in the social structure, the working class, so as to turn it away from violence and convert it to their beliefs. This tactic was far more astute than its equivalent in France, where violence was rampant, and where the centre of gravity of society—the bourgeois-peasant alliance versus the workers—depended as much on force, from June 1848 up to the Commune, as on universal suffrage (Bédarida 1979, pp.132-3).

The rise of the trade-union movement towards the end of the nineteenth century did seem to constitute a response likely to threaten this assimilation, but

one should not minimise the impact of mid-Victorian integration, even though it was incomplete and transitory. There is no doubt that it has profoundly influenced British society right up to our own times by providing a code of conduct that is accepted by all. The resulting consensus included an emphasis upon personal respectability (tinged with puritanism), a predilection for democratic and parliamentary methods (renouncing indiscipline and bursts of violence of a Chartist or Jacobin type), and the adoption of many of the ideals of the ruling class (ibid., p.133).

The development of the education system, of amateur and professional sports, and the modern mythology of the Royal Family, all helped in the creation of the consensus that characterises modern Britain. The cinema, born at a time when the aspirations to class collaboration of working-class political forces were already being institutionalised (the formation in 1900 of the Labour Representation Committee, which was to become the Labour Party in 1906), did not yet have the place among the ideological apparatuses that it was to acquire in Britain during and after the Second World War. But it did play what was then a unique premonitory role and can be seen as a kind of emblem of that class situation, thanks to two socio-cultural phenomena—Rational Recreation and one of its key components, the Magic Lantern—which made a decisive contribution, throughout the nineteenth century, to British 'social control'.

From the 1840's on, and especially after the final defeat of Chartism in 1853, the ruling classes launched a grandiose campaign whose aim was no more nor less than the control (or as we would say today, co-optation) of the totality of the leisure-time activities of the workers. This battle was not won in a day, far from it, and its story, as told by Peter Bailey (1978), will perhaps help us to a better understanding of the place initially occupied in the British cinema by middle-class artisans, of the tolerance of 'anarchistic' themes in that cinema, and also of the rapid 'deproletarianisation' of British films and British audiences after 1906 (with the introduction, for example, of a national censorship system, for which there was to be no equivalent in France until the First World War).

'The concern to police the amusements of the poor had a long history in English life,' explains Peter Bailey (ibid., p.17), but from the middle of the eighteenth century this concern grew apace, particularly among those presiding over a rapidly growing industrial production. 'Principal targets were animal cruelty, sabbath-breaking and intemperance' (p.18). In fact, for the ruling strata the main problem was to prevent workers' pastimes (animal sports in the streets, in particular) from encouraging large gatherings of the 'dangerous classes', on the one hand, and, on the other, preventing the abuse of alcohol from fostering riots—which were only too likely, given the extreme poverty of the period—and undermining the health of the worker battalions. The new police forces, created around 1840, were soon assigned as their principal task the repression of the traditional pastimes of the inhabitants of towns and villages: 'The players and spectators of street games were prosecuted for obstruction, trespass, breaches of the peace, vagrancy and desecration of the sabbath.... In clearing the streets, they [the police] not only threatened to deprive the working class of its last resort of public assembly, but also cut off many of its diversions by moving on the street performers' (p.21). Those who set themselves up as the defenders of these festivities (and others such as fairs and annual holidays), arguing 'that they provided a safety valve for the discontents and frustrations of a hard-driven working people[,] found no support among the middle classes, particularly since this traditional licence encouraged recrudescences of saturnalia which they found offensive to their sense of station and social order' (p.22). However, the working population discovered a form of resistance.

This was the 'singing saloon' (not to be confused with the French *caf'conc'*, for, despite certain similarities, in Britain it was primarily the customers who produced the music). 'The singing saloons were called into being by the working classes, and the working classes asserted a remarkable degree of popular control over them' (p.307). These saloons, offering both drinks and songs, soon became the music-hall, the first version of which— before the essentially repressive reforms of 1885—retained all the specificities of the singing saloon: the constant participation of the audience in the show, frequent exchanges between performers on stage and customers in the hall. And the reforms, when they were introduced under pressure from the ruling classes, consisted precisely of the suppression of the consumption of intoxicating liquor in the auditorium and the prohibition of performers addressing the audience and the audience joining in the choruses of the songs.

This wide movement in favour of *rational recreation*—i.e., a recreation whose contents and forms had lost any subversive character—also had other aspects, ones which were not simply repressive. One of the most important was the creation, from 1850 on, of Working Men's Clubs. For Henry Solly, the founder in 1862 of the CIU (Working Men's Club and Institute Union), 'the achievement of a well-ordered and harmonious society depended upon educating the working classes to recognise that the existing system offered the best, and indeed the only guarantee that the interests of both capital and labour would be well and equitably served' (ibid., p.110).

Alongside the Working Men's Clubs, alongside the early lending libraries, and a few People's Palaces, the temperance movement grew with great vigour. Led in particular by the Methodist Church (whose popular roots made it especially suited to a task in which its terroristic, guilt-instilling methods found fertile ground), this movement, based on the monstrous ideological inversion whereby alcohol is made the main cause of poverty, took a variety of forms: lectures, soon illustrated by magic-lantern projections and addressed to adults or to children, the opening of coffee houses to encourage the consumption of non-alcoholic beverages, the publication and distribution of a vast literature, etc.

Finally, one of the main objects of this battle was the participation of the 'better classes' in popular pastimes. On the one hand, the aristocracy, whose 'decadent' pastimes were still suspect in the eyes of a middle class steeped in the cult of work, were to take up new forms of recreational activity (rational ones, of course) capable of providing a model for the working strata. The development of modern sport in the nineteenth-century public schools was intimately linked to this notion. On the other, the middle class itself was to share the pastimes of those that toiled beneath its yoke. This last project, not surprisingly, remained more or less a dead letter, beyond a certain symbolic participation of owners in the working men's clubs. However, in the decades preceding the reform of the halls, both the reformers and the proprietors of the music-halls themselves, who, for material reasons, shared their aspirations in this respect, produced a stream of propaganda claiming that the well-off were frequent attenders at the 'halls'. In fact, nothing could be further from the truth (ibid., pp.155-6).[1] Only in the 1890's did certain music-halls built in city centres set out to draw an audience consisting more or less exclusively of members of the middle classes wishing to slum but also to keep their own company.

This wish to create *mass pastimes* able to appeal to rich and poor together and thus to promote the reabsorption of class conflicts—*The Times* of October 15th 1883, for example, complained that music-halls 'intensify the tendency of the nation to become two' (cit. ibid., p. 160)—became, however, perfectly realisable with the development of the cinema, both in Britain and, under slightly different conditions, in the USA.

Indeed, the history of the development of popular leisure in Britain in the nineteenth century as I have outlined it briefly here leads directly on to that of the British cinema in two distinct aspects: cinema as a genuinely popular spectacle (music-hall, fairground), and cinema as a spectacle aimed at the people but in middle-class hands from the outset.

For, in the early stages it was at music-halls and fairgrounds that the lower classes made the acquaintance of the cinema; and at least one of the most important producer-film-makers of the period came from their ranks. Moreover, most of these film-makers were formed in the magic-lantern business, and many of them were to adjust the content of their films to the tastes of a popular audience, even when their forms prefigure Griffith or DeMille.

It is very unfortunate, especially for cinema historians, that a thorough history of the magic lantern in Britain remains to be written. For its role was absolutely crucial. The American film historian Charles Musser argues (1982) that there is not a history of the cinema beginning, say, in the Grand Café in 1895, but rather a history of projected pictures going back (in the West) to the middle of the seventeenth century, in which the invention of the cinema is only one stage.[2] Restricting ourselves to Britain alone, it seems that the inventions of the 1890's were often seen there as representing no very major break in continuity. When Cecil Hepworth, an important English cinematic pioneer and the son of a famous professional lanternist, first saw a projection of moving pictures (filmed by Birt Acres) in 1896, he was not particularly impressed and it was only months later that he realised the significance of the phenomenon (Hepworth 1951, pp.26-7). After all, magic-lantern shows in Britain had attained a remarkable level of sophistication and already included important kinetic features, be it the mechanical animation of coloured drawings achieved by a variety of ingenious devices incorporated into the glass plates, or the spectacular transitions known as 'dissolving views' obtained by superimposing several lantern beams on a single screen.

Moreover, mixed shows including lantern slides and films remained common, and not only in Britain, for a long time. In his valuable memoirs (ibid., pp.31-2), Hepworth describes a show of his that he called *The Storm*, consisting of half a dozen slides followed by a forty-foot film: 'The sequence opened with a calm and peaceful picture of sea and sky. Soft and gentle music (Schumann, I think). That changed to another seascape, though the clouds looked a little more interesting, and the music quickened a bit. At each change the inevitability of the coming gale became more insistent and the music more threatening; until the storm broke with an exciting film of dashing waves bursting into the entrance of a cave, with wild music (by Jensen, I think).'[3]

There is no doubt that the temperance movement deserves the credit for giving a decisive impetus to the development of the magic lantern in Britain and conferring on it the truly industrial scale it acquired in the last few decades of the Victorian era. Beyond the enormous networks of customers it provided, such as the Band of Hope (a movement for the early indoctrination of the children of the poor with the temperance message), a lay magic lantern movement also grew up. Smith and Hepworth, for example, only ever seem to have presented purely entertaining or instructive shows in lecture halls like that of the Royal Polytechnic Institution in London. But temperance lanternists were quick to realise that to draw and retain their popular audiences—who were often illiterate, and hence inaccessible to the flood of temperance literature that had been issued since the 1840's—it was not enough to show them 'documentary' pictures, usually drawings illustrating the history, manufacture and awful consequences of the consumption of beer, gin, etc. One had to make up a varied programme in which, say, a brief comic monologue (five or six slides painted with prettily coloured pictures) was followed by a 'Chromatrope' (an ingenious kaleidoscope-like effect animated by a slow, hallucinatory gyratory movement[4] thanks to the rotation of one sheet of glass over another), then a spectacular transformation deriving from Daguerre's dioramas and achieved by the slow superimposition of two or even three light beams from quite technologically sophisticated projectors (e.g., a sunlit railway station—night slowly falls—the signals change to green and a train passes). Also common were 'travel' series, which constituted the main substance of lay lanternism, but also an important proportion of the complementary programme of the temperance lanternists, and gave rise directly to the exotic (and colonialist) scenics of the early cinema.

But the turning point in the history of the magic lantern, and also a product of the temperance movement, was the introduction (by the Bamforth company) towards the end of the 1860's of 'life models'. These were fairly long series of slides (some as long as fifty or more)[5] made by photography and subsequently hand-coloured. The scenes illustrated were posed by real people in often quite elaborate artificial settings. The stories told were of a highly edifying kind, usually with unhappy ends, and usually (but not always) directly illustrating the ravages of alcohol. In my opinion there can be no doubt that the spectacular 'break-throughs' of British film-making in the very early years, i.e., the astonishing premonitions of the IMR it exhibits, derive from the tradition of life models—which, although they were exported and widely exhibited in the USA, France and elsewhere, seem almost all to have been made in Britain.

The magic-lantern show did, of course, remain essentially an illustrated lecture. The texts published to go with the series often have several hundred words for each slide, so a twenty-minute lecture may have required only a dozen pictures (by comparison, modern tape-slide presenters regard ten seconds per slide as a maximum). From the few indications that we have, it seems that this very prolix style often served as a model for the first film lecturers. But at any rate, it seems likely that, helped by the lecturer, the relationship the magic-lantern spectator maintained with the projected pictures was an *exploratory* one, a feature that was, to a certain extent, to characterise the cinema in its most primitive form.

However, as the life models developed, staging techniques emerged that prefigure not so much the primitive mode, but more the central procedures of the IMR that superseded it.

The most important of these is a certain ubiquity of the camera. In many of these slide sequences, the spectator follows a series of moments in a single setting rendered by pictures of different shot-scale and sometimes even from different angles. Usually, it is true, the changes of shot-scale and angle are pretty small, of an order that the IMR was explicitly to condemn for the crime of 'lèse-continuité'. However, I am convinced that the reason why the (British) Gaumont film-maker Alf Collins, in a 1905 film called **When Extremes Meet**, could change the angle from which the same subject was shot at a time when such a figure was simply unthinkable in any other producing country,[6] is the lanternist 'legacy'. One might also refer to the changes in shot-scale (cut-ins) in **Rescued by Rover** (1905), changes which are quite small—from 'long shot' to 'medium shot'—and thus quite

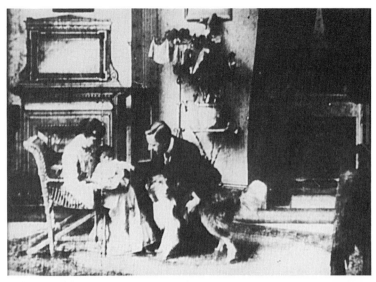

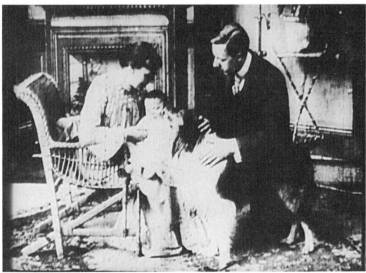

Fig. 7: **Rescued by Rover** (Hepworth, 1905). An early example of a cut-in match, reminiscent of similar strategies in magic-lantern Life Models.

comparable to those observed in many life-model series. On the other hand, from the few samples I have been able to see,[7] insert close-ups do not seem to have been very common in life models. It does seem that Smith's famous film **Grandma's Reading Glass** (1900?)—a series of insert close-ups showing what is seen after views of the act of looking—derives from a lantern show, but that was the presentation of a 'trick' rather than a life model in the strict sense. More pertinent here is the set called *The Auction*. It consists of a series of close-ups of lots displayed in a sale room, commonplace objects—mattresses, shoes, etc.—in a particularly advanced state of decrepitude, which the last verse of the brief poem accompanying the pictures describes as the effects of a poor wretch who fell victim to alcohol. The last picture of the series shows us *full length* the character supposed, presumably, to have delivered (off-screen) the sinister words of the commentary, a kind of preacher-cum-auctioneer who stands forth before the spectators to point the moral.

Generally speaking it seems that the many experimental uses of insert close-ups in early British films—especially those of Smith—come not directly from lantern-slide practices but as an extrapolation of them. Moreover, it seems even that there was a kind of taboo against the close-up for the lanternists, at least if we can believe the following article from the *The Optical Magic Lantern Journal*:

> Size, independent of anything else, has the power to affect an audience—or the more educated and intelligent portion of it—pleasantly or unpleasantly, as it may be suited to the subject shown. Pictures exhibited much above their normal size have a more or less grotesque appearance, especially if containing figures. Landscapes pure and simple only on rare occasions give rise to criticism in this respect; but take flowers, figures, or anything of such dimensions that they can be easily compared or exaggerated. The screen proclaims their unreality, which is at once strikingly apparent (Moore 1894, p.56).

It seems legitimate, on the one hand, to see here a suggestion as to why the cinema so slowly accepted the insert close-up (generalised only after some twenty years), but also as to why the 'film

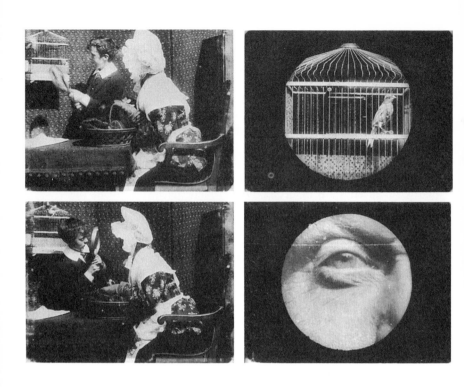

Fig. 8: **Grandma's Reading Glass** (Smith, 1900).

portrait' so easily became an autonomous and important genre, following **Repas de bébé**. Indeed, one can easily imagine that the author of these lines would have had no trouble with the photographic portrait inaugurated some fifty years earlier, examples of which were common in lantern shows of the 'collage' type (e.g., portraits of John Wesley in the many series of disparate pictures illustrating the exemplary career of the founder of Methodism). As the article suggests in passing, the difficulty arose when there was *comparison*, when the close-up was inserted into a context which established a scale of reference. We are dealing here, in fact, with an index of the strength of the resistance offered by the exteriority of the 'pre-institutional' projected picture, an exteriority that implied a unique point of view and had to give way to a degree of internalisation (identification of the spectator-subject with the viewpoint of a mobile camera) for the IMR to emerge.

At one time—exactly when I cannot ascertain, but it was certainly well before the turn of the century—certain published lectures still contained remarks referring to the pictures as such: 'Here is a typical picture showing us Scrooge in all his miserliness ....' 'At the rear of this picture we see the door behind which sits Mr. Smalley, Scrooge's clerk....' (examples drawn from a life-models adaptation of Dickens's *A Christmas Carol*). This practice remained current in travel series in which, generally speaking, there was no continuity effect fusing the pictures into a 'seamless' whole, and comments of the type 'here is a picture of the Pantheon' were more or less unavoidable—it was neither necessary nor possible to tone down the exteriority of the picture. But I am absolutely convinced that professional lecture-writers had quickly realised, especially with life models (drawn subjects, particularly the comic ones aimed at children, seem to have used the designatory mode more frequently), that allusions to the picture as such destroyed the nascent diegetic illusion.

****

Almost all the 'visionary' pioneers of British production were familiar with photography and the magic lantern: Hepworth,

Smith and Williamson were photographers and lanternists, R.W. Paul dealt in photographic materials and projection equipment in Brighton, Mottershaw did the same in Sheffield, while the Bamforth company had been one of the most important names in the manufacture of lantern slides for many years. The contrast with the socio-professional origins of the first recruits at Pathé's, for example, is striking (see pp.72f. above). When the British historian Roy Armes (1978, p.17) states that 'from the beginning films were entertainment artefacts made by bourgeois manufacturers for the urban working classes,' he is simply summarising an obvious fact. There is a striking contrast both in manifest content and in 'language' between the predominantly populist cinema of France and what has to be called the middle-class cinema of Williamson, Hepworth, Smith and co.

When Smith, in 1900, filmed fragments of a pantomime based on **Robinson Crusoe** acted by middle-class Brighton children—it seems he was commissioned to film dozens of them—he was not content to frame the proscenium 'à la Méliès', but inserted a medium close-up of the girl playing Robinson standing on a raft while a painted backcloth unrolls behind her. And Williamson, doing his bit towards the conditioning of public opinion against the anti-imperialist rising known as the 'Boxer Rebellion', deployed an alternating editing system close to shot-reverse-shot in the 1903 version of **Attack on a China Mission**.[8] In the same year his fine comedy **The Dear Boys Home for the Holidays**, as well as giving an astonishingly naturalistic depiction for the period of a life style which is manifestly that of Williamson himself (the actors are his own family), is organised according to a remarkably precocious system of *contiguity syntagms* (cf. p.209 below), prefiguring Griffithian topography. Georges Sadoul suggests (1973, t.II, p.249) that the class character of this filmmaker's work is tempered by a certain 'social tendency': 'Williamson, Haggar and Mottershaw generally side with the humble, as does R.W. Paul.' Haggar, certainly, in his origins and vocation was an authentic representative of the populist fairground cinema whose British version I shall discuss below, but neither Paul nor, especially, Williamson can be located anywhere but in the ideological space of a completely conformist middle class, the class of which he, Smith, Melbourne-Cooper and Hepworth especially

Fig. 9: **Attack on a China Mission** (Williamson, 1900?), the single-take version.

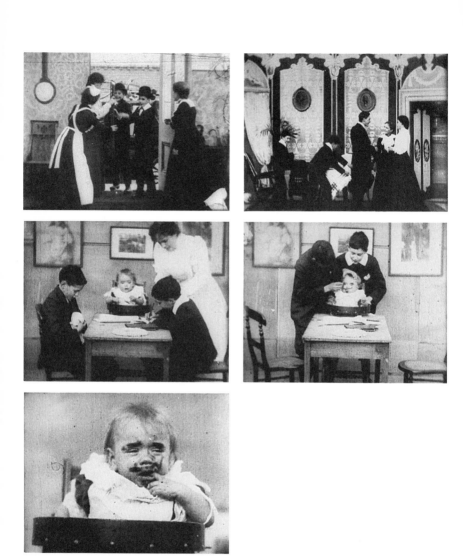

Fig. 10: **The Dear Boys Home for the Holidays** (Williamson, 1903).

were in life the worthy representatives. The films I have just discussed provide abundant evidence of this. In support of his claim, Sadoul cites three films: **Wait till Jack Comes Home** (1903)—an old working-class couple, victims of misfortune, are saved from despair by the long awaited return of a now prosperous son; **The Deserter** (1903)—a soldier steals out of the barracks to say farewell to his parents, and is then acquitted by a magnanimous court-martial; and **A Reservist before and after the War** (1902)—an indigent old soldier steals a loaf, and a policeman takes pity on him. Yet none of these films is at odds with the ambient discourse of sympathy for the poor, the sentimental support of the system of charity that had been part of a class strategy in operation since the middle of the previous century.

As for the films of R.W. Paul—whose main innovations lay in the domain of trickwork and occurred before 1900—**Goaded to Anarchy** (1905) is in the tradition of Pathé's **Le Nihiliste** or Biograph's **The Nihilists**—the revolutionaries are conveniently far away, in Russia—whereas a film like **His Only Pair** (1902)—children outside a window jeer at a poor child whose mother must patch his trousers before he can go out again—is an example of a quite obscene miserabilism.

A remarkable film of Williamson's which I shall discuss at length below (see pp.219ff.), **The Big Swallow** (1901), has a much more subtle inscription of its class origins. A dandified gentleman approaches the camera, making threatening gestures intended to indicate to the 'photographer' that he does not want his picture taken (the problematic of the ownership of the image, once again, discussed above, p.69, in respect to the French film **The Clumsy Photographer**). His open mouth moves into extreme close-up, and then, by a childishly simple but effective trick, he seems to 'swallow' camera and photographer. Finally he backs away, licking his lips.

This film is an important example of the series of what might be called 'experimental gag films', in which the three great middle-class innovators—Smith, Williamson and Hepworth[9]—and others, too, promote one or other of the problematics that were to appear later as essential issues of the IMR but were still at this time far from the concerns of the great majority of filmmakers. I shall examine a few of these films for their heuristic importance at the appropriate time. Here let me merely cite a few titles: Hepworth's **How It Feels To Be Run Over** (1900), in which a motor car apparently runs over the camera, raising the whole problematic of the *centring of the subject* but in a different light from that of **The Big Swallow** (cf. pp.202ff. below); Smith's (?) astonishing **Masques and Grimaces** (1901?), in which the juxtaposition by editing of a series of shots of a clown's head wearing different make-ups and making different faces constitutes in fact an exercise in *action matching*, which was only to enter the institutional vocabulary twenty years later! One might also mention the film preserved in the National Film Archive, London, under the title **Ladies' Skirts Nailed to a Fence** and produced around 1900 by the Bamforth company, or Lewin Fitzhamon's **The Other Side of the Hedge** (Hepworth, 1905), two extremely precocious examples of 180-degree matches promoted into pivot-gags (see p.226 below).[10]

Let me be explicit: I am convinced that the class origins of these film-makers as much as their lantern experience lay behind the astonishing inventions in which their work abounds. They were steeped in middle-class culture, frequenters of theatres and museums, familiar with the great nineteenth-century novels. It is inconceivable that they would approach representation in the same way as, say, Zecca or Hatot. Smith was, of course, like Méliès, a presenter of semi-popular shows, and his series of little scenes in medium close-up (a genre he seems to have been the main proponent of, following Lumière but preceding Zecca, who copied many of his films in France) drew on urban folklore, and on music-hall in particular.

Thus, in this cinema, unlike the Danish cinema after about 1906—i.e., a cinema made by members of the middle class for an already largely middle-class audience—we have a cinema intended for popular edification, made by members of the middle class for the working masses[11] and which only the latter deigned to watch until around 1909-10.

For in Britain, too, there is abundant evidence that the cinema's earliest audiences were almost exclusively poor ones. The most eloquent testimony to this is probably a silence—that of *The Times*. After duly greeting the Cinématographe Lumière at its first presentation in London in 1896, there was not one further mention of the cinema in the prestigious newspaper of the upper middle classes for eight years. When this silence was finally broken in 1904, it was only to publish a letter from Friese-Greene complaining that the new edition of the *Encyclopædia Britannica* did not do him justice! In fact *The Times* did not mention the cinema in its own right until 1906, when the American producer-distributor Charles Urban, a specialist in 'actualities' (the only genre to find favour with the middle classes in Britain, too), invited the press to a showing of views—in particular a bull fight filmed in Spain—which he had thought it ill-advised to screen for wider audiences. Whereupon the *Times* columnist naturally congratulated him for this act of paternalistic self-censorship.

In Britain as in France and the USA, the earliest permanent purpose-built cinemas date from 1906 or 1907. Until then films had been screened more or less anywhere, 'in village halls, in church halls, as part of the variety programme in music-halls, in schools, in empty shops with the front windows knocked out and replaced by porticos, in tents, and by travelling showmen in magnificent portable theatres.... The largest of these held about 800 people' (Field 1974, p.16). Thus in many respects the situation was substantially the same as that we have observed in France. A document written by the actress Leonora Corbett and once preserved in the British Film Institute Library gives a revealing glimpse of the class character of these shows. She explains that she and her sister used to wander about her home town, the industrial city of Sheffield (an important centre of film production at this time), and one day came across

a huge tent on an empty lot, inside were rows of benches, perhaps half a dozen or so, a very shabby affair, same as the district, the term 'bug show' crops up in my mind, which conjures up the idea of shabby little places in run-down areas where some type of entertainment was held, this tent seemed to us to be in that category, and coming from a theatrical family and no doubt for other reasons, we would not dare go in, nothing was acceptable but legitimate theatre, especially moving pictures, anything else was looked upon with scorn. However, when we saw the bill 'moving pictures', we took a chance on being punished and went in....

Then, lo, they saw their own mother on the screen. When they told her this afterwards, she was too touched to punish them, although she had never spoken to them of this inadmissible aspect of her professional activities:

> Yes! mother 'stooped' to work and to allow us to work in these films, we needed the money, I received two shillings for one day, when the children asked me why I was away from school, I would not tell them, one day the teacher called me to the front and questioned me, going into great detail.

Thus, in Britain too the cinema was 'the poor man's theatre', despised by 'decent people'. At a time when 'on an average, the working man spent as much on drink as he did on rent,' the 'penny gaff' (which often cost less than a penny in fact) was 'the cheapest evening's entertainment that could now be obtained. For one could not spin out half a pint of beer to last a whole evening, and gin, on which one's grandfather could have got "drunk for a penny, dead drunk for twopence," now cost threepence a tot' (Field 1974, pp.17-18). Thus, 'the social centre for the lower classes began to move from the pub to the picture theatre' (Low 1948, p.32). And these historians' claims are complemented by the experience recorded by the inhabitant of a 'classic slum':

> Cinema in the early years of the century burst like a vision into the underman's existence and, rapidly displacing both concert and theatre, became both his chief source of enjoyment and one of the greatest factors in his cultural development.... Many women who had lived in a kind of purdah since marriage (few respectable wives visited public houses) were to be noted now, escorted by their husbands, *en route* for the 'pictures', a strange sight indeed and one that led to much comment at [my parents'] shop. Street corner gossip groups for a time grew thin and publicans complained angrily that the new fad was ruining trade: men were going to the films and merely calling in at the tavern for an hour before closing time. The disloyalty of it! (Roberts 1973, pp.175-6).

In other words, until 1908 or 1909, the situation in Britain would seem to have been much the same as that in France, except that the higher standard of living enjoyed by British workers (especially in terms of working hours) presumably allowed them to go more often to the cinema at an earlier date. But where content is concerned, did this working-class audience see there only the edifying pap produced by Hepworth, Bamforth and company? Not quite.

For there were film-makers active far from the respectable districts of Hove or Walton-on-Thames, in the mining districts and industrial regions—South Wales, Sheffield—simultaneously producing films that seem almost to come from another world. The one we know most about today is William Haggar, most of whose films seem unfortunately to have been lost, although the chief survivor, **Charles Peace** (1905), is certainly one of the true masterpieces of primitive cinema anywhere.

Born in 1850, Haggar was the illegitimate son of an Essex housemaid. He never went to school but became a travelling musician and then stage hand in a fairground theatre. Finally, in 1900, he opened a large itinerant cinema booth, Haggar's Bioscope, and shortly thereafter made his first films. Haggar's cinematic career was almost entirely confined to South Wales, the clientele of his booth consisting mostly of coal miners, and it was for this clientele that he made his films. 'Our well-tried motto [was] "stick to the coal",' his daughter recalls in her memoirs (Richards n.d., p.20), where she also evokes the year of the great strike that forced them to try their luck in less industrialised areas in England, where they nearly starved.

Entering production at a relatively advanced age, Haggar remained a traditional craftsman, his only ambition being to make films for his own exhibition requirements. That is to say, his films were made to measure for his popular audience. A startling agreement he made with (British) Gaumont guaranteed him developing and printing in exchange for world exhibition rights in the films he provided; Haggar only took for himself a few prints which he showed in his booth—which seems to have been the largest in Britain during the fairground period. Meanwhile, Gaumont distributed his films throughout the world without even acknowledging their paternity. We are certainly still a long way from the age of star producer-directors, though the Urban company, which also distributed his films (under what conditions I do not know), was more correct, for its catalogue attributes the films he made to his name.

The artisanal character of Haggar's production was not peculiar to him in Britain. Smith, Williamson and, initially, Hepworth all worked in this way, using the various members of their families as actors, as Haggar did. In general, what distinguishes British cinema from French and American at this period is its artisanal character. This was, moreover, to be its undoing.

I shall analyse **Charles Peace** later in relation to its representation of space and its embodiment of the 'primitive mode of representation'. But in the way it makes the notorious criminal a kind of superman, both villainous and sympathetic, fascinating and brutal, obstinate and epic, it is much closer to **Au bagne** and the French populist cinema, prefiguring even the Zigomars and Fantômases, than it is to the **Modern Pirates** of Arthur Melbourne-Cooper, another gentleman-film-maker from the Brighton region. In this strange fantasy for the children of the gentry, bandits who are completely dehumanised—primarily by the ultra-long primitive shot-scale—traverse the countryside in a motor car disguised as a dragon, devouring whole flocks of geese and even a bobby before they are captured by the police.

The Peace character, by contrast, is a kind of acrobat-clown straight from popular music-hall (his face is made up in the same way), and the way he ridicules the police, in particular, makes him a character manifestly close to the popular audience—who are also assumed to be quite familar with the historical Peace's deeds, although he had been executed some fifty years earlier. At any rate, this seems to follow from the allusiveness of the extremely fragmentary inserted captions (see pp.173ff. below).

The few other surviving films of Haggar's and the catalogue descriptions of the lost ones suggest that, although **Charles Peace** may have been its maker's most ambitious film, it was by no means a passing accident, at any rate in its class content. **The Salmon Poachers—A Midnight Melée** (1905), a lost film, showed 'the poachers surprised fishing in the moonlight by police in a boat. A chase ensues, with many policemen thrown into the water. In this film, directed for a popular audience, the smugglers [sic] outwit their pursuers and escape' (Sadoul 1973, t.II, p.244).

Fig. 11: **Charles Peace** (William Haggar, 1905). Once again, the notorious burglar foils a police attempt to arrest him.

Authority baffled was a recurrent theme in Haggar's films, e.g., **Bathing Not Allowed** (1905), in which urchins deprived of their swim by an angry squire and a policeman took their revenge by tipping them into the water, or **Brutality Rewarded** (1904), in which a gentleman who had mistreated an old beggar woman was punished by the crowd. Although in his 1903 film **A Dash for Liberty; or, The Convict's Escape and Capture**, order was restored—as its sub-title suggests—the main title clearly locates its sympathies on the same side as the Zecca-Nonguet film discussed above. A film like **D.T.s; or, The Effect of Drink** (1905) constituted an unusual variation on the temperance film, insofar as the drunkard who had a terrifying vision in a crisis of *delirium tremens* and swore never to touch another drop was a high-society clubman.

Of course, the openly anarchistic moral of **The Salmon Poachers**, based on an old image of the rebellious poacher,[12] was exceptional even in this populist cinema. Nor is there any evidence that this lost film reflected Haggar's own ideology. In a film on a similar theme he made in 1903 and which has survived, **Desperate Poaching Affray**, the law wins out, by contrast. But the brutality of the film's action is astonishingly realistic: game-keepers, landowners and policemen fall like flies under the cornered poachers' fire, and the final fight in a pond is an unusually violent one. Moreover, this film has very advanced editing and camera movements for the time, both during the chase and in this astonishing final fight, in which the editing even contains an adumbration of shot-reverse-shot, extraordinarily rare at this time,[13] showing that even a film-maker as remote as Haggar was socio-professionally from the gentleman film-makers had learnt the lantern lesson.

We know little about Frank Mottershaw except that he was a photographer in Sheffield, that he founded the Sheffield Photo Company there in 1899, and that the latter soon became the site of an equally familial and artisanal cinematic production activity. Whatever may have been his own social origins, it seems likely that the populist or even popular character of his productions results from the fact that they were addressed in the first instance to a local audience of workers and craftsmen (the Sheffield Photo Company entered cinema by way of distribution and exhibition before it began production). His films are remarkable especially for their crude violence, stripped of any sentimentality, a characteristic feature of Haggar's films, too, but one absolutely lacking in the films of Hepworth, Williamson et al., or indeed in French populist cinema, which is on the whole fairly good-natured. During the now famous **A Daring Daylight Burglary** (1903), a policeman is knocked off a roof in a fight and killed; the ambulance that rushes up finds only a corpse to take away—all shown without the slightest melodramatic effect. Morality is safe, of course: a little boy had alerted the police as soon as the burglary started—informing has traditionally been encouraged in Britain in the name of social consensus—and at the end of a breathless chase the malefactor is caught. But the perfunctoriness of the victory of the forces of order clearly links this film to Haggar's. Other films of Mottershaw's, seemingly lost, alas, went considerably 'further', i.e., reflected the anarchistic ideology of **The Salmon Poachers**. In **An Eccentric Burglary** (1905) and **The Eccentric Thief** (1906), malefactors appeared and disappeared at will to provoke the police. In **The Bobby's Downfall** (1904), a tramp fastened a sleeping policeman to a lamppost with his own handcuffs. However, Mottershaw remains above all the great pioneer of the chase (see pp.147ff. below), a genre he went on exploiting for years. Although he and Haggar do not seem to have ever engaged in systematic 'experiments' like the middle-class lanternists, their cinema, too, shared for a time in the great innovatory movement of British cinema as a whole.

This populist tendency is found elsewhere, notably in some of the films made for Gaumont by the prolific Alf Collins: **In Our Alley** (1906), 'scenes of slum life'; **A Lodging House Comedy** (1906), in which the boots revenged himself on a dandified drunk; but above all the quite exceptional film **The Eviction** (1904). Here, inhabitants of a workers' slum turn upon the bailiffs and policemen who come to evict them. At the end of a fight which is violent rather than comic, and a chase in which it is the 'robbers' who expel the 'cops', the bailiff is ridden in a wheelbarrow. The Gaumont catalogue does, of course, describe these tenants as Irish, which allows the subversive violence to be attributed to a reputedly turbulent race while no doubt encouraging the secret admiration of more law-abiding English workers. Another film of

Alf Collins's, **When Extremes Meet** (1905), is just as subversive in its way: a drunken cockney couple provoke a middle-class couple and have the last word in the ensuing fight (the clergyman who tries to separate the combattants is arrested by a policeman!).

One of the greatest obstacles facing the historian is the apparent loss of most of the films of Haggar and Mottershaw—particularly regrettable being that of the latter's **The Life of Charles Peace** (1905) and **Robbery of the Mail Coach** (1903) which seems to have been the model for Porter's **The Great Train Robbery**. It is surely no accident that the well-off heirs of such as Hepworth and Williamson had the means and the desire to preserve their ancestor's work which those of Haggar and Mottershaw lacked (although there may be other contributory factors, too). Nevertheless, an important chapter in the history of the early cinema still remains to be restored to the light.

****

All historians agree that the decline of the British cinema dates from around 1906, a decline which is both industrial and 'artistic'. I have no reason to dispute the matter. It is clear that the age of neologisms was long past by this time, and that it fell to the Americans—whose cinema had anyway been just as experimental on occasion since 1902, as we shall see—to take over from the British in the construction of the IMR. Remaining far too artisanal in comparison with the enormous resources available to trusts like Pathé and (soon) Edison and Biograph, and self-financing only to a small degree because of the fragmentation of production, the British industry gave up the struggle against the foreign invasion: 'Production stagnated in Great Britain after 1906 and by the time of Robert William Paul's retirement in 1910 foreign domination of the industry amounted to 85 per cent, with France (40 per cent) and the United States (35 per cent) in the forefront' (Armes 1978, p.27). This massive invasion of foreign-produced films was accompanied by a socio-economic development with a precise counterpart in the USA, as we shall see. This was a powerful dual effort on the part of the establishment as a whole to raise the standing of the cinema for both economic and ideological reasons. Four years after the inauguration of the first Board of Censorship in the USA, the industry set up a self-censorship committee in Britain. Along with this effort to purge films of elements that might make them offensive in the eyes of the middle classes went an attempt to raise the quality of the audience (the former being naturally one of the preconditions of the latter):

A little booklet on how to run a cinema, published in 1911 by *Kine Weekly*, makes it clear that the better sort of proprietor was a paragon of probity and public spirit by the standards of his day. He was concerned for 'the labouring classes', though he had a romantic longing for the approbation and patronage of 'the carriage trade'. He was firm, but kind to his staff, especially the female staff.... As for the films, good quality is to be preferred at all times to 'trashy comics' [at the time these would mainly have been French films] (which the carriage trade will not accept anyway), and a special effort must be made to make the Sunday programme appropriate to the day, otherwise how will one still the outcry against the Sunday opening of picture houses? In all this one can see that rectitude was backed by self-interest (Field 1974, p.39).

Everything suggests that by 1913, with an unprecedented visit to a cinema by the Prime Minister (the Liberal Asquith), with a major complimentary article in *The Times*, with the proliferation of luxurious Picture Palaces, a decisive step had been taken in the fight for the creation of a socially mixed audience, a mass audience in the sense also understood in the USA. A visitor from France in 1912 was astonished to find there were 500 cinemas in London, many being luxurious and well-appointed. Even more significant is his fascinated description of the English audience: 'We never observed the slightest disturbance or talking. All the audience's attention was fixed on the screen and not until the end of the film did they hiss the thief and (always) applaud the policeman' (*Le Cinéma*, May 17th 1912). It is easy to imagine how this contrasted with the restless and noisy popular audiences of Paris. Everything suggests that British cinema, *taking over from rational recreation*, followed the general movement of British society closer and closer to a kind of peaceful coexistence between antagonistic classes—a process hardly affected by a general strike in 1926 which nothing since has even approached in scale.

Is it true that 'the 1912 coal strikes ... failed to lead to the usual violence because the strikers spent their temporary freedom at the pictures,' as Rachel Low (1948, p.32) tells us was suggested at the time? Whatever the answer, there is no doubt that the development of the British cinema as a whole inscribes it in the apparatus of social control born in the nineteenth century which has done so much to make British society the model of social-democratic liberalism.

There are striking parallels with the USA, which we shall now turn to examine, but also fundamental differences, arising from those already distinguishing these two great capitalist countries, one on the decline and more and more dependent on its colonial empire, the other now beginning its real rise, having escaped from that empire more than a hundred years earlier.

NOTES

1 One cannot help thinking of the articles in the American trade press around 1908 that claimed a large middle-class attendance in the nickelodeons, when such was still by no means the case.

2 For my reservations on this point, see pp.247f. below.

3 Porter, when he was an exhibitor at the Eden Musée, New York, was responsible for similar mixed projections.

4 The resemblance between these literally fascinating motifs and those used by hypnotists is quite striking. One cannot but be reminded of the name '*Fascinateur*' given by the Church in France to those who deployed their magic lanterns in the context of the great crusade against working-class secularisation (see p.77 n.13 above).

5 It is important to stress that these large glass plates, especially when they were in colour (either option was available), were quite expensive. That is why few sets consisted of more than a dozen slides.

6 As late as 1904, to obtain a similar camera ubiquity, Biograph technicians had to invent a whole motivating anecdote in **The Story the Biograph Told** (see p.248 below).

7   In David Francis's important collection.

8   However, this famous film remains something of a historical mystery. The 1903 Williamson catalogue (included in the Urban catalogue of the same date) unquestionably shows in both text and stills an alternation between one set-up (returned to several times) of a large house in front of which the fights take place, and another (also repeated) showing a gate through which come, first, the Chinese rebels and then the marine riflemen running to the rescue. However, the film with this title preserved in the National Film Archive in London—which can be dated with certainty, it seems, to 1900—contains only one shot: that of the house, in front of which all the action of the film takes place (Chinese and marine riflemen arriving from a never revealed off-screen space). Moreover, there are no visible discontinuities in this film. Comparison with the stills in the catalogue shows that it is the same picture. For the time being explanations of this mystery must remain hypotheses; the most plausible is that in 1903 Williamson re-issued the film with the addition of a new shot, and a new editing. This hypothesis, which I owe originally to Charles Musser, seems to be corroborated by the fact that 1903 is the year of Mottershaw's **A Daring Daylight Burglary**, Hepworth's **Firemen to the Rescue** and Haggar's **Desperate Poaching Affray**, all three of which are remarkable for their precocious editing experiments.

9   Even Sadoul, in his eagerness to issue a certificate of progressiveness to the English school that we have him to thank for restoring to prominence after thirty years' oblivion, does not try to hide the openly reactionary ideology of someone like Hepworth. **The Aliens' Invasion** (1905), a lost film Sadoul describes from the catalogue, was a shameful denunciation of the customs of the hateful foreign workers who were (already!) arriving to steal the bread from the mouths of indigenous British workers (this is a subject others also treated at this time). Elsewhere (see p.163 n.14 below) I describe the edifying portraits of the nice middle classes and their dear animals offered in **Rescued by Rover** and **Black Beauty**.

10 The '180-degree matches' that have been discovered with such amazement in more or less contemporaneous American films such as **Next!** and **Off His Beat** (see p.233 n.26 below) involve changes in the sets and are in fact a direct (but precocious) extrapolation of 'primitive autarchy'. Hence they are not evidence of the same 'experimental awareness'. However, it is true that comparable films, experimenting with other figures, were produced in the USA in the same period (**The Gay Shoe Clerk, A Subject for the Rogues Gallery**, etc.).

11 With a fairly predictable repertory, ranging from the temperance film inspired directly by lantern slides—R.W. Paul's **Buy Your Own Cherries** (1904), Cricks and Sharp's **Drink and Repentance—A Convict Story** (1905)—to the patriotic and imperialist film—Walturdaw's **How a British Bulldog Saved the Union Jack** (1906). The long series of films about the misdeeds of scrounging tramps, fake blind beggars or cripples, etc., is not only to be laid at the door of these middle-class film-makers, for Haggar seems to have made a large number for his working-class spectators. It is conceivable that these films—which generally give a 'humorous' presentation of the obsessive fantasies of the middle

classes about the lumpen strata (think in particular of the many films in which the tramp steals a baby's milk!)—were perhaps highly valued by members of the 'respectable' poor, flattered by a confirmation of the fact that they were not quite at the bottom of the social ladder.

12 In the era of the Chartist rebellions, especially, 'trouble-makers' sacked from the factories for their part in working-class agitation often poached for a living.

13 And still very uncommon in 1911 when Griffith, for example, introduces a similar one almost furtively in **Fate's Turning**.

Business is Business: An Invisible Audience

The development of French cinema before the First World War—or rather its relative non-development—cannot, of course, be reduced to the history of the class struggle in France or the relatively slow industrial growth of that country: relatively autonomous cultural factors like middle-class and aristocratic elitism or the exceptional strength of popular counter-ideologies, *factors which are nonetheless class-based*, were also determinant.

As for the more contradictory situation of British cinema, it seems to me a faithful reflection of the development of the ideological struggle in Britain at the time, when, thanks to homogenisation strategies such as Rational Recreation, the viewpoint of the ruling classes achieved hegemony, but working-class culture was acquiring institutions that guaranteed its *persistence*, most notably with the creation of the Labour Party.

In the USA, whose vanguard role in the development of the IMR is outstanding, class relations were equally important, but also more 'violent', in the sense that the path the cinema took there implied the rejection of a whole social stratum despite the fact that most of its audience for more than five years came from that stratum.

****

In 1849, New York was the scene of an incident that symbolises a crucial turning-point in the history of American show business: the Astor Place Riot.

This was an extremely violent clash between the forces of order and a lower-middle-class crowd protesting at the presence on a New York stage of a Shakespearian actor named Macready who, two years earlier, had roundly criticised the famous American actor Edwin Forrest, then on tour in England. Underlying this was a confrontation between two conceptions of the theatre associated with two social groups: Macready represented the cultivated, snobbish, aristocratic tradition originating in the detested former colonial centre, Britain, and his indigenous supporters were the urban big bourgeoisie and the landowners; Forrest, by contrast, represented the taste of the 'ordinary people', a variety of clerks, artisans, farmers and workers. One of the objections 'men of taste' had to Forrest was that he took liberties with 'the divine Shakespeare' precisely in order to bring him within the reach of the masses.

At this time and in this place such things were taken very seriously: the incidents that took place outside the theatre between demonstrators and the police, and inside it between opponents and supporters of Macready, resulted in the little matter of 31 deaths and 150 injuries. Far more was at stake than the immediate issue, for the riot

> played an important part in accelerating the development of show business. Before 1850, most theatres in America tried to offer entertainment packages with something for everyone. More and more conflicting patrons and acts were crammed into the same theatres. Like a balloon, stage entertainment stretched and stretched. Finally it exploded. The Astor Place Riot was the pin-prick that did it. It symbolised the irreconcilable conflicts between the desires, values and needs of middle- and upper-class Americans (Toll 1976, p.23).

It was, in fact, a decisive step on the road to the constitution of the 'mass audience', excluding only the intellectual elite, that reached its apogee in the cinematic institution of the 1930's. In scale this was a specifically American project, although the aims were close to those of Rational Recreation. This schism cleared the way for the growth of 'popular' arts owing little to the tastes of the great East Coast families who held real financial, industrial and political power. But the forms of spectacle that then grew up in a leisure sphere distinct from that of the ruling classes still served the interests of one or another of the latter's components. The creation before the Civil War of the minstrel show—a sequence of acts sung, danced or declaimed by white actors in blackface—was explicitly aimed at defusing the liberal bad conscience of the North by proving how 'happy' the slaves were; similarly, vaudeville, born at the time of the great rural exodus at the turn of the century, sought to convert the uprooted villagers to the values of urban and industrial civilisation, including the new and more intensive forms of exploitation they were subject to in the cities.

About the same time as the Astor Place Riot, there began to reach the USA the first waves of the immigration that, lasting until the First World War, would constitute, along with the earlier wave of forced immigration from Africa, the American working class. And like the blacks, the immigrants were long to remain outside the mass audience for whom the new forms of spectacle were created: in succession to the blacks, indeed, they became its ideal Other.

After the Northern victory in the Civil War, when the minstrel show had lost much of its ideological credibility, the blackface artists turned to another form of 'soft' racism, ridiculing the 'eccentricities' of the Irish, the Germans, the Scandinavians, etc., whose arrival on the labour market was disturbing to indigenous Americans, even if they did not regard them as direct competitors. And the vaudeville comics, unrestricted by the minstrel format (in particular, its black make-up), were to make anti-immigrant racism[1] the mainspring of their humour.

The immigrants, of course, long constituted a super-exploited stratum with minimal leisure time and minimal material means to profit by it. But they needed distractions nonetheless, and found them, sometimes at the cost of great material sacrifice. However, it was not 'indigenous' forms of spectacle that they turned to. Let alone its explicitly xenophobic content, a form such as the minstrel show, for example, born three decades before the first great wave of immigrants, quickly became a highly coded spectacle, shot through with cultural allusions only meaningful to native Americans and depending to an important extent on wordplay. As for the melodramas presented by itinerant companies in the 'opera houses' of the small and medium-sized towns and appreciated by an audience of farmers, shopkeepers, etc., they too required some knowledge of English and local customs.

The same was true of vaudeville, although it was the 'popular' show par excellence, particularly in its form, at least in the 25 years of its reign (1880-1905):

> But one must not suppose that the greater part of a vaudeville audience, except perhaps for some of New York's East Side theatres, was made up of immigrants directly off the boat. The leisure time, the price of a ticket, and the frame of mind required to appreciate a vaudeville show were not available to the impoverished, unknowing newcomer. For him the immigrant theatres and cheap variety shows could offer more than the gilded palaces and highly paid performers of the circuits. Vaudeville was not prepared to initiate the Italian or the Slav directly into the American way of life, because it made so few points of contact with the ethnic culture of any one group (McLean 1965, pp.40-41).

Deriving from the lowly music-hall (which, after 1880, became 'burlesque', see below), American vaudeville is a fast-paced grouping of all sorts of turns, from hypnotism to trained animals, from singers to acrobats, from juggling to the comic sketch. After the famous Tony Pastor had 'purged' it of the 'vulgar or licentious' character it had inherited, it became the 'family' show par excellence, able to gather together that mass audience— containing both workers and members of the lower middle class, both men and women—aspired to by all the entrepreneurs of spectacle at the end of the century and then sought by the first magnates of American cinema.[2]

Albert McLean, in his provocative study of vaudeville (1965), has shown that the latter's role was to further the acclimatisation of the masses born in a traditional, obscurantist village culture but brutally transplanted to the cities by an accelerating industrial revolution. In particular, these new office workers and (petty) civil servants were to be initiated into a kind of scientistic humanism, a faith in the greatness and superiority of Man (this was the function especially of the trained animal acts, the hypnotists and the 'demystified-magic' turns presented by the great Harry Houdini) capable of filling the gap left by traditional religious beliefs. Let me repeat, it had to be a resolutely decorous show, in order to attract 'respectable ladies' and especially to overcome the puritan distrust of stage shows as such, which was widespread in rural America at the time.

Films could be viewed in a number of different types of location in the USA between 1894 and the nickelodeon boom of 1906—penny arcades, circuses, amusement parks, waxworks shows—but there can be little doubt that the preponderant exhibition site at this time, at least until the emergence of Hale's Tours, was the vaudeville house. However, if the cinema was to an important extent addressed to what McLean calls the 'new folk', it was so rather clumsily—especially after 1900—and in a format, in the broad sense, that hardly suited it. That is why I am inclined to agree with those protagonists in the current debate among American scholars (see p.139 n.4 below) who hold that in this early stage the cinema passed the vaudeville audience by.

For if ever there was a cinema that can be described as primitive in the pejorative sense of impoverished and crude, it is that of the USA before 1906: visual flatness (in both senses), poor composition, and in general what the modern eye can only perceive as an irritating ugliness, can be said to be the almost absolute rule, from Dickson's **Barber Shop** (1894) to Dawley and Porter's **Rescued from an Eagle's Nest**, which may be said to close the primitive period in the USA in 1908. In the same period, by way of comparison, French films, while just as primitive morphologically, had, even in their frontal long-shot pictures, produced plastic solutions such that films like **Histoire d'un crime** ('Story of a Crime', 1901) or **Voyage dans la lune** ('A Trip to the Moon', 1902) seem very beautiful to us today.

The only explanation available for this ugliness or even quasi-illegibility in the appearance of such films as **A Career in Crime** (Biograph, 1900) or **Ten Nights in a Bar-Room** (Biograph, 1901), or even the first Porter spoofs such as **Terrible Teddy, the Grizzly King** or **The Finish of Bridget McKeen** (both 1901), seems to be the absence of the impact on American cinema of a graphic tradition comparable to the one in which Méliès was formed, or that of illustrated magazines like *Le Petit Parisien*, from which **Histoire d'un crime** derived its visual style. Popular newspaper illustration certainly flourished in the USA. But although both the form and the content of these comic drawings and strip cartoons may have influenced the cinema, they had no graphic influence properly speaking, presumably because of the socio-cultural formation of Porter and his colleagues. The discrepancy between the admirable drawing of Winsor McCay—which Méliès or Zecca could certainly have reproduced—and the crude design, clumsily imitating French imagery, of a film such as **Dream of a Rarebit Fiend** (1906), whose title Porter took from one of McCay's most famous strips,[3] is striking. This backwardness of American cinema in comparison with that of Europe long persisted. Compare Griffith's pictures with those of Perret or Feuillade, say, or those of Barker with those of the Westerns Durand shot in the Camargue, or even those of **Foolish Wives** with those of **La Dixième symphonie**.

It is not hard to imagine that these drab, unconvincing, and only rarely coloured pictures must have seemed even paler in the gaudy, eye-catching context of the vaudeville. Even in this respect the suggestions that the primary function of films there was as 'chaser'—to empty the house between shows in a continuous performance—seem trustworthy.[4] French films were, of course, already being imported into the USA, and it would seem likely that coloured prints of Méliès's *féeries* would have been more successful from this point of view (but they would often be shown in pirated, and hence monochrome prints). But Méliès's films, like the rest of French films, were culturally very remote from this audience. One would expect the erotico-infantile symbolism underpinning the *féeries* and comics to disturb the American lower middle class far more than their French counterparts, not to speak of the anarchistic populism of the early French output.

By contrast, American films of this period are plainly and explicitly addressed to the vaudeville audience, and in their content they indisputably partake of the vaudeville spirit. Before 1900, scenic subjects, travel films or actualities, predominated, both for Biograph and for Edison. This genre had an indisputable place in the hybrid vaudeville spectacle, if only as a demonstration of a new wonder of the industrial revolution, a new conquest for Man. But it was hard to maintain its novelty value, especially after the end of the Spanish-American War as a ready source of cinematic spectacle. So film-makers turned to the

Fig. 12: The New Folk: the respectable vaudeville audience in 1908.

'composed view'. The result was the most moralising and edifying films the primitive cinema ever saw, films perfectly matching the spirit of vaudeville and its audience, at least in principle.

This moralism went far beyond classic themes such as temperance (omnipresent nonetheless) or the principle that crime does not pay.[5] A quite astonishing number of films pretend to intervene 'instructively' in all the aspects of urban everyday life, with the manifest intention of assisting in the adaptation of all the newly arrived country bumpkins to urban technology. The result was a series of 'genres' which seem to be absolutely unique to the USA.

There were films warning against the dangers of gas, such as **They Found the Leak** (1902), in which a group in nightshirts venture into a dark cellar with a lighted candle to look for a gas leak, paying for their imprudence with a visually derisory but appropriately deadly explosion. Another example is Porter's minor masterpiece of black humour, **Another Job for the Undertaker** (1901), in which the obligatory bumpkin enters a hotel room and totally ignores a large notice advising him not to blow out the gas jet that lights the room; alas, he is illiterate; he does blow it out, goes to bed—and there follows a stock shot of a funeral procession.[6] A less macabre variant on the same theme is **The Light That Didn't Fail** (1902), in which the bumpkin, after a series of comic attempts to blow out the electric light, wraps it in his carpet bag to get some darkness to sleep by. Here the title is a comic allusion to Kipling's famous story *The Light that Failed,* just the kind of joke to flatter the vaudeville audience and its modicum of culture.

The theme of the bumpkin arriving in the city and finding a technological civilisation beyond him or disorientating customs is very widespread. One of the most popular series was that of Uncle Josh, a character whose advanced age could only add to the degree of his amazements. In **Uncle Josh at the Moving Picture Show** (Porter, 1902), the hero is in a stage box watching various filmed tableaux from the Edison catalogue projected onto a screen of stretched cloth; his amazement and his naive belief in the projected picture are so strong that he tries to kiss the dancing girl, is terrified by the train advancing towards him, and finally, trying to get to grips with a 'seducer', tears down the screen to reveal behind it a furious projectionist. Here was an auto-reflexive demonstration of one wonder of technology quite in the spirit of Harry Houdini's very materialist demythifications of his own 'magic'. As for the sucker who conceives the unlucky notion of having a drink with a prostitute, he quickly learns **How They Do Things on the Bowery** (Edison, 1902): she drugs his whiskey and relieves him of his wallet and watch, and as he leaves the bar he is arrested, presumably for vagrancy!

The cleverness of these warnings lies in the fact that they make vaudeville customers laugh at the expense of those they might once have been but no longer want to be, their cousins newly arrived from the country. By laughing at them the new citizens could feel that, by contrast, they were well integrated into urban life.

This is not the only way these films bear the imprint of their main intended audience. These members of the lower middle class were also interested in the professional activities of such guardians of property as the firemen and police of a great city (**Life of an American Fireman** and **Life of an American Policeman**, Porter 1903 and 1905, respectively). And although the vaudeville audience was socially homogeneous, it was sexually mixed. A film like **The Unfaithful Wife** (Biograph, 1903), in which the wife refuses to give up her lover and flouts her husband until he kills her and commits suicide, could have appealed to the fantasies of both sexes in a period when women were acquiring a quite new independence that threatened male domination. In **The Burglar** (Biograph, 1903), it is the wife who catches the intruder, while the husband hides behind her.

On the other hand, it seems highly unlikely that the many literal filmings of vaudeville turns could have had any other use, presented in the context of a live show, than to empty the house indeed.

But however substantive the affinities between this audience and the films it saw at the vaudeville, it was a quite different audience that flooded into the nickelodeons when, from 1906, the latter took over from the over-specialised Hale's Tours.[7] For at least four or five years, the bulk of the urban nickelodeon audience consisted of immigrants. Is it ('merely') for this reason that the vaudeville audience did not go for several years, and that it required concerted efforts to give them a taste for cinema as an essential step towards the constitution of a mass audience?

****

How did immigrants satisfy their leisure needs at the turn of the century, living as they were in a country in which everything was strange to them?

In some great urban centres where there was a sufficient concentration of immigrants, foreign-language theatrical companies flourished until the turn of the century. Was the disappearance of most of these troupes a result of the increasing accessibility of the cinema show, or rather an effect of the phenomenon of Americanisation in general? Whatever the case, it seems that, although the poorest immigrants—the sweat-shop workers—did go to these theatres, they had to make considerable sacrifices to do so, for in 1898 seat prices were four or five times those of the future nickelodeons (see Corbin 1898).

Men among the immigrants are also known to have frequented the low-level variety shows known as 'burlesque', or rather '*burleycue*', the Americanised pronunciation helping to distinguish between the classic nineteenth-century burlesque—a theatre of parody with European origins—and the striptease and clowning show for men only[8] that emerged from it late in the century.

Then there were the penny arcades, amusement parlours containing rows of slot-machines of all sorts. People spent a few hours in them between supper and bed or visited them on rest days at only a tiny cost and even in the hope of winning a derisory prize or a few cents to enable them to stay longer. As we know, the first phonographs (with cylinders and earphones) appeared here, as did the first Kinetoscopes and Mutoscopes in the period when Edison and the founders of Biograph thought that moving pictures would be most profitable on an individual-viewings basis. When, subsequently, collective viewing sessions were organised with the Cinématographe and the Vitascope, they took place in tiny halls at the back of the penny arcades, and it was here that cinema strictly speaking was discovered by the same poverty-stricken immigrants who were already the main clients of the arcades.

They also encountered films in other places, at the circus, in amusement parks, perhaps even at the vaudeville. But what were they looking for and what did they find? Other than its low prices, what attracted the immigrants to the cinema? For throughout the period concerned, except for a few films made after 1910-11, precisely at a time when the audience was beginning to broaden, the American cinema only addressed immigrants as Other, when it deigned to acknowledge their existence at all.

It is generally held that 'the movies became for immigrants a powerful experience of the American culture which was often denied to them, surrounding them with images, fantasies, and revelations about the New World' (Ewen 1980, p.S51). An Italo-American chronicler of the period described this experience: 'Cold chills crept up and down his back as he witnessed thrilling scenes of what he thought was *really* American life' (Mangano 1917, p.7; cit. Ewen 1980, p.S51). Today, however, it seems more probable that the penny arcades, like the nickelodeons, were above all a social meeting-place, a haven of conviviality.

For if an immigrant, of no matter what origin, occasionally encountered a picture of a member of his own or one of the other new ethnic groups in these early films, that picture was hardly a sympathetic one. In **Hot Mutton Pies** (Biograph, 1902), a Chinaman is selling them on a street corner. His customers discover they are really made of catsmeat and chase after him. Immigrants, it is clear, will eat anything. In the unusual **The Heathen Chinese and the Sunday School Teachers** (Biograph, 1904), utterly ridiculous fat Chinamen run a laundry, visit an opium den, and inexplicably become the objects of the consuming passion of a group of women Sunday-school teachers. The racism—and sexism—of this film are almost surreal (but the obsession with miscegenation aroused by young women engaging in educational mission work at the time is evidenced by a number of newspaper articles). This film is dually inscribed in the ideological space of vaudeville: while making fun of these women's stubborn commitment to an impossible task of 'humanisation'—these people can never be 'like us'—it also attacks a kind of religion associated with the village which vaudeville saw it precisely as its mission to combat. As for Porter, his astonishingly realistic depiction of the execution by electric chair of the Polish anarchist Czolgosz (**Execution of Czolgosz, with Panorama of Auburn Prison**, 1901) is very much in the age-old tradition of public executions, the aim being both to intimidate the immigrant masses and to satisfy lower-middle-class curiosity.

Finally, that 'benign' form of racism, *ethnic humour*, is echoed in the filming of a turn subtly entitled **Levi and Cohen, the Irish Comedians** (Biograph, 1903).[9]

By about 1906, when the proletarian audience had begun, with the proliferation of nickelodeons, to become much more important for the cinema than its vaudeville-based middle-class audience, Biograph produced a series of films dealing with the 'world of work' often seized on for their 'social realism'.[10] The best known of these nowadays are **The Tunnel Workers** and **Skyscrapers**, both made by Frank Dobson in 1906. In the former, the conflict is essentially sentimental (the hero saves a rival's life in an accident), and the characters have no ethnic marks, but in the latter it is unmistakably the immigrant who is the Other, and his extreme perversity—he is quarrelsome and treacherous—that propels the action. This is a conflict between a vindictive dishonest worker with foreign features called Dago Pete, and an immaculately upright foreman with an Anglo-Saxon profile: sacked by the latter for fighting, the wretch tries to avenge himself by planting a watch he has stolen in the foreman's house. Order and truth are restored thanks to the testimony of a little girl; Dago Pete is taken away by the police and the foreman is re-instated.

With the exception of a few rare films produced more towards the end of the nickelodeon era,[11] the cinema continued to ignore the existence of those who were its main customers for a crucial five-year period and more.

The historian Russell Merritt (1976, p.72, n.18) has surveyed all the summaries of films published in *The Moving Picture World* in 1907 and 1908—i.e., at a time when the nickelodeon was well established and its audience well defined. I indicated his results above (p.62). Out of 1,056 American films issued in a twenty-month period, only eight dealt with 'immigrants or the poor', while seven others made by Pathé and Gaumont in France dealt with similar themes.

Those who made the films continued to aim essentially at the audience of the vaudeville theatres, even if that had never been anything but a captive audience and hardly ever ventured into the new specialised houses. And those responsible for creating and running the latter shared the same attitude:

The five-cent theatre may have been widely regarded as the working man's pastime, but the less frequently reported fact was that the theatre catered to him through necessity, not through choice. The blue-collar worker and his family may have supported the nickelodeon. The scandal was that no one connected with the movies much wanted his support—least of all the immigrant film exhibitors who were working their way out of the slums with their theatres. The exhibitors' abiding complaint against nickelodeon audiences—voiced with monotonous regularity in trade journals, personal correspondence, and in congressional testimony—was that moviegoers as a group lacked 'class' (ibid., pp.65-7).

Adolph Zukor, a founder and first president of Paramount, began his cinematic career as a Brooklyn exhibitor in one of the many store-front theatres, showing films in the Hale's Tours format to audiences presumably already consisting of other immigrants less well off than himself. His business prospered and 'we were compelled to remove the cars which had lost all their attraction and put seats in our stores, thereby increasing the number of spectators' (Zukor 1930, p.39).[12] Soon he opened a dozen cinemas in the New York region. 'The novelty of the chase pictures began to wear out, too, and about 1907 or 1908 we found ourselves where we could not carry on the business profitably. And anyway, no one had any money left' (ibid.). Zukor is alluding to a brief recession that naturally first affected the least favoured strata, precisely the ones that were mostly immigrants and provided much of the nickelodeons' clientele. This recession also affected the other industrialised countries (see p.56 above), but in the USA it served as a pointer for those who were to become the vanguard of the nascent film industry. Recessions pass, but was it wise, from a business point of view, to rely entirely on such a fragile audience, one which a brief bout of unemployment would drive from the cinemas en masse? Would it not be better to attract a different audience? Here is Zukor again: 'I had taken about fourteen leases and found myself where I had to go through bankruptcy to get out of the leases or else continue in business. I chose to continue in business' (ibid.).

What he did was to import from Europe the three-year-old Pathé **Vie et passion de Notre Seigneur Jésus Christ** (1906 or 1907) and attempt to conquer a new market:

> We arranged for an organ and a quartet to play and sing appropriate music. I did not dare open in New York. So we tried it first in Newark. We were on a street adjoining a big department store and opened up Monday morning. A great many of the bargain hunters—I mean the ladies—dropped in early to see and hear the performance. As they walked out, I stood at the door eager and anxious to hear the comments. People with tears in their eyes came over to me and said 'What a beautiful thing this is' (ibid., pp.39-41).

The choice of a religious subject shows how, even in this experimental period, Zukor was concerned to attract both an immigrant Christian audience and a lower-middle-class audience of rural origin. The quotation also emphasises the importance to this generation of entrepreneurs of the conquest of a feminine audience as a guarantee of bourgeois respectability. Russell Merritt (1976, p.73) writes:

> The problem was how to lure that affluent family trade.... The answer, at times conscious but more frequently a matter of convenience, was through the New American Woman and her children. If few professional men would as yet, by 1908, consider taking their families to the nickelodeon, the women on a shopping break, or children out from school, provided the ideal life line to the affluent bourgeoisie.[13] .... In a trade hungry for respectability, the middle-class woman was respectability incarnate. Her very presence in the theatre refuted the vituperative accusations lodged against the common show's corrupting vulgarity.

This appeal to women soon manifested itself in the content of the films themselves too: 'Female protagonists far outnumber males, dauntless whether combatting New York gangsters, savage Indians, oversized mashers, or "the other woman"' (ibid., p.73).[14]

As I have said, for these entrepreneurs the ideal audience was the puritan audience of vaudeville. It is therefore hardly surprising that the cinema that had hitherto fought against often petty local censorship and the campaigns of the various legions of decency turned now to organising its own censorship system. Between 1906 and 1909 there is a remarkable change in the content of films. Edifying though they may have been hitherto, their warnings against pickpockets and other perils of the city went with a certain element of voyeurism vis-à-vis vice and shocked a bien-pensant audience by nakedly revealing an urban society in which crime and violence were already out of control (cf. especially the astonishing Biographs **A Rube in the Subway**, 1905, and **The Streets of New York**, 1906). Griffith's approach to crime a few years later—a member of the middle classes successfully defends himself against the tramp's invasion—bears witness to an idealisation, a concealment of reality that was to become the rule for more than fifty years, until the end of the reign of the Hays Code.

Other innovations were also intended to attract a respectable audience. The institution of uniformed ushers still in force in large exclusive houses in the USA today was created, providing a kind of pseudo-police force whose averred function was to control the noisy, popular elements of the audience and to reassure its middle-class component. Some exhibitors attempted, as Marcus Loew did in 1907, to combine vaudeville turns with films in the cinema show, a practice that lasted until the end of the silent period.

Zukor then decided to hand his cinema over to a consortium and go into production. Having heard that Sarah Bernhardt was an enormous hit in a play called *Elisabeth d'Angleterre*, in 1911 he followed in the footsteps of the Film d'Art (it is significant that in this drive to 'raise the level' of the cinema he thus made a second appeal to France, the mythical land of culture), invested in the filming of the play, and launched the film in the legitimate theatres of several large towns. It is true that this decision to

Fig. 13: At a time when the nickelodeon owners were anxious to improve the tone of their clientèle, the presence of an automobile in front of the theatre was felt to deserve a letter in the trade press. Here the prosperous car-owner has come to see a programme featuring a documentary, the preferred fare of the 'better cultivated' film-goer.

Fig. 14: An early squad of uniformed ushers, whose presence, it was hoped, would keep the *hoi polloi* in line so as not to disturb their 'betters'.

desert the nickelodeons for a more luxurious context, reserved hitherto for live actors, was overdetermined by the constitution of the Edison Trust and its attempt to eliminate 'independent' competitors. But the fact that Zukor felt ready to take this unprecedented step with this new product confirms the intention behind his whole early career: to attract the middle classes, if need be by seeking them in their more usual haunts.

Zukor and his generation of entrepreneurs were zealously assisted by the trade magazines that began to appear around 1907, whose editors were often very farsighted and among the first true film critics anywhere. Their analyses dealt with all aspects of production and exhibition, script content and directing technique, cinema furnishing and programme composition. And everything written in *The New York Dramatic Mirror* or *The Moving Picture World* was to one purpose: to make the cinema a major industry by creating for it a mass audience. And in order to massify an audience that (for the time being!) only comprised the 'dregs of society', one could only aim 'higher'. W. Stephen Bush, a columnist for *The Moving Picture World*, constantly appealed to 'the coming ten and twenty cent moving picture theatre,' in the words of the title of an article of his (Bush 1908a): 'Scattered all over the Union are numerous places today that have broken away from the sacred nickel, have offered more than the average nickelodeon (may Heaven forgive the man who invented this abomination of a name!) and are making far more money by charging more and are in addition blessed with a better and cleaner patronage.' He listed the conditions on which each exhibitor could enjoy these enviable results: '... better music, ... better films, ... good stage effects, ... the printing of attractive programmes, the making of artistic signs, intelligent advertising, good lectures,' the last being for Bush and many others the most certain way of holding a middle-class clientele—but also the sign of a certain conservatism (see pp.133ff. below).

If Bush was principally concerned with the context in which films were presented, he and other columnists also had prescriptions as to the content of films, pointing out what should be repressed in the name of 'good taste', providing a 'guide' for existing or future censorship. Discussions of this topic in the press almost always turned on a hypocritical protection of the working classes against dangerous influences—unpunished crime, violence, smut, vulgarity—and rarely admitted that the crucial issue was to avoid shocking the new customers. It was these press discussions that eventually resulted in an institutionalised self-censorship.

But in content as in 'language', the major contribution of these columnists was to single out the tendencies and even latencies that had to be encouraged to bring about the birth of the institution as we know it:

> No one ever looks twice at a man's picture. As a mere thing of beauty, he is usually unmanly; as a creature of forceful character, he is usually unlovely. We look to woman for what beautifies existence, and, as interest in picture plays is stimulated by what is seen, it becomes centred on the heroine of the story. To suit the role, she must be lovable. Thoughtful appreciation of what is required by the role and good taste in things feminine count, but, when she delights the eye and stirs the irresponsible pulses of responsible men with a dazzling array of potent womanly attributes, she wins because she represents the ideal creatures of one's heartaches and dreams (Harrison 1910).[15]

In fact, a decisive step towards the emergence of the IMR in the USA was indeed marked by the final abandonment of male actors playing women's parts, and the premises of the star system in the occasional appearance in emblematic close-ups at the beginning or end of the films of beautiful heroines.

When they recommended the adaptation of more Shakespeare plays (Bush 1908b) or attempted to protect the audience against populist vulgarities from France or naturalistic audacities from Denmark,[16] these columnists were always helping to create the conditions for the socio-economic broadening that enabled the American cinema to become an industry.

But in the last analysis, the transformation of the cinema depended on those in charge of production and direction, the Blacktons, Griffiths, Bitzers, etc.

At Biograph it seems that when Griffith first joined them they had already developed a reassuring dramaturgy deriving from the homogenised melodrama still surviving at the beginning of the century and familiar to Griffith from his theatrical experience. Its predominant feature is an idealisation of idyllic village life, a 'perfect' order of family and community troubled momentarily by some dramatic event. The latter often comes from the city in the form of a kind of lumpen criminality (the hobo), sometimes actually seen climbing down from the rods of a railroad car, as at the beginning of **The Lonedale Operator** (1911). At the end family and community order have always been restored. There is a striking contrast here with a film marking the high point of American primitive cinema, **The Kentucky Feud** (1905), in which rural order degenerates into absurd and absolutely unredeemed butchery and country dwellers are seen as Other, as in the French populist films. Soon such 'lapses' would no longer be possible. Even before Griffith, the 'village' theme existed in germ in the cinema.

It can already be found in 1905 in **The White Caps** (Wallace McCutcheon and Porter for Edison), an exceptionally elaborate film for its period, especially in its editing. Ten years before **The Birth of a Nation**, the aim of this film is to idealise a kind of Ku Klux Klan, seen as the guardians of rural morality, here providing protection to a woman and her children, regularly beaten by a drunken husband. The last is whipped, tarred and feathered, and ridden out of town on a rail! (Such white caps did indeed proliferate in Mississippee at the turn of the century, but their target was primarily the black workers of large Jewish landowners whom these small white farmers blamed for difficulties really imposed on them by an unjust credit system.)

Most of Griffith's Biograph films are explicitly addressed to two audiences: towndwellers who, although they may only have reached the city recently, still clung to a nostalgia for the 'lost paradise' of the village; and the rural audience itself, which was beginning to grow much more rapidly than was the case in France, for example.

Griffith was a member of a new generation of film-makers whose origins and cultural horizons contrast strikingly with those of Porter and Bitzer, say. In particular, their background was 'artistic' rather than technical.

The son of a Southern doctor who had been a Civil-War hero ruined by Reconstruction, Griffith was by 1908 so déclassé in relation to all his antecedents, so much a *man of the interstices*, that he seems cut out for the part he was to play in this period of sociological transition in the history of the American cinema. Fascinated at an early age by the American popular theatre, that offshoot of European melodrama, with its feeble texts and promotion of the actor's performance, Griffith joined a very modest stock company when he was twenty. In twelve years he became familiar with all the levels of popular theatre of the period, from tours only nominally distinct from vagrancy, to the status of author of plays staged in a large Washington theatre, via a period of acting in and staging the dramatic sketches that formed part of the vaudeville show. In conformity with the 'edifying' character of vaudeville, these sketches were usually digests of prestigious texts, a genre Griffith successfully pioneered in the cinema: his adaptation of Browning's verse play **Pippa Passes** (1909) was the first film to be reviewed in *The New York Times*.

This connection between Griffith and vaudeville perhaps helps to locate the latter as a transitional spectacle, not just in that it had an 'educational' address to an uprooted audience, but insofar as it helped that audience to get over its prejudices against the theatre (*of representation*) by injecting it in small doses in the form which was to be recognisable from around 1908 in the films of Griffith and Blackton.

The founders of Vitagraph, James Stuart Blackton and Albert Edward Smith, both of whom had come from England with their parents as young men, were also prepared by their class origins and culture to respond to the new needs of a new audience.

Admittedly, Blackton, who made all the company's output for several years, went rather too far in his admirable film **And the Villain Still Pursued Her; or, The Author's Dream** (1906). This extravagant surrealistic parody, reminiscent of Tex Avery, is at least twenty years ahead of its time in the history of American comedy, and proves once and for all that if the cinema had been open to the country's finest talents—and one could ignore the criteria that prevailed in it—American cinema could have been as 'sophisticated' as that of Denmark. But in the USA there were other fish to fry.

More suitable were the 'art films' that Vitagraph began to make in 1907 with productions such as **Francesca da Rimini; or,**

Fig. 15: Albert E. Smith at the camera during the filming of **The Bargain Fiend** at the Vitagraph Brooklyn studio in 1907.

The Two Brothers, already more modern (in their use of space) than their slightly later French equivalents. They also began to make films explicitly addressed to the desired new strata: the office workers who are the protagonists of a pretty love story like **The Romance of an Umbrella** (1909) and the minor intelligentsia (**A Friendly Marriage**, 1911).

Simultaneously with these transformations in content (and format: the films became longer and the narratives more articulated), basic changes began to occur in the mode of representation. Griffith popularised the medium close-up, the alternating syntagm, and the insert, while Vitagraph began to abandon frontality, experimenting with shot-reverse-shot and actors with their backs to the camera, and tried out edge lighting.

The profound connections between the search for a 'new audience', the economic growth of the cinema, and changes in content, on the one hand, and on the other, the profound changes that were to take place in the mode of representation,[17] seem to me to be inscribed in the discourse of those who stubbornly defended all these advances:

> **Rescued from an Eagle's Nest** is a feeble attempt to secure a trick film of a fine subject. The boldness of the conception is marred by bad lighting and poor blending of outside photography with the studio work, which is too flat; and the trick of the eagle and its wire wings is too evident to the audience, while the fight between the man and the eagle is poor and out of vision. The hill-brow is not a precipice. We looked for better things (Anon. 1908).[18]

The anonymous author of these lines, like Gorky twelve years earlier, has listed the various deficiencies of the 'primitive mode of representation' that had reigned since Lumière: its lack of depth, centring, and continuity, in other words, of *presence* and *verisimilitude*.

Nevertheless, in subsequent years it was possible for other contributors to *The Moving Picture World* to take Porter and his outdated primitivism as a model:

Fig. 16: **The Romance of an Umbrella** (Vitagraph, 1909).

A great many of the pictures that are made ... would be all the better ... if the figures were placed farther away from the camera. The Rex releases are examples, to our mind, of the proper thing to do. Here Mr. Porter works on a large stage, and places his camera at a considerable distance from his actors. The result is that he avoids abnormality of size, and when you see the pictures on the screen, they express the proper sensuous impression of size (Anon. 1911).[19]

A number of articles published between 1909 and 1912 (e.g., Anon. 1909a; Hoffman 1912) mourn the loss of the body in this way and demand the maintenance of the primitive tableau. The reason is that *The Moving Picture World* is one of the sites of a struggle between the two systems of representation, and it is not surprising that it should often contain 'false solutions' to the problems facing the new spectators, unused to the screen and, what is more, confronting a ceaselessly shifting 'language': 'If you have seen a picture ten times you can be of great help to the man who sees it for the first time. You can explain and point out things that at the first exhibition of the release even a man of average intelligence and good education might very easily miss.' Thus William Bush (1911),[20] appealing for the nth time in *The Moving Picture World* for the extension and development of the lecturer. In fact, we find many proposals—some carried out, others not—made in the name of an improvement in the 'quality' of the audience[21] but objectively contradicting the currents that were to result in the internalisation, ubiquitisation and centring characteristic of the IMR, one of them being this extension of lecturing, another a system of projection with the lights up intended to make cinemas less dangerous places, also conceived of in France (see Gunning 1981).

But a handful of columnists, some of them anonymous but others whose names we know—Frank Woods, Louis Reeves Harrison, Rollin Summers—succeeded in laying down with astonishing clarity the bases for a true *pragmatics* of the IMR.

These men dealt with almost all the 'obstacles' separating the cinema as it was at the beginnings of their critical careers from a quite different cinema they could only anticipate, of course, but whose gestation did indeed follow the lines they had foreseen and promoted. I am often amazed at their foresight in seizing on the most basic questions posed by this transition period: 'The most conspicuous offense committed by motion picture producers and players against this quality of reality is the tendency that nearly all of them have at times to play to the front, thus betraying unconsciously that they know they are being pictured, and giving the impression to the spectators that they are going through their parts before an audience which is not seen in the picture, but which appears to be located in front of the scene' (Woods 1910). A man who, in the same article, compared the 'shock' experienced by the spectator as the result of a look at the lens with that felt by a hypnotic subject when the hypnotist snaps his fingers to wake him from his trance, was not going to preach the maintenance of lecturing or projection with lights up. We are dealing with an absolutely basic understanding of the 'historical tendency' (cf. p.232 n.23 below). The same can be said of the writer who argued against lecturing on the basis of essential features of the bourgeois naturalist theatre—closure, linearity—which the cinema was soon to assimilate using its own means: 'The acted drama must explain itself. Its story must be unfolded bit by bit, without explanation, from a prologue or lecture. The moving picture play should be similarly constructed' (Summers 1908, p.212).

Thus these men clearly saw the need to make 'composed views' conform to certain norms of representation that constituted a *second nature* for them as cultivated individuals—a respect for temporal linearity, a rigorous logic of cause and effect, the necessary presence-absence of diegetic space, all questions that will be central to the next few chapters of this book and which they approached with an openness especially valuable to the modern investigator:

> It seems equally justifiable to use the device of the printed message, and if it is presented in such sequence that curiosity is aroused as to its contents it will probably be received by the audience without substantial loss of illusion. Printed explanations thrown on the screen before scenes are not at all similar in principle and are entirely crude and unjustifiable. They destroy the suspense and interest by outlining the scope of the scene in advance (ibid.).

The practice condemned here in 1908 was one that was to survive in Griffith's films until many years later and to reach delirious heights in an internationally successful film like **Cabiria** (1914). In many European films it remained throughout the 1920's one of the last survivals of the primitive period.[22] This suggests how much these columnists were ahead of their times on occasion. Frank Woods, in a section of anonymous reviews he wrote along-side the column he signed 'The Spectator' (Woods 1909b), went so far as to give detailed advice as to the construction of scenarios and even editing:

> The first few scenes of this picture [**The Jilt**] appear to be disconnected and drawn out to greater length than the nature of the scenes warrant. The affection of the two college boys could have been shown with less detail; their grief at parting is overdone, and a scene in which one of them saves the other from footpads appears wholly unnecessary. By economising the points noted, there would have been room in the reel to introduce the woman who turns out to be the 'jilt' with more clearness.

These calculating recommendations show that Woods—who eventually became a Hollywood producer—had a perfect under-standing of the economy of centring (around the *persona*, around the feminine body) that the Institution would come to espouse. He wrote about the editing of a sequence located in a theatre in **The Sales Lady's Matinée Idol** (Edison) as follows (1909a):

> Another view of the balcony is now presented and to under-stand the conduct of the audience we are obliged to imagine that they are witnessing the railroad scene previously exhibited. Here is where skill in preparing the film for exhibition would have made this picture a model of its kind. If short scenes had alternated back and forth between the stage and the balcony, showing the progress on the stage and the effect on the bal-cony audience concurrently, the effect would have been greatly increased.

This passage dates from early in 1909, several months before Griffith's first use of shot-reverse-shot in a theatrical context (**A Drunkard's Reformation**, released April 1909). This shows how imbricated was Griffith's work with Woods's.

The rapid move towards the IMR characteristic of American cinema at this time was capable of consummation earlier than is usually realised. A film that came to my notice shortly before this book was finished has shown me that at least one film-maker in America was capable, if only intermittently, of a hallucinatory anticipation of the codes of the *film noir* of the 1940's. That is a sufficient indication that the Institution and its Mode of Representation first achieved fruition in the USA. **The Bank Burglar's Fate**, directed by one John G. Adolfi, was released by the independent studio Reliance in 1914. The very elaborate use of shot-reverse-shot near the end of this film, when the detectives are monitoring, from one café table to another, the activities of the gang of bank robbers they have been tracking down, is already six years ahead of the average Hollywood film. But the close-up that opens the film, a portrait of a gangster casing the joint before the 'job', leaning against a shop window which reflects the street he is surveying, constitutes a reflexive use of off-screen space which can be said to sum up the procedures of the IMR as a whole, and might have been signed by the Raoul Walsh of the 1940's. Other sequences from the film produce the same feeling, the close-up completely escaping its *primitive autarchy* (see p.149 below). This is a first (?) completion of the itinerary embarked upon after 1908 by Griffith, Blackton and others. Comparing it with a film like Billy Bitzer's **The Kentucky Feud** (see below), a totally primitive product whose editing consists only of the arrangement of its tableaux and their titles, one can only conclude that the cinema was never again to change so profoundly as it did between 1905 and 1914 in the USA, not even perhaps with the introduction of sound.

****

Fig. 17: **The Bank Burglar's Fate** (John G. Adolfi, 1914).

It now seems clear, too, that this movement towards the IMR is partly the responsibility of film-makers capable of drawing criteria for their innovations from bourgeois culture and with a 'natural' propensity, quite independent of any purely economic motive, to address their own class. This hypothesis is corroborated by the counter-example of France discussed above. We have seen that the middle classes' contempt for the cinema there produced a historical delay, and also that this could be contrasted with the farsightedness of the middle class in Britain. We might also have explored the astonishing Danish cinema, the first in the world made by members of the middle classes for members of the middle classes, ahead of Hollywood in a number of fields (lighting, even editing). Or the better known Italian cinema, in which innovations and the embourgeoisement of the audience went hand in hand, once aristocratic patronage took over control.

But can we, for all that, claim that what I am tempted to call a 'primitive mode of representation' was truly the 'property' of 'the lower classes'? It was certainly invented by members of the middle class—Méliès, Lumière, Alice Guy—but, for seemingly diverse reasons, they from the start adopted into their practice popular forms (the picture postcard, the strip cartoon, conjuring, music-hall) that transmitted a tradition very remote from the bourgeois theatre they went to as members of their class.

In the USA at this time, on the other hand, a form of spectacle more closely related to the music-hall and the *caf'conc'*—the theatres of the poor in Britain and France respectively—than to the bourgeois theatre was the preferred entertainment for a whole new petty bourgeoisie, newly arrived from the villages and suspicious of the theatre for puritan reasons.

It also seems well established that this American lower middle class was less fond of the earliest films than the masses of Britain and France.

But one should, I believe, be very suspicious of the temptations of a populist reading here. On the one hand we know nothing at all about the real reactions of the popular audiences of the period. Were the classic historians right in claiming, for example, that early audiences quickly tired of the forms of early cinema? On the other hand the popular forms that clearly overdetermine the mode of representation of these early films are anything but 'pure'—they are often forms created from bits and pieces by the middle classes for the masses.

Finally, given that this mode of representation is largely defined only *negatively*—in a strict morphological sense it is *unmarked*—this overdetermination may have been partly a matter of contingency, for this early 'system' is also the 'simplest' way a film camera could have been used.

NOTES

1   Which the immigrants eventually internalised as an ethnic rivalry—'we Irish are better than you Poles'—that is the source of the divisions and weaknesses of the American working class from its origins to this day (see Arnault 1976, pp.230-31, and 1972, pp.132-3).

2   Need it be pointed out that, although the cinema audience has become diversified and specialised in recent years in the industrialised countries, this 'expanded target' remains the ideal of American commercial television, vigilant in its efforts to produce an endless chain of 'least objectionable programmes'?

3   Of course, starting in 1911, McCay himself drew for animated films which are amongst the earliest masterpieces of the genre.

4   Robert C. Allen (1980) claims that the vaudeville audience was immediately very taken with films. But one senses in his book a need to over-rate the role of vaudeville—and with it the American middle class's fascination for cinema from its birth—arising from the internal logic of a US doctoral thesis. Charles Musser (1984), on the contrary, points out in support of the idea that films served to empty the vaudeville houses between shows that they often stayed on the bill for as long as five weeks, whereas the variety programme changed weekly and the audiences were regular attenders.

5   The earliest criticism appearing in the trade press already attacks the 'immorality' of certain French films, and the censors later banned series such as **Fantômas** and **Zigomar**.

6   **The Finish of Bridget McKeen** (Porter, 1901), subsequently copied by Smith in Britain (see p.197 below), is based on the same model.

7   What was the composition of the audience for Hale's Tours? In principle, it was just as true of the USA as of Europe that the 'scenics' almost exclusively projected in them were such as to attract the middle class. But in the great centres of immigrant settlement it seems likely that the latter provided much of that audience.

8   Elizabeth Ewen (1980) tells us that the cinema, unlike the tavern and the burlesque, was considered 'permissible' for the women of the immigrant

populace, and that they took considerable advantage of this permission. But was this true before the First World War? The testimony used to support the claim all dates from after 1918, a period when women from better-off strata had also begun to go to the cinema.

9 These 'Irish' comedians are hopeless, and they are bombarded with tomatoes *that come from behind the camera*. This precocious example of the staging of 'reverse-field space' is one among a whole series of US films that are 'experimental' in the same sense as some British ones. But the latter's experiments are concerned with editing earlier and more often than the American ones.

10 They are somewhat similar to the Pathé films of the series including **Au bagne** and **Au pays noir**, insofar as they combine 'scenic' views with composed views. At the beginning of **Skyscrapers**, we see real labourers at work in documentary shots not directly matched with the first shot of the fiction. A few modernist-inclined scholars have tried to make a film like this a kind of prefiguration of the discontinuities characteristic of modern cinema (Godard, Solanas, Sara Gomez). But at this time, clearly, the distinction between fictional and real on the screen was still extremely fluid (think only of certain 'actualities' by Méliès or Pathé such as the two versions of the Mont Pelée eruption reconstituted in the studio but exhibited as documentaries). Even such striking (to our eyes) mixtures of material as, e.g., **Un Drame en mer** ('Tragedy at Sea', Velle, 1905) may not have been perceived as such by regular viewers of the period, or rather the mixed character was *non-pertinent* in a show consisting of discontinuities from beginning to end. If this is so, then the shots that introduce **Skyscrapers**, although they seem to us to have all the marks of 'documentary' (people look at the camera—but the spectators in exterior scenes and even the actors themselves often looked at the camera at this time), are quite unambiguous to the historian: they prefigure a standard and even essential procedure of the future Institution, i.e., the incorporation of stock shots or other material photographed 'live' into the diegetic flux without any visible break in continuity.

11 Still later is the famous film **The Italian** (Reginald Barker for Thomas Ince, 1915): Beppo, a highly exploited Italian immigrant, sees his child die as a result of the insanitary conditions of the ghetto and the cruel indifference of a political boss. However, at the last minute he abandons his attempt at a horrible revenge—to bring about the death of the boss's small daughter—and goes to meditate over the grave of his own son. But the fact that the film is narrated as a kind of tacit flashback by this same Beppo, now decently housed and dressed, is reassuring: the poverty is only temporary, no human tragedy is final in the land of free enterprise! (Tom Gunning has suggested to me that this man was not intended to be Beppo, but the actor who played him, George Beban, *in propria persona*. Be that as it may, the textual effect and its ideological implications are the same.)

12 The origin of the text translated into French in Zukor (1930) is not stated; it is close to, but not identical with Zukor (1927). In the translations in the text of this book, I have followed the wording in this last source except where the French version materially differs [Translator's Note].

13 It is surely suggestive of the differences between the status of middle-class women in France and the USA—then as now—that their going to the cinema hardly had the same effect in France, where the masculine and feminine spheres are more strictly segregated.

14 Even in 1917, when luxury cinemas had been built in residential districts inspired by the decor of the upper-class country club, free gifts of perfume were still being offered at the doors to attract women customers (see Gomery 1978).

15 It is surely a further sign of the 'backwardness' of French cinema that, with the exception of the voyeuristic films made for men only, the heroines of French films are often far from constituting sex objects, right up to the end of the First World War.

16 The Danish cinema, early brought under the control of remarkably able figures from the bourgeois theatre, was the first cinema made by highly cultured people for their social peers, i.e., the first middle-class cinema in a full sense. And these artists familiar with Strindberg, Ibsen and Bjørnson broached themes like sexual passion, adultery, and unwed mothers, and hence were denounced as pornographic in the USA. Of 32 films copyrighted by Nordisk in the USA in 1911 and 1912, only two or three were actually distributed (see Bergsten 1973, pp.27-8).

17 Tom Gunning (1981) argues along essentially the same lines, noting in certain of Griffith's films the characteristics of an emergent 'middle-class language'. Charles Musser (1983), on the contrary, insists that the technico-economic instance is the most important: it was not the wish to replace a popular audience with a middle-class one that caused the change in 'language' but the simple economic logic of the transition from the artisanal to the industrial stage within the cinema itself. But insofar as we are considering a product for which ideology was, as it were, the very substance (what the audience bought was above all sensation, emotion and experience, it was *ideal*), I find the 'economic last instance' hard to apply in a conjuncture as overdetermined as this one. And we should not underestimate the importance for the consolidation of the socio-economic situation in the USA of the apparent obliteration of class distinctions and the establishment of every possible *instance of consensus*.

18 I am grateful to Charles Musser for drawing this text to my attention. I am even more grateful to him for a conversation which enabled me to improve the present chapter enormously.

19 An ironic fate for Porter, who was surely far in advance of his contemporaries between 1900 and 1906, and yet was so far 'behind' them in 1911 that he could be proclaimed the standard bearer of the enemies of the close-up! But is it too venturesome to suggest that the constitution of the cinematic subject via camera closeness, ubiquity, etc., demanded a new self-awareness on the part of the director? In his memoirs, Arthur C. Miller, recalling his move to Rex with Porter, remarks that the latter 'was a pretty thorough mechanic and ... it was the mechanical aspect of film-making that interested him the most' (Balshofer & Miller 1967, p.45). The time did come (in 1911, in fact) when Porter 'began to realise that directing was a full-time job, and concentrated on

it more than ever before. Nevertheless, it was a struggle for him to stay away from the camera. He ... found it necessary to be able to perform all the duties that went into making a moving picture, including the developing and printing of the film' (ibid., p.49). Miller concludes: 'However, the day of specialisation had arrived, and, of course, D.W. Griffith was the great example in the directing field as was Billy Bitzer as a cameraman' (ibid.). Surely artisanal ubiquity had to cease for the oneness of the director-subject to be conveyed, via the ubiquity of the camera, to the oneness of the spectator-subject.

20 The fact that Bush himself was a professional lecturer does not mean that his calls for a wider use of lectures were not approved by the editors of *The Moving Picture World* and hence by a proportion of the trade and the audience (as is evidenced by letters published in the trade press of the period, not only in New York but also in London).

21 It is patent in all their articles on the subject that Bush and company explicitly linked the lecturer to the search for a 'respectable' audience; see especially the announcement of a visit to a cinema by a rather high-class lady lecturer, a certain Madame Lora Bona (Anon. 1910a & 1910b).

22 In the films of Abel Gance and other Frenchmen, as in those of Eisenstein and other Soviet film-makers, this 'primitive survival' was a factor of pedagogic distantiation, a last rampart against institutional *absorption*.

Passions and Chases—A Certain Linearisation

A *large-scale narrative form* first appeared in the cinema extremely early—but only a very elementary one. It is found in the boxing matches filmed for the Kinetoscope, first by the Latham brothers, then by Raff and Gammon. They consisted of series of one-minute shots (the length of a round) that could be viewed one after another through a Kinetoscope peephole by inserting a coin for each round. The culmination of this genre came in 1897 with the live shooting (all the previous ones were re-enactments) of a fight between Corbett and Fitzsimmons with a camera deriving from the Kinetograph, the Ceriscope. After 'editing', the film attained the then quite unprecedented length of fifteen minutes. Despite the 'documentary' character of these films, they present one of the premises of what was to become the narrative concatenation of institutional editing, especially in the suspense built up from one episode to the next *for the spectator with a knowledge of the codes of the boxing match.* In this we are still at the heart of the primitive system; continuity and sequentiality are dependent on a competence outside the system of the film: he (or she) who does not know the meaning of the sequence of rounds, the rules of boxing, the secrets of tactics and strategy, will only perceive a series of exchanges of blows, repeated again and again until the final knockout, if such there be.

By a *large-scale narrative form* I mean one that bodies forth articulations of the signified by means of articulations at the level of the signifier, one in which discontinuities in the picture produce narrative meanings (in contrast, particularly, to those discontinuities which are due to accidental stoppages of the camera and are common in the films of the early years, when such jump cuts were just semantic noise, whereas those of Godard, say, are meaningful). Narrativity could of course unfold *ad libitum* in the primitive tableau, but once a single narrative articulation was revealed by a discontinuity of the signifier, a decisive threshold had been passed. This has happened for Porter, for example, with **The Finish of Bridget McKeen** or **Another Job for the Undertaker** (see p.139 n.6 above), whereas it has not in **Grandma's Reading Glass** (see p.89 above) despite the number of its shot changes, because the latter only function descriptively and to satisfy the scopic drive, but are not narrative in the strict sense.[1]

The first manifestations of this *biunivocal concatenation* in the context of fiction properly speaking were the four versions of the *Passion Play* shot in 1897 and 1898—two in Paris (by Lear, and later by Georges Hatot for the Lumière company), a third in Bohemia by the American William Freeman, and a fourth in New York by Paley and Russell. The first two were more than ten minutes long, already an exceptional length for the period, but the others were close to or longer than half an hour! Given that no story other than that of the Passion of Jesus Christ attained such a length for more than ten years, it seems clear that we are dealing with a privileged phenomenon, and one whose deeper meaning I am convinced has hardly been brought out by the classic histories of the cinema.

In fact what we have here is a brilliant illustration of the fundamentally contradictory nature of the primitive cinema, in which one step 'forward' so often implies two steps 'backwards'. The best way of grasping the nature of the system that was to emerge from the interweaving of all the advances of this kind that can be detected between 1897 and 1914 is to look more closely at this contradiction.

The origin of these various versions of the Passion story was quite directly 'theatrical': the cultural and touristic success at the end of the nineteenth century among a bourgeoisie now travelling en masse of folkloric spectacles like those of Oberammergau in Bavaria and Hořice in what is now Czechoslovakia (the latter was the Passion play filmed more or less *in situ* by Freeman). It is important to emphasise that this was a theatrical form descending directly from the mediæval mystery plays and still at the turn of the century having only minimal connections with the naturalism of the bourgeois theatre. Zdeněk Štábla, who has written a study of Freeman's film, describes the Hořice Passion Play as follows:

From the text of the Passion play, which was first published independently in 1892, it appears that two kinds of stage techniques were used, depending on the nature of the scenes and tableaux. Most scenes were of the traditional dramatic variety, where the conflict between the individual characters was expressed mainly in the form of dialogue. There were about fifty of these tableaux, or to be more precise, brief acts and scenes. The so-called 'live tableaux' were of a completely different nature. These were introduced by a *commentary* given by the choirmaster. There were 26 of these tableaux grouped together in a number of sequences alternating with the dramatic scenes. *They were more like pantomime than drama and were much better suited to the purposes of filming* (1971, p.19).[2]

And in fact all the versions of the Passion play filmed between 1897 and 1907 consist of a series of tableaux vivants, preceded (separated) by the title of the tableau (ibid., p.3n.), and usually, one assumes, described by a lecturer (here arising quite logically from the original spectacle).

Of course, the beginnings of an explanation for the existence of these filmed Passion plays can be found in this affinity between two silent arts. But this form of mime appeared before any other because the story of the Passion was an almost universally familiar one. Clearly, this was what allowed the promoters of these films to go so decisively beyond the limits of the Lumière or Dickson sequence shot and offer their audiences a long-lasting spectacle made up of a large number of tableaux vivants *linked together in a sequence which everyone could be assumed to know*. It should be emphasised that almost any sequence of tableaux from one of these films—e.g., in the Lumière **La Vie et la Passion de Jésus-Christ**: 'The Adoration of the Magi', 'The Flight into Egypt', 'Arrival in Jerusalem', 'Betrayal of Judas', and so on for a total of thirteen numbers—would be completely lacking in narrative meaning for any spectator ignorant of the basic teachings of Christianity. In most cases the pictures contain no intrinsic pointers to what makes one necessarily follow on from the previous one. Once Christ has grown his beard, at any rate, the sequence of the pictures could be radically altered without at all troubling a spectator who did not already know, say, that 'Arrest of Jesus Christ' follows 'The Holy Supper' and precedes 'The Resurrection'. Without a whole set of external referents, the innocent eye would see a kind of spiritual landscape, like the purely 'topographic' spectacle that ecclesiastical stained glass might offer to the pagan eye. By contrast, for Christians—including non-practising ones and non-believers brought up in a Christian tradition—these pictures follow an ineluctable order, the Order of orders, one might say, the progression of the most exemplary of all lives, the linearity of which, guaranteed by its sacramental gestures, can be seen in the West as founding any possible linearity. In fact, the Passion story was capable of establishing the principle of narrative linearity in the cinema a long time before a 'syntax' had evolved to provide for it also at the level of the relation between signifier and signified rather than at that of the referent alone, as is the case here (where the semiosis is the same as that in the boxing match).

But at the same time—and this is a precocious manifestation of the kind of law of mutual inconsistencies that governs the whole development of the primitive cinema—all these versions of the Passion story crystallise and exaggerate the fundamentally non-linear characteristics of the 'primitive tableau', the 'Lumière model'. The tangle of contradictions these films gave rise to was to take more than twenty years to unravel.

The imagery used in these Passion films, as in the 'popular' representations they reproduced, came from the Saint-Sulpician imagery of contemporary religious paintings. This borrowing added to the acentric, 'panoramic' constraints often attendant on the reading of this kind of painting a further series of constraints deriving from the introduction of movement into a flat picture. And here neither colour, three dimensions nor speech helped compensate for the increase in reading difficulty. Georges Sadoul's judgement of the Lumière Passion film (1973, t.I, pp.372-3) is dismissive: 'All they did is to photograph a series of theatrical scenes, without in any way adapting the acting, the composition, the costumes or the staging for the cinema, inevitably giving an impression of confusion and complication on the screen.' This is in fact the impression inevitable to a modern eye faced with very many films made in the first decade. But it is not necessarily the one always felt by regular viewers of the period, to whom the primitive cinema itself offered a certain 'perceptual education' (see p.155 below).

At all events, by 1897 there is no doubt that those who exhibited these Passion films to audiences, notwithstanding the familiarity of the story, felt the need to have their projections accompanied by lectures modelled both on magic-lantern lectures and on the folkloric plays' own commentaries. These lectures had two functions: to sort out the 'confused' iconography, and to remind those in the 'flock' who might have forgotten them of the individual details of the 'greatest story ever told'.

I shall return to this 'impression of confusion' in relation to the issue of what I call the *linearisation of iconographic signifiers*. For the moment I want to trace the development of the narrative linearisation, the installation of a biunivocal 'cause-and-effect' chain clearly initiated in these first Passion films.[3]

****

In 1897, the British pioneer George Albert Smith shot a film of forty feet or so in front of a windmill on the downs near Brighton and called it **The Miller and the Sweep**: in front of his mill, a miller carrying a sack of flour accidentally bumps into a sweep with a sack of soot. A fight follows, in the course of which the miller is blackened with soot and the sweep whitened with flour. Up to this point the film consists of a typically mechanical low music-hall gag of a type reflected in other British films.[4] But towards the end of this short film, the miller runs out of frame pursued by the sweep (or is it the other way round?) and at the same moment a small crowd whose off-screen presence has in no way been signalled hitherto cross the screen after the two protagonists and the film only ends when the last of them has left the frame.

One would surely be wrong to claim this as the first *chase film*. For a start, there may have been earlier ones in Britain or in France. Then again, insofar as chase films have a privileged position in the history of the cinema from around 1903 it is because they contain several shots. Nevertheless, given the whole later development that culminated in the IMR, this film made by a film-maker distinguished by his visionary powers points to the historical need which was answered by the chase film.

It has been suggested (Salt 1982) that this nascent chase and the cinematic genre itself derived from the European tradition of vaudeville, in which it was indeed customary to organise a chase with a number of characters crossing the stage and supposedly continuing in the wings. This is in fact an example of the naturalistic tendencies gradually invading all European theatre at the turn of the century. But in the cinema it acquired a more explicit and broader meaning. To see in it no more than a mechanical consequence of a 'theatricality' not yet overcome would be to suggest that the extraordinary explosion of chase films in the following years was an 'inexplicable fad'. On the contrary, it represented the second great gesture towards the linear chains of the future IMR.

In **The Miller and the Sweep**, the entry and exit of the small crowd 'coming from nowhere' already suggests, in a way impossible for a chase in a theatre, *where audience and actors occupy the same space*, the existence of a *latent* domain adjacent to the profilmic space of the primitive single set-up. It indicates an *elsewhere* that could be linked to that space by a relation of spatiotemporal succession, but only by virtue of a concatenatory principle that would constitute the first step on the way to the *physiologically rational ubiquity* of the Institution, still inconceivable in 1897.

One first major advance towards the discovery of this principle was made with the first chase films properly so-called, which made use of the notions of both temporal succession and (more or less close) spatial proximity, without yet codifying the rules that would eventually anchor these successions and proximities in the spectator's body. That is why the chain of the chase films is still basically committed to *primitive externality*.

The British film-maker Williamson's **Stop Thief!** (1901) presents a chase structure which, while still extremely rudimentary, does nonetheless *extend over three shots*. The first shot of the film shows the motive for the chase—a tramp steals some meat from a butcher's boy—and its beginning; the second, the chase going on—pursued by the boy and several dogs, the tramp runs along a street; the third, its end—when the tramp hides in a barrel centre frame, is caught there by the dogs and dragged out by the butcher's boy.

It could be said that the device used in **The Miller and the Sweep** created a tension (in a sense **Arroseur et arrosé** had already created the same tension). The primitive cinema then proposed two resolutions of that tension. The first, maintaining the autarchic tableau, is embodied in a 'remake' of the Lumière film by Smith called **A Practical Joke** or **A Joke on the Gardener** (1898). Here the whole chase is confined to the frame, taking place round a tree. The film is a *retreat* from editing. But is it of any importance that the first known cinematic chase that adopts the other solution, i.e., editing, contains not two but three shots?

A bipartite structure in which the signifiers of 'beginning' and 'conclusion' would be positively delimited by the linking of shot to shot, whereas that of 'continuation' would be principally an absence, would perhaps have constituted a violation of the 'laws' of narrativity which, as we know, demand this tripartite structure. Thus it is clear that these laws were in force from the most remote premises of the IMR.

At any rate, the second shot does contribute *duration* to Williamson's chase, the installation of what Christian Metz has called 'frequentative or durational editing' (1966, pp.121-2; cf. 1972, pp.65 & 120, 1974, pp.121-2, 127 & 131-3), and in particular it creates interstices in which the chase can be inferred to be continuing.[5] A series of only two shots would have given the impression of a chase stopping as soon as it had started. It would only have consisted of an exit from one space followed by an arrival in another, an effect equivalent to that of the classical ellipsis of the shot of the stairs, eliminating rather than designating the ascent of those stairs.

These few suggestions prove, I think, that institutional continuity was born with the chase, or rather that the latter came into being and proliferated so that continuity could be established.

But in one absolutely critical respect the primitive chase remains within the Lumière model, in what I have called the *autarchy of the primitive shot* which still links it to the picture postcard.[6] This autarchy reveals itself in two ways. First, for many years, and in every producing country, even when there are a large number of participants in the chase, each shot is obligatorily extended until they have all left the frame; and each shot also usually shows the entrance into frame of all the participants. Billy Bitzer's **Tom, Tom, the Piper's Son** (1905), which seems so pedantic in these respects that one wonders whether it might not be a parody of this 'tic' of the chase film, appeared just as 'cuts on action' began to be seen in Britain and France. This can be said to be the beginning of the emergence from the 'primitive sphere', of the disappearance of that autarchy.

The other sign of primitive autarchy is more negative, marked by an *absence* which helped to maintain the *externality of the spectator subject* that I shall be discussing at length later (pp.165ff.). In Williamson's film, the characters leave the first shot on the left, enter the second one on the left and leave it on the right, and enter the third one on the right. In other words, there is as yet no observation of the 'rule' of *direction matching* that was later to guarantee a certain continuity (abolishing primitive autarchy) and to help to centre the spectator-subject.

But despite this externality, despite the primitive autarchy that follows from it, showing a series of shots of people running after one another was already to create a far greater sense of continuity than static tableaux could. And this was the role of the chase: to extend the film experience, to initiate a certain 'imaginary' production of duration and succession exploiting an off-screen space which although it was still amorphous would eventually make possible the diegetic production characteristic of the institution. But at the same time the chase was to give rise to the first continuity matches, in other words, the first concatenations of an indexical kind, as opposed to those already coded in the symbolic (the lecturer's speech for the Passion films) or iconic modes (to use Peircean terminology—see pp.209 & 231 n.10). Almost everywhere and at the same time film-makers decided to organise the direction of their chases or runs along binomial lines: towards the camera/away from the camera. The dog's run in **Rescued by Rover** is towards the camera while it is following the beggar woman who has kidnapped the baby, and away from it while it is returning home. Such innovations organise the shots geographically, linking them together by connections that are visual but also purely indexical.

It is perhaps nearly tautological to say that classical editing's system of spatial concatenation is based solely on the indexical order, while its temporal concatenation (succession/ellipsis, flashback, simultaneity) is based as much on the iconic order (night versus day, changes of clothes) as on the symbolic order (intertitles, dissolves, close-ups of clocks). But this distinction does perhaps make it easier to pose correctly certain questions of the history of film stylistics, questions which are beyond the scope of this book. Why is it, for example, that the only symbolic codes that have ever been specific to the cinema—all those special effects known as opticals (fades, wipes and dissolves in the sound period, but also irises and vignettes in the silent)—have often become marginal or vanished entirely today (from the Institution, of course)? And why, with the exception of the opening fade-in and closing fade-out which still persist (and in a few cases dissolves), straight cuts have become the rule for all shot changes, temporal modes being differentiated via the non-specific codes of the cinema, the only other specific code still 'in force' being the one governing diegetic topography, i..e., precisely the *indexical match* (matching direction, position or eyeline)? And above all, why is it that the processes of internalisation and naturalisation seem to be ever increasingly refined at the stylistic level without changing the IMR one iota as an infrastructure?

Insofar as these questions belong to the history of stylistics, they are beyond the scope of the present study. But to the extent that they suggest that the disappearance of the 'punctuations' of the pre-talky era was the object of a long drawn-out 'struggle' (which lasted until the 1950's in Hollywood) precisely because they were the last traces of the process of building the IMR— whose naturalising vocation was better suited to the indexical mode than to the symbolic—their invocation is not perhaps out of place here.

****

As we have seen, the transposition to the cinema of the codes of the Passion play or painting could not but aggravate the 'crammed', 'confused' character already noted in Lumière's urban scenics. This aspect of the primitive tableau, which seems to demand a *topographical reading*, is absolutely crucial for the definition of the features of any 'primitive mode of representation'. After 1900, certain efforts were made to simplify, to strip down the primitive long shot in order to make it easier to read (efforts which recall Dickson's black backgrounds at Edison). But even a film-maker like Porter, who shows this concern for simplification very early, sticks to the long shot 'crammed with signs' until 1906 (**Life of a Cowboy**). This is a kind of picture whose content can only be exhausted—sometimes even simply read—by a modern spectator, at any rate, after repeated viewings. Let me cite some other examples drawn from the American cinema, which was, of course, 'behind' the French and even British cinemas in compositional terms at this time, but nevertheless addressed significant audiences both inside and outside the vaudeville theatres.

A Rube in the Subway (Biograph, 1905) shows in a single shot a highly ingenious set with trains that arrive and depart to the left and right of a central platform at the end of which a stair ascends. In this very small space a considerable crowd walks up and down, and in their midst the rube gets involved in a series of minor comic incidents which most modern spectators are absolutely incapable of deciphering at one viewing of the film. True, the rube character does appear in a number of films, so assiduous film-goers of the period could perhaps have registered him as the centre of the diegesis.[7]

Then there is the first shot of the fine film photographed by Bitzer already referred to, **Tom, Tom, the Piper's Son**, which I first discovered in the important work Ken Jacobs has made from it. The shot shows a village square completely filled by a market crowd and dominated by an acrobat in a white leotard and tights. Experience shows that the story enacted in this tableau is rarely readable to the modern eye at one viewing. Jacobs's film, which *analyses* this scene for many minutes as if under a microscope is a good simulation of the process the eye conditioned by the modern Institution wants the film subjected to. It provides the elements whereby its components can be linearised, torn from their simultaneity[8] to bring out not only the narrative centre of the picture but also all the signs around, during, before and after it that constitute its site, occasion, etc.

This shot seems all the more significant when one realises that three years later Bitzer was to become Griffith's preferred cameraman and that one of the first pieces of advice he is supposed to have given the new director (for his first film, **The Adventures of Dolly**, 1908) was not to put his camera too far away from his subject (Bitzer 1973, p.66). It might seem to follow that this first shot of **Tom, Tom, the Piper's Son**—which was a very popular film on its release—soon came to appear to him to be a mistake. And yet he was still to make what I regard as one of the authentic masterpieces of the primitive cinema, **The Kentucky Feud**, characterised by exceptionally and uniformly long-framed shots in which this topographical reading is a constant requirement.

What was its *status* in 1905?

At about this time, in his reflections on art, Rodin proposed the following analysis of Watteau's *The Embarcation for the Island of Cythera*: 'In this masterpiece the *action*, if you will notice, begins in the foreground to the right and ends in the background to the left.' There follows a description of each of the *successive scenes* in the painting, which he demonstrates detail the stages of one and the same *galante progression*. 'You see, then, that an artist can, when he pleases, represent not only fleeting gestures, but a long *action*, to employ a term of dramatic art. In order to succeed, he only needs to place his personages in such a manner that the spectator shall first see those who commence this *action*, then those who continue it, and finally those who complete it' (1912, pp. 81-4).[9]

This 'guided-tour' approach to the composition and reading of pictures systematised in the perspective organisation of the Renaissance is still very fashionable among certain photographers today, but it is more or less discredited for modernists. Even when it no longer adheres to a directly narrative model, it implies a linear arrangement of the visual signifiers in a biunivocal causal chain, in other words it implies their succession in time ('the spectator shall first see this, then that'). It can be said of the Institutional cinema that when its principles of composition and lighting were definitively established at the end of the 1920's, the IMR had, thanks to the addition of movement, succeeded in what classical painting had only adumbrated, namely, *the harnessing of the spectator's eye.*

But Rodin's argument is also useful insofar as it clearly emphasises the profound kinship between the linearisation in diegetic space-time of the 'simultaneous signs' of the primitive tableau—achieved by the medium close-up which isolates or *excerpts* (1904-12)—and the simple narrative linearisation already proposed half a decade earlier by the chase film.

In contrast with this linear model, it is striking how many tableaux and even whole films were shot in all the major producing countries up to 1914 (think of scenes from **Fantômas** or **Judith of Bethulia**) which demanded a topographical reading by the spectator, a reading that could gather signs from all corners of the screen in their quasi-simultaneity, often without very clear or distinctive indices immediately appearing to hierarchise them, to bring to the fore 'what counts', to relegate to the background 'what doesn't count'.[10]

****

As I have suggested, the lecturer represents the first attempt to linearise the reading of these pictures, which were often both too 'autarchic' to be spontaneously organised into chains and too uniformly 'centrifugal' for the eye to pick its way confidently through them. The lecturer served both to bring order to the perceptual 'chaos' of the primitive picture and to impress on the narrative movement a supplement of 'directional necessity' or concatenatory momentum. In their ratiocinatory pedagogy of the eye, Rodin the critic and the lecturer of the magic lantern, and later of the film, were closely allied.

However, the presence of lecturers at an increasing number of projection points between 1897 and 1908 or 1909[11] could not but have had one contradictory effect, eventually resulting in their demise. This effect was one of 'non closure' and distantiation, in contradiction with the project of *diegetic presence*, of a certain transparency of the signifier in which the linearising drive is a crucial component: reading the story as it were alongside the diegesis, the lecturer produced a disjunction in the signifying process similar to that produced by the narrator in the Japanese doll theatre (see Burch 1979, pp.72-4).

But lecturers were surely *more than crutches* for film-goers while they still held their place. In the long term they surely taught film-goers how to read the vast, flat and acentric pictures I have described. The regular spectator before 1910 surely learnt to be more alert to the screen than the modern spectator, more on the look-out for the surprises of a *booby-trapped surface*. The commercial failure of Jacques Tati's hilarious masterpiece **Playtime**, whose images frequently share this primitive topographism, confirms that we have lost the habit of 'keeping our eyes open' in the cinema.

****

I have noted (see p.26 above) the appearance in Dickson's, Demenÿ's and then Lumière's work of the *portrait*[12] as an autonomous genre in the three great producing countries. This phenomenon represents a first impulse towards diegetic presence and the constitution of character in the cinema. But the main difficulty facing those film-makers whose historic task was to adapt to the cinema the essential gestures of classical theatrical, novelistic and painterly representation was not that of filming their actors from close to; this was something they had always done. It was that of integrating these close-ups and medium close-ups into the film, of presenting one after another long-shot tableaux and closer views, of achieving analytically the linearisation of the primitive tableau into a succession of pictures that would cut it up and organise it, making it *legible*.

Today we can easily embrace the itinerary of the process by which iconic signifiers were linearised: for some twenty years the primitive tableau, hegemonic in France until the First World War and still preponderant in the USA after 1910, guaranteed the co-presentation of all the components of a scene. Even a tableau showing only two characters offers an exchange of looks, for example, as a single unit with a complex meaning (*x* looks at *y* before/while/after *y* looks at *x*). Division into two or more medium close-ups, quite apart from the greater proximity of the faces it provides, makes it possible to organise, to simplify this 'action' (*x* looks at *y*/*y* does not look at *x*, then looks at *x*/*y* meets *x*'s look, then turns away, etc.).

A situation that the pure primitive cinema could not resolve 'plausibly' was that of the voyeur (or voyeuse). The co-representation of a man or woman looking and the object he or she looks at never plausibly establishes the invulnerability of that look. I am thinking, of course, of the archetypal voyeur film with the husband hidden behind the curtains, but also, as late as 1913, of a dramatic scene (the gipsy woman Lyduschka watching Balduin in Stellan Rye's admirable **Der Student von Prag**, 'The Student of Prague'). This archaism is often found in Griffith's Biograph films, in which it already constitutes an obvious deficiency: the supposed tramp hidden behind the bureau spying on the middle-class family in **The Lonely Villa** would be much more convincing if he were presented in a 'shot-reverse-shot' pattern which would introduce the principle of biunivocal concatenation by counterposing two linked terms in a perfectly clear way: the seer/those seen.[13]

The concatenation of tableaux emerging directly out of the primitive chase was *generalised* between 1904 and 1908[14] (from the latter year, think of Henri duc de Guise fleeing from room to room ahead of his assassins in the famous film by Le Bargy and Calmette). The great pedagogue, in this respect as in others, was Griffith at Biograph. In film after film, he links one autarchic tableau to the next with endless exits and entrances through lateral doors, perfecting this type of match to a degree which wholly satisfies the modern eye, making these doors a demonstrative materialisation of that 'abstract' notion, the direction match. By contrast, the linearisation of iconic signifiers, implying the crucial identification of the spectator-subject with the camera, took a dozen years to achieve complete realisation. It is presumably because of this discrepancy that the fact that these are two aspects of one and the same problem tends still to be ignored today, either by privileging the role of the scopic drive in the introduction of the 'close-up', despite the massive overdetermination of the latter process, or by hypostasising a figure like the point-of-view shot as a specifically subjective shot, which is almost meaningless in a system in which *every shot is subjective* (see p.251 below).

Similar screen-notions have hidden from specialists the fact that the emergence of the alternating syntagm was also part of this process of linearisation.

I have already alluded to the existence of a threshold beyond which the syntagm of *temporal succession* (e.g., **Another Job for the Undertaker**, before-after relationship) became that of *spatial succession* by way of the primitive chase and the gradual introduction of the indexical signs of position, direction and eyeline matching (which were in their turn to provide a basis for the unity of the spectator-subject, see pp.209ff. below).

Another threshold was crossed when it became possible to 'deduce' from the relationship of succession between two tableaux in the time of the film (of its reading) the idea that they were diegetically simultaneous. For the alternating syntagm derives quite directly from what I have called the syntagm of succession (which in turn is based on the 'arbitrary' and not yet signifying juxtaposition of the autarchic tableaux of the earliest period).

The reader will not be surprised to learn that the earliest attempts to show two simultaneous actions occurring in two different places produced the co-presence of the two actions in the same tableau: in Williamson's **Are You There?** (1901) a curtain end separates two protagonists talking to one another on the telephone. This type of visibly arbitrary material convention had to be replaced by a different, purely syntactic type.[15]

Now that contemporary stylistics allows almost any temporal relationship—flashback, ellipsis or simultaneity—to be expressed by a mere shot change, to the exclusion of dissolves and other optical effects, the emergence of the alternating syntagm has to be seen as the foundation-stone of modern syntax. But in the historical context its main significance is that it was the moment at which it was realised that any diegetic topography could be reduced to the linear model.

Let me try to isolate the 'morphological moment' at which this originary fissiparity arose, i.e., at which a distinction began to be made between two meanings attributable to the transition between two biunivocally concatenated shots: in the first case, which we have already examined at length, what is signified is that the time of the second shot is linked to that of the first by a relation of posteriority; in the second, that a series of shots seen *repeatedly* in alternation with another series implies a relationship of simultaneity with the latter.

It seems fairly certain that the first standardised manifestations of the alternating syntagm (I regard the doubtful case of Williamson's **Attack on a China Mission**, see p.107 n.8, as precocious and isolated, whatever the date of the lost version) are found *in chase films* made in France around 1905. In **Les Chiens contrebandiers** (see p.78 n.20) the successive stages in a chase are no longer simply shown in order, as in **Rescued by Rover** or **Tom, Tom, the Piper's Son**. There is a shift from one participant to the other, sometimes showing the dogs outwitting the customs officers, sometimes the customs officers searching for them, sometimes the smugglers on the lookout to ensure their dogs' success. In **The Cripple and the Cyclists**, a modern version of the fable of the tortoise and the hare, we are shown two runs in parallel, so we never know until the last shot which will win, the cripple in his little cart who knows the short-cuts, or the athletic but over-confident cyclist who imprudently stops at cafés en route.

It was the highly linear logic of the race situation that made it the privileged point for the development of the alternating syntagm in all its forms. Griffith, of course, became the great teacher in this field, articulating hundreds of 'switchbacks' in dramatic last-minute dashes to the rescue, the most famous being those at the climaxes of **The Birth of a Nation** and **Intolerance** (a film whose overall structure is a variant on the alternating syntagm in which History takes the place of the chase or race).

This great advance towards the linearisation of diegetic topography is less important as a specific figure—repeated alternation has become relatively rare since Griffith—than insofar as it lays the basis for the simultaneity embodied in a whole series of more or less conventional juxtapositions which are immediately perceived as signifying 'meanwhile'.

****

It is therefore clear that important aspects of the codification process that was to culminate in the IMR—often described by previous authors as a series of discrete phenomena—were in fact different manifestations of one and the same *linear drive.*

Some readers may reckon that by insisting here on 'vulgar' aspects of linearity I am in some sense forestalling any analysis of the 'deep linearity' of the institution, the indeed very complex relationship between the levels of the signifier and the signified that is constitutive of the transparency effect, an effect we all know today is only a *trompe-l'œil*, at least under the scalpel of Theory. But my investigations have convinced me that this general linearity is based, historically at least, on quite simple principles, the ones I have stated in this chapter and others I will state later. I hope for the moment that I will be granted the benefit of the doubt on this point.

NOTES

1 I am referring to the minimum conditions of narrative as defined by the semiotics of narrative since Propp: beginning—continuation—conclusion, which can, of course, all be contained in a single shot, and are in **Arroseur et arrosé**, for example.

2 My emphasis. I should make it clear that the main purpose of this monograph is to prove that Freeman's **The Horitz Passion Play**—surely the first American production shot overseas—really was made in Bohemia and not, as some historians have claimed, in a studio in the USA.

3 It should be emphasised that the Passion film remained an important genre until at least 1907 when the most spectacular of them all was made for Gaumont by Alice Guy and Victorin Jasset, a symbolic collaboration of one of the earliest pioneers of the primitive cinema and an innovator of the next period.

4 In the same year the British company Walturdaw produced a film called **Black and White Washing** including a similar exchange of complexions—in this case between races—caused by substituting shoe blacking for soap.

5 Durational editing in fact has two sides, being only a special manifestation of ellipsis. The dissolves in a desert journey (Metz's example) constitute what I have called 'indefinite ellipses', major ellipses of relatively long but indeterminate duration—the fact that time has passed is *designated*. Here, on the

contrary, we have two 'measurable ellipses', 'invisible' minor ellipses only connotatively signifying the passing of time, as opposed to the denotative mode of the major ellipsis (see Burch 1973, pp.4-8).

6 Many French chase films are in fact a series of postcards filmed in the Lumière manner and intended to form a series of the type 'Parisian trades' or 'sights of the capital'. A Gaumont film of about 1906, **Le Coup de vent**, is a perfect illustration of the genre (a country bumpkin loses his hat as he leaves the railway station and his 'trip to town' becomes a race from tourist sight to tourist sight chasing his flying headgear). **The Trusting Cabman** (see p.78 n.21 above) and **The Clumsy Photographer** (p.67), which are not chase films, adopt the same schema. A spontaneous expression of primitive autarchy, the schema embraced all the comic genres.

7 The same is true today. Costa-Gavras is supposed to have claimed that the use of actors very well known to French audiences in **Z** was intended to help spectators distinguish immediately between a plethora of characters (Alain Resnais in conversation at the Institut de Formation Cinématographique in 1969).

8 Of course, having analysed the film's pictures in this way, Jacobs does not try to re-establish the 'ideal' linearity but instead to build a form that maintains the tension between signified and signifier (the modernist option) instead of reabsorbing it as the editing of the IMR would do.

9 Noted down in 1911, this commentary of Rodin's also confirms the 'universality' of the three necessary narrative components.

10 A sorting process performed today and long since by techniques of lighting, framing, camera placement, movement and colour, all of which fuse together into a 'natural' centring.

11 According to Charles Musser (personal communication), a first decline in lecturing occurred in the USA after the turn of the century. The practice grew again with the rise of Hale's Tours in 1904-5, and then declined again around 1908-9. In France, by contrast, the practice seems to have been fairly regularly maintained for the whole fairground period.

12 'Close-up' or 'medium close-up'? For my purposes here they are equivalent insofar as both isolate the faces of one or more individuals as such, detaching them decisively from the background, from any surrounding faces, and from *their own bodies*.

13 Of course, the first 'keyhole' films constituted a first linearisation in this sense as early as around 1900, but it was to be ten years and more before the *mediating agent* (the telescope, keyhole, etc.) which evidently located the object seen *in a different space* could be dispensed with.

14 The British film-maker Hepworth was perhaps the first to go beyond the chase in films based on the journey—apparently uncertain and hence suspenseful—made by a trained animal whose cleverness ensures a happy end to a dramatic situation. By making the journey the centre of the story, Hepworth was in fact demonstrating his mastery of continuity. In his company's **Rescued by Rover** (directed by Lewin Fitzhamon), the story's concatenation is articulated around the journey of a dog tracking the kidnapper of his master's little daughter,

returning for the father, and leading him back to the house where she is being held to save her. In **Black Beauty**, it is a horse that goes to seek help after its master has been knocked down by tramps in a wood.

15 The shift was not made without hesitations. At Biograph in 1904 there was an attempt to show the simultaneity of two scenes by superimposing them (**The Story the Biograph Told**). It is not a very convincing experiment, and it is doubtful if it was often repeated.

Building a Haptic Space

Some twenty years ago, a group of writers associated with the magazine *Tel Quel* who were interested in the cinema as well as the plastic arts came, via a somewhat tendentious reading of Pierre Francastel, to constitute 'Renaissance space' as a *bad object* and the *avowed surface* of modernism as a *good object*. Marcelin Pleynet, Jean-Louis Baudry and others decreed that the optical properties of the photographic lens (and hence the cinematic lens), a monocular technology arising directly from bourgeois ideology,[1] were a kind of 'original sin' of the seventh art, a historical fatality adhering to its very being and that only disruptive practices could free it from.

Those who put forward these theses could appeal to the great relevance of the studies carried out in a spirit close to Marxism by Pierre Francastel and Erwin Panofsky on the social and historical dimensions of the emergence of perspective in Western painting, linked as it was to the symbolic and technological needs of the new mercantile classes. Moreover, at the time these theories flourished in France (in *Tel Quel, Cinéthique*, and *Cahiers du Cinéma* from 1968-73), the early cinema, that of the years before 1906, was still too little known for them to have access to the essential pieces of evidence. It was not realised that for some twenty years the cinema had followed a path which in basic respects 'began again' from the universe of primitive (or naive) art and only fully rejoined the 'classical' representation of space between 1910 and 1915.

It was difficult—and it still is—for the non-specialist (and it should be emphasised that it is non-specialists that we have to thank for asking these questions in the first place) to avoid reducing all early films to the Lumière model where the representation of space is concerned.[2] It was difficult—and it still is, all the more so insofar as Renaissance perspective has indeed exercised a hegemony over the institutional representation of space in the cinema for nearly three quarters of a century, a hegemony all of us internalise as something always already there. This is, of course, an illusion: this hegemony was the fruit of more than twenty years' work, in a sense a recapitulation of the decades of work which went into the constitution of monocular perspective in painting.

Attempting to rebut this metaphysics of original sin, Jean-Patrick Lebel remarked (1971, pp.23-4) that 'painting, in relation to "reality", is in fact a complete reworking. There can be no "reflection" insofar as it is the painter who reconstructs on a canvas an illusory "real" space by organising lines and colour relations.' But he shares the same blind spot as those he is criticising when he goes on: 'This ... is not the case in the cinema. It is not the film-maker but the passive recording apparatus of the camera that reproduces the object or objects filmed in the form of a reflected image constructed according to the laws of the rectilinear propagation of light rays.' For before those laws could be inscribed in a picture that adapted to the cinema the pertinent features of the Renaissance, certain shooting conditions had to be assembled, certain others excluded. Now, this set of choices, though everyone has internalised them today, did not arise spontaneously; it too *has a history*. This history has been completely forgotten today, to the point that any return to certain primitive practices in this respect will seem avant-garde (Godard, Akerman in **Jeanne Dielman**).

An exploration of the surviving corpus of films from the earliest period, still so little known, and also a closer examination of the period from 1906 to the First World War, reveals that as a whole this cinema is deeply *split* where the representation of space and volume is concerned. On the one hand, in fact, and especially in films deriving from the Lumière model, one finds a perfect adaptation of the rules of perspective codified by Alberti. However, the perseverance of primitive autarchy in particular, but also the fragmentation of programmes, mean that it is impossible to talk of a hegemony of this type of picture over the early cinema.

For the material conditions of production at that time—but also the popular models that so marked early cinema, from chromolithographs to strip cartoons, from shadow puppets to the

Folies Bergère—helped induce in all the makers of composed views—in studios but also sometimes in the open air—a superb indifference to what seems to us today the three-dimensional vocation of the cinema. Years before **Caligari**, decades before Godard, their films demonstrate the objective capacity of the cine camera to produce a representation of space closer to that of the middle ages, of Epinal (or of classical Japan) than to that of the painter Millet, to cite the model deliberately chosen by Billy Bitzer.

The factors contributing to the visual 'flatness' of so many film tableaux before 1906—and in certain places until 1915—are five, I think:

1 a more or less vertical illumination suffusing the whole field in front of the lens with a completely even light;
2 the fixity of the camera;
3 its horizontal and frontal placement;
4 the very widespread use of painted backdrops;
5 lastly, the placing of the actors, always a long way from the camera, often spread out in a tableau vivant, all facing front, and without axial movement of any kind.

Thousands of films produced during the period I am referring to might serve to illustrate this important tendency and its objective resistance to illusionistic perspective, but the *œuvre* of Georges Méliès undoubtedly provides the clearest model; he was not only principally responsible for the development of this tendency, but, in an article published by his close friend Maurice Noverre (1930) and presumed to reflect his ideas, actually outlined its *theory*:

> What is there to say about contemporary views, in which the lens is supposedly following characters *from real life* and photographing them unawares? .... What is there to say, too, about sets that move horizontally or from top to bottom allowing different parts of a room to be seen, characters who suddenly grow larger or whose hands and feet become enormous so a detail can be made visible? We shall be told, of course, that that is modern technique! But is it the right technique? That is the question: is it natural?

It is clear that for Méliès, a living fossil from the primitive period 25 years later, what is 'natural' is still the externality of the spectator-subject. He perceives a tracking shot as a movement not of the spectator's point of view but in the pro-filmic field, a close-up as an increase in the size of something in that field. In 1930, as a spectator, Méliès still saw himself as sitting in a fixed position in front of a flat screen, which was indeed the mental position of his audiences 25 years earlier. And as much as the exhaustion of a certain style it was the fundamental challenge to this imaginary placement represented by American and Danish films that drove Méliès into bankruptcy in 1912.

L'Homme à la tête en caoutchouc ('The Man with the Rubber Head'), made in 1901-2 when Méliès was at the height of his success and creativity, can be seen as a practical demonstration of this theorem. It is a film with a single trick described as follows by Georges Sadoul (1973, t.II, p.61): 'A chemist [Méliès himself] in his laboratory places his own head on a table. Attaching to it a rubber tube connected with a giant pair of bellows, he begins to pump the latter as hard as he can. Thereupon his head begins to swell until it becomes truly colossal....' Sadoul gives this account of the trick mechanism: 'The head swells against the black background produced by a wide-open door. On this reserve was superimposed a view of Méliès's head shot with the camera tracking in and out.' In fact it was Méliès, seated on a rolling trolley, who moved closer to the camera on an inclined plane, but what matters to me here is that the camera set-up prevents the movement in depth being perceived as such, it appears on the screen as a two-dimensional movement only, as an enlargement or shrinking of the head.

It is enough to inspect any collection of stills from Méliès's films in their black-and-white versions (a historically important facet of his work irrespective of the question of tinting, see pp.171ff. below), or to view a reasonably large body of the films to have ample evidence of the fact that for Méliès the perceptual flatness of the picture on the screen was the only cinematic 'truth'. Although he used 'close-ups' in his films much more than is often realised, they always signify 'large size', as in **L'Homme à la tête en caoutchouc**. He only recognises one possible shot scale, that of the 'proscenium' long shot. It is undeniable that this

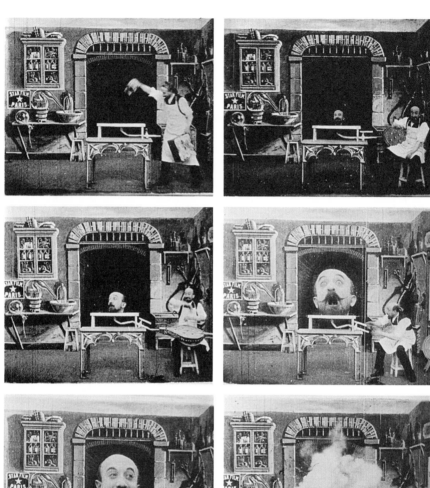

Fig. 18: **L'Homme à la tête en caoutchouc** (acted and directed by Georges Méliès, 1901-2).

attitude derived from a theatrical 'prejudice', but the rigid transfer to the screen of the 'uniqueness of the theatrical viewpoint' in fact radicalises the latter. By adopting a rigorously centred frontality (a viewpoint the spectator at the theatre rarely has, in fact, since only a few seats in the stalls provide it), and mostly suppressing the perspective box of the stage *à l'italienne*, Méliès considerably increases both the effect of visual flatness and the spectator's sense of externality. The pictures Méliès presented are less like that archetypical theatre than they are like the two-dimensional representations of it offered by nineteenth-century woodcut-printed posters.

Moreover, Méliès was quite prepared to introduce into his tableaux two-dimensional mobile props to represent objects. Think in particular of the banquet in **Barbe Bleue** ('Blue Beard', 1901), in which servants file past, one carrying an enormous turkey, another a roast sucking pig, like placards on a demonstration. Nor should it be forgotten that the studio Méliès built at Montreuil was the first in Europe with a glass roof, a form of lighting that was to dominate the cinema for fifteen years. It is undeniable that technological and economic obstacles to the rapid development of appropriate electric lighting co-determined this 'choice', made by all studios until about 1906. But a comparison between Méliès's tableaux and traditional popular pictures (*images d'Epinal*, woodcuts, etc.), which in turn descend from mediæval traditions completely ignorant of Renaissance perspective, demonstrates Méliès's almost systematic refusal of that perspective. And this is true of all the genres he initiated, from the *féerie* or trick film to the reconstituted actuality (e.g., the famous **Le Sacre d'Edouard VII**, 'Special Coronation Film', 1902).

For Méliès was the film-maker of the tableau vivant as it was practised (and still is practised) in French spectacular variety shows as well as at the Théâtre Robert Houdin. Many shots or whole films are presented as no more nor less than a series of stages leading up to an *apothéose* (see p.193 below), the term used in the popular theatre of the time for one of these tableaux vivants, seemingly modelled on the coloured prints adorning our great-grandparents' albums.

It will be objected that, in films like **La Civilisation à travers les**

ages ('Humanity Through the Ages', 1908), Méliès's tableaux set out to copy the chiaroscuro used by salon painters like Prudhon (as Georges Sadoul has demonstrated—1973, t.II, p.281), or that his backdrops in tableaux such as 'The Foundries' in **Voyage dans la lune** are perfect reproductions of the codes of perspective. But in the primitive cinema and in Méliès's films in particular, the painted backdrop is patently ambiguous, both in its peculiar stylisation and in its fixity, and especially in the way it divides the profilmic space into a narrow zone of action in the foreground ('lateralising' the actors' movements) and a zone the characters cannot enter but supposed to extend back behind them.

This ambiguity of the painted backdrop is more frequently and better illustrated by Zecca and his collaborators at Pathé. Georges Sadoul (1973, t.II, p.187) retails the following exemplary anecdote: 'Zecca painted some of these sets, e.g., that for **Un Duel abracadabrant** (['A Mumbo-Jumbo Duel'] no. 676 [in the 1902 catalogue]). The backdrop represented a sloping street. Zecca could not get the perspective of its paving-stones right, so he turned them into a heap of stones on which he boldly planted the sign "Street Closed".' And in his first famous film, **Histoire d'un crime** (1901), one of the most spectacular tableaux shows the opening of the double doors leading to the courtyard in which the Guillotine has been set up. This prospect is, of course, a painted backdrop, and as the doors open, their shadows fall on it. Here, as often in the primitive cinema, I am inclined to attach importance to mistakes, meaning-effects that the film-makers failed to notice or believed their audiences would fail to notice. I do not think they are any the less symptomatically important for that, since if ever there was a phenomenon with causes as unconscious as they were conscious, it is the way the cinema in some sense recapitulated the history of the pictorial representation of space in the West.

Moreover, Zecca achieved effects with his backdrops whose poetry is no longer simply that of a lapsus. For example, the astonishing little fantasy film **Tempête dans une chambre à coucher** ('A Bewildered Traveller', 1901), a striking anticipation of Magritte's 'visual puns', with its strange reshuffling of pictorial codes: the character whose movement endows him with apparent solidity seems to be caught between two surfaces—the waves in

Fig. 19: **Histoire d'un crime** (Zecca, 1901).

the foreground and those seen through the doorway—and these two planes seem to meet, denying that solidity. Once again, **Caligari** is not very far away (see p.183 below).

With the erection of Pathé's new studios in 1904, it became possible to use much wider backdrops, and Zecca and Nonguet's camera began to 'scan' these in smooth panning movements. In **Au pays noir** (1905), for example, the second tableau, 'On the Way to the Pits', shows the miner and his sons leaving their home, passing a shop whose proprietor they greet, then moving on again against a painted landscape followed by the pan through at least 60 degrees to arrive at last at the pithead, located at the extreme left of a grandiose mining landscape. In **Au bagne**, a similar tableau shows the convicts at hard labour; a group carrying a beam emerge from the prison gates right and move left, followed by the pan; this pauses as they put down their load, but then resumes its right to left movement as a second group of convicts carrying bales and sacks enter right and cross to the gangway to a ship which they ascend. These two tableaux, executed in dramatic detail by Lorant-Heilbronn, contain painted 'extensions' of three-dimensional elements (the water between the quay and the ship in the hard labour scene, railway lines at the pithead) and are thus reminiscent in a number of respects of devices used by Daguerre in his dioramas. The interest and indeed beauty a modern eye sees in these scenes arises from the unexpected cohabitation in a transition period of two modes of representation: for us it is impossible not to see (especially because of the camera movement, which authoritatively proclaims the absence of any real depth by the same movement with which it reveals the landscape) that we are dealing with a *composite picture*. Such pictures may (perhaps) have produced a greater illusion at the time, but the inevitable comparison with the many scenes shot out of doors at the same period[3] could not but have drawn attention to this ambiguity, if only subconsciously. And there is no doubt that the development within the studios—and especially at Gaumont—of a negotiable and even spectacular depth of staging (the films of Jasset and Perret of 1911-13) was greeted as an undeniable advance. For the nascent Institution demanded the homogenisation of the signifier: primitive discontinuities were a hindrance to it.

The role of colour should also be evoked. This was initially an ambiguous one where the representation of spaces and volumes is concerned. In France, in particular, colour played an important part in Méliès's films and in Pathé's trick films and *feeries*. In the earliest years this was primarily to make the characters stand out against a monochrome background by tinting them in bright colours, i.e., to counteract the flattening effect resulting from uniform lighting, camera placement, etc. However, the irregularities initially inherent in hand tinting and then in hand-cut stencils tended rather to emphasise the surface effect (Dufy-like flat tints), while successfully making the picture more legible and endowing it with great plastic charm. The perfecting (in about 1906) at Pathé of a less laborious system of mechanically-cut stencils allowed a more precise registration and the multiplication of tinting in many more films. With this improved Pathé-Color process colour had already acquired its institutional function as a 'supplement of reality' (and 'beauty') even before Smith's first Kinemacolour experiments in 1911 (and the latter proved short-lived, whereas Pathé-Color flourished until the end of the silent period).

But with the earliest forms of tinting an effect of aerial perspective also appeared in the backgrounds of the pictures in the vistas of blue sky that came to characterise some painted landscapes. A comparison of the black-and-white and the hand-tinted versions of a 1903 film like Méliès's **Le Royaume des fées** ('Fairyland, or, The Kingdom of the Fairies') suffices to show how much relief could be added by tinting the background.

However, one should not imagine that the French primitives, even the *feeries*, were 'like the cathedrals' (whose façades were, we know, originally a riot of colours). For not everyone saw them in polychrome versions. In fact the purchase price—and later rental—of a coloured copy was such that many small fairground exhibitors could hardly afford them. Their customers had to be content with the black-and-white versions. Méliès himself attached what is surely a conceptual importance to the latter. As we know, the sets in his Montreuil studio were themselves black-and-white, painted in grisaille to provide better control of the greyscale on black-and-white film. This grisaille of Méliès's is revealed by the black-and-white versions of his films to belong unquestionably to the lineage of the surface arts (*camaieu*, stained glass, bas-relief).

Méliès was surely aware of the depth colour gave to his pictures. But this does not seem to have been his main concern. On the other hand, there can be little doubt that by far the greater number of early film-makers, especially in Britain and the USA, were consciously aware of a 'need' for depth. Chase films, in particular, are full of shots showing the protagonists wading towards the camera across a river or lake (there are striking examples in **The Great Train Robbery** and **Rescued by Rover**). Similarly, the publicity for a film often contained references to 'smoke effects', because the latter, which were achieved at considerable trouble in some films, particularly by the use of smoke cartridges and the choice of dusty roads for cavalcades, created a fine aerial perspective.

These endeavours, and the fact that they were drawn to the audience's attention, show both the sense of inadequacy induced by the visual flatness of interior tableaux—for which the exteriors were intended to compensate—and how difficult film-makers and audiences found it to 'forget' they were dealing with a flat backdrop, a materially flat and hopelessly external picture.

France saw the earliest and most spectacular development of staging in depth, as early as the first chase films whose visual system derives directly from the Lumière scenic (**Arrivée d'un train à La Ciotat**, etc.). And France, where primitive frontality persisted for so long and the introduction of American-style editing was so long delayed, saw the development—especially at Gaumont with Feuillade and Perret, and at the new Eclair company with Victorin Jasset, a refugee from Gaumont—of a dramaturgical exploitation of vast sets quite 'modern' in their effectiveness.

In all the producing countries, the chase film was almost always shot in exteriors[4] and thus along the lines of the scenics, with staging in depth. But it was in France that there was very early a systematic effort to make the characters explore all the corners of the perspective box. Rather like a conjurer putting his wand in the hat to show that it is empty, French directors used characters to show that none of the space visibly represented is on a painted backdrop, that it can all be entered and touched, is 'haptic', to use the technical term psychologists of perception have derived from the Greek word for touch and juncture. Pathé's fine film **Le Brigandage moderne** ('Modern Brigandage', 1905) is entirely constructed on this principle: the victims' automobiles, the policemen's bicycles and the brigand's motorbike come and go in all directions, and at one point a policeman climbs a telephone pole. There is a particularly significant shot in which the police tie a rope across the street to capture the motorised brigand and hide from him by hiding from us—they leave the screen. This sort of exploitation of off-screen space, fairly common in the films of Feuillade, Perret and so on, further serves to emphasise the circumscribed, geometrical nature of the perspective box. This method of staging is *a three-dimensional version of the autarchy of the primitive tableau.* For, despite the later contribution of artifical lighting, these pictures—Jasset's **Zigomar** series, Perret's **L'Enfant de Paris** and **Le Roman d'un mousse**— remain strangely and splendidly geometric, like demonstrations of a perspective so academic that it is 'unnatural'. This is partly due to the often still very flat lighting, but the most important factor is the continuing French insistence on a strict frontality that is already being rejected by the Americans and the Danes.

The whole visual history of the cinema before the First World War—and not only in France—thus turns on this opposition between the 'Mélièsian' affirmation of the surface and the affirmation of depth already implicit in **Arrivée d'un train à La Ciotat**. This contradiction was to be reabsorbed, in a sense, between 1915 and 1920, as the result of a compromise. This involved the suppression of the flatness of the painted backdrop, etc., but also that of 'extreme' primitive depth,[5] which was not to be rediscovered until twenty years later by Renoir and then in the USA by Welles, Wyler, etc.,[6] afterwards becoming a standard element of the institutional 'vocabulary'. There is one British film that embodies this primitive dichotomy, alternating interior scenes which affirm the surface at least as much as Méliès's films, and exterior shots skilfully exploiting depth of field. This is William Haggar's masterpiece **Charles Peace** (see pp.99ff. above).[7]

On the one hand this film contains interiors so stylised as to put C. Gordon Craig to shame—schematic structural details drawn onto walls, the moon pinned to a backcloth behind the window, a complete lack of side walls coming towards the

Fig. 20: **Le Brigandage moderne** (Pathé, 1905).

Fig. 21: **Charles Peace** (William Haggar, 1905).

camera. In striking contrast to these interior tableaux (to which might be added another studio-shot scene of a rooftop fight), there are scenes of violent action—fights, chases—filmed in exteriors and arranged to make admirable use of depth of field. Despite the 'naivety' of film-makers at this time and all that might be said about Haggar's humble origins, I am tempted to hold that this contrast between interiors and exteriors is not an accident. Given that Peace alone of all the film's characters wears a music-hall clown's make-up, I am even tempted to see in this coexistence of two types of representation of space a pendant to the coexistence of two forms of popular art and the unbridgeable gulf between two 'social temperaments', Peace being a kind of force of nature astray in an insipid lower-middle-class milieu.

No doubt I am reading too much into this film.

Nevertheless, **Charles Peace**, while offering a real demonstration of primitive types of space, is an admirably harmonious work in its very discontinuities. That is why I am inclined to see in it one of the earliest examples in the cinema of a complex form, one of the first (objective) achievements of a specifically filmic æsthetic, if only because it makes more systematic use than others of the collage principle, and because, no doubt involuntarily, it suggests a certain self-reflexivity.

****

Another essential aspect of this gradual 'conquest of space' is the mastering of lighting. Here, too, at the the outset, in the period of painted backdrops and small studios, the forces at work seem massively and unilaterally technological: the absence as yet of appropriate electrical lighting equipment. But I do not think matters are so simple.

If we consider the primitive cinema as a system we have to conclude that it was only partly for technological and economic reasons that lighting *as an articulated code* was only introduced into the cinema after some twenty years. It was also because the overall logic of the primitive system was compatible with a uniform and essentially flat lighting.

Leaving aside a few experiments at Edison and Biograph (the filming of the Jeffreys-Sharkes boxing match in 1899), and Méliès, too, from 1897, the very first uses of electric light were intended to produce one-off dramatic effects, only appearing once or twice in any given film. For example, in **Falsely Accused** (Fitzhamon for Hepworth, 1905), a dark lantern holding a small arc-lamp casts a beam across the walls of a set when the villain is committing his nocturnal crime. But when the studios began to install electric lighting equipment, they remained content for several years to arrange it so as to suffuse the stage with an essentially uniform light. At Biograph, whose New York studio was electrically equipped as early as 1905, the racks of fluorescent tubes with which it was equipped seven years later still reproduced the daylight effect that the same firm was obtaining simultaneously on its open-air stages in California. The arrangement of the tubes on one of the walls of the stage as well as the ceiling to light the set laterally as well as vertically, although by no means ensuring the relief produced by modern lighting, does undoubtedly facilitate the reading of the picture. And the similar system used around 1911 at Vitagraph (see **A Friendly Marriage**) secured even better effects of the same kind. But note Billy Bitzer's description (1973, p.77) of the lighting arrangements at the Californian stage he installed on his arrival in 1910: 'On the lot we constructed a large wooden platform and covered this area with white cotton sheets on pulleys, so that we could adjust the amount of sunlight needed for the camera.' For this purely quantitative concern was to predominate in the USA, and in most countries (other than Denmark and Italy, seemingly) until around 1915.

At no point in his career could Billy Bitzer be described as the most advanced of cameramen. Linda Arvidson (1925, pp.128-9) claimed that he refused to help in the dawn and dusk lighting effects that frame **Pippa Passes**, and they were shot on Griffith's instructions by one of the other cameramen who worked on the film, Arthur Marvin and Percy Higginson. Before 1912 their colleagues at Vitagraph and particularly certain Danes—who had already proved adept in the use of chiaroscuro *obtained by means of daylight only*—were ahead of everything being achieved in the normal run of things at Biograph. And some of the 'inventions' in **Intolerance** had become commonplace in the Italian cinema several years earlier. Nevertheless, his trajectory and the commentary on it he has left us seem to me to have a real value by reason of the typicality they can be said to exhibit.

In the second year of their collaboration, Griffith and Bitzer began exceptionally (and this for a long time) to use light for 'special effects', often obtained with much effort. The final tableau of a film whose importance I have emphasised elsewhere (see pp.218ff.), **A Drunkard's Reformation** (1909), a tableau showing the reconstitution of the nuclear family after the crisis brought about by the husband's intemperance, is lit (by a single lamp located in a fireplace) in a chiaroscuro style reminiscent of Greuze or even Georges de la Tour. The introduction here of a relief at odds with the general context of the film is striking. Although some of Bitzer's experimental effects did have a directly narrative function, most of his endeavours were intended to introduce effects of relief, even if he himself, like most of his contemporaries, simply described them as aiming at *expressiveness*. He calls his experiments in backlighting inspired by Millet's *The Gleaners* 'new' and 'splendid'. One imagines he would have similarly described the backlighting fringing a character's hair in medium close-up that he began to experiment with around 1912. This suggests the unconscious status of the obstacles to the development of the institution and the slight awareness those working towards that development had of the real nature of the edifice they were building.

The story Bitzer tells us (ibid., p.85) of his 'invention'—totally accidental, he claims[8]—of the artistic vignette, even if it is apocryphal, suggests the intimate but confused aspirations entertained by many cinema workers: 'Their pleasure [that of the Biograph bosses] knew no bounds.... They thought the shaded corners took away the hard sharp edges and added class to the picture.' In fact, the purpose was once again to give the image relief, on the one hand by detaching the figure from a darkened background, on the other by destroying the rectangularity of the frame, a reminder of the notion of a surface.

Indeed, until wide-aperture lenses producing out-of-focus backgrounds became available and lighting equipment allowing backgrounds to be darkened had been perfected, the vignette continued to serve these same aims of relief. But it was to survive these technological changes by a number of years, and only really disappeared with the talky. For the vignette fulfilled a double, perhaps a triple role. While toning down the 'hard sharp edges', it also drew the eye away from the form and limits of the frame, it ensured one more centring effect, tending to conceal the fact that the cinematic picture results from a discontinuity and a choice. In other words, it weakened the sense of a primitive 'autarchy' of the picture, creating the feeling that beyond the peephole whose contours fade out like the edges of the ocular field, there really is boundless space.

Bitzer's museum trips suggest the distance between his era and that of Porter, who drew his inspiration from strip cartoons. But although Bitzer was one of the earliest pictorial specialists, he was also poorly educated. His efforts, like those of the Vitagraph cameramen, to get away from primitive lighting, were a long way behind those of the Danes, the Italians and even the French (especially where composition was concerned), for reasons of national culture and/or class. In Italy, especially, where aristocratic patronage paved the way for a rapid embourgeoisement of audiences and film content, particularly spectacular advances were made, as is revealed by stills from the famous film **Sperduti nel buio** ('Sunk in the Mire', 1914), which has unfortunately been lost but makes the experiments undertaken a year later by De-Mille in **The Cheat** seem crude by comparison.

If the lighting in **The Cheat** caused a sensation in France, no doubt that was less for the night effects—already standard practice among the Danes and better done by them, too—than for the use the film makes of shadows, which have the effect of extending pro-filmic space into the off-screen area (see p.212). But I think that, in addition to its class content[9] and Hayakawa's performance, one key to the extraordinary impact of **The Cheat**, especially on the elite from which was to emerge the next generation of French film-makers, lay in the photographic angles selected by DeMille, which systematically avoid frontality and horizontality. The characters do mostly stand facing the camera—whereas at Vitagraph, at Ince with Barker, and elsewhere, actors had been encouraged to offer three-quarter back views to the camera for several years—but the camera never quite faces a wall and, notably, the lens axis is never quite parallel to the floor. There had been high and low angles, and also oblique angles, in very many exterior shots in films by Griffith and others for at least five years. But what was new about what DeMille did (though I have no reason to think he initiated the approach) was that in all his interiors the camera films the set from a doubly oblique angle, with respect to the back wall and with respect to the floor, towards which it is always slightly tilted. The contrast with the primitive cinema is a striking one: there the camera is always arranged facing the set and strictly parallel to the ground. There is the same contrast with the interiors—and many exteriors—in Griffith's Biograph films. But from now on floors, table-tops, etc., were to display their surfaces as broad parallelograms, to multiply the signs of linear perspective across the visual field: a profusion of convergent lines were to be presented to the eye to prove that what confronts us really is a haptic space.

Another result of this new positioning of the camera is that there was much less empty space at the top of the screen, a type of composition that tended to flatten Griffith's pictures in particular, creating the impression of the background toppling towards the spectator over the characters' heads.

****

Need I emphasise the role played in France and then in the USA and elsewhere by the actors beginning to move in the axis of the lens as the sets became deeper and habits of laterality lost their hold? As for the introduction and generalisation of over-the-shoulder shots and the general use of foregrounded elements, I must admit that although I would locate that introduction around 1920, a chronology of the phenomenon still remains to be written, as far as I know.

Although, as is clear, it is by no means a *sine qua non* of the production of a 'haptic' space—movement of actors, camera placement and lighting are already sufficient, even in the absence of editing—the final factor I shall consider is often presented nowadays as the main guarantor of this 'hapticity'. I think this is an error of perspective. But I also think that this may be where camera movement of the tracking type makes its most specific and semantically 'original' contribution.

Cabiria (1914), the first film to make frequent use of tracking shots, demonstrates the topographic and semantic equivalence of camera movements and continuity matches (see p.156 above) while emphasising the essential peculiarity of this type of movement as an imaginary experience: its confirmation of the effect of volume. For although the slow forward, backward and sideways tracks of Fosco-Pastrone's *carello* did indeed adumbrate the topographical figures of *static continuity* in editing (axial matches, contiguity matches), they only adumbrated them, they were only the rough equivalents of figures mastered three years earlier in American editing. But it is precisely their failure in this respect (or rather, their backwardness) that reveals what seems to me to be the original feature of this type of movement in the Institution. Moreover, this engineer-turned-producer-turned-director was well aware of it: '... the camera movements were used to create stereoscopic effects. Focussing proved very difficult. All the more so in that I emphasised the impression of relief by sometimes using curved rather than straight tracks.'[10]

However, if neither 'primary identification' with the camera nor the constitution of a 'haptic space' necessarily depend on camera movements, if they can ultimately be established without them, it is the case that movement represents the point of contact of two composite systems, one that centres the ubiquitous subject (see pp.202ff.) and one that constitutes the effect of a 'haptic' space. Here at one go we have both an analogue of the 'motionless voyage' in diegetic space and the *tangible* proof of the three-dimensionality of 'haptic' space. This is no doubt the source of the tendency to privilege movement in connection with one or other of these basic functions when these are provided by far more complex means.

Finally, as an additional interference, this double dynamic affirmation of the centrality of the spectator-subject and of the 'hapticity' of space produced by the modern tracking shot (**L'Argent**, 1927) itself came to reinforce the static affirmation already long constituted by the combination of the network of monocular perspective with the network of eyeline matching in reverse shots—the whole forming a complex system converging on a single unique point: the spectator-subject (see pp.202ff.).

****

It is amazing that it is precisely at the point when these networks of depth were being set up and the surface of the cinema screen was finally becoming 'transparent to the voyager-subject' like Alice's looking-glass, that a German psychologist who had emigrated to the USA and seen a wide-ranging selection of recent American films was capable as early as 1916 of giving a remarkable account (Münsterberg 1970, pp.21-4) of the contradiction between surface and depth that had divided primitive cinema, that **Charles Peace** had so well illustrated and that was at last in the process of reabsorption in the earliest years of the mature Institution:

> But while regular motion pictures [as opposed to hypothetical stereoscopic ones] certainly do not offer us this complete plastic impression, it would simply be the usual confusion between knowledge about the picture and its real appearance if we were to deny that we get a certain impression of depth. If several persons move in a room, we gain distinctly the feeling that one moves behind another in the film picture.[11] .... We believe that we see the persons really in the foreground.... *Nevertheless we are never deceived; we are fully conscious of the depth, and yet we do not take it for real depth.* Too much stands in the way.... The size and frame and the whole setting strongly remind us of the unreality of the perceived space. But the chief point remains that we see the whole picture with both eyes and not with only one, and that we are constantly reminded of *the flatness of the picture* because the two eyes receive identical impressions. And we may add an argument nearly related to it, namely that *the screen is seen as an object of our perception* and demands an adaptation of the eye and an independent localisation.... *We certainly see the depth, and yet we cannot accept it.* .... It is a unique inner experience, which is

characteristic of the perception of the photoplays. We have reality with all its true dimensions; and yet it keeps the fleeting, passing surface suggestion without true depth and fullness, as different from a mere picture as from a mere stage performance.

Although this description uses the same terms as the analysis of the comic illusion offered by Octave Mannoni (see p.251), it seems to invert them. For Mannoni, that illusion amounts rather to 'I know but all the same ...', i.e., to the accepted victory of the illusion, the bracketing off of the demystificatory knowledge, which was to be the main result of the Institution at all levels. Perhaps we are dealing with a conjunctural effect—for Griffith in 1916, the codes of relief, especially those of lighting and movement, had not yet taken their ultimate form. Or, perhaps, more simply, Münsterberg is parading the critical spirit he thinks proper to the scientist.

But it is well known that Modernism eventually institutionalised a certain tension between surface and depth such as Münsterberg evoked ('and yet it keeps the ... surface suggestion without true depth and fullness'). And indeed, as early as 1919, the first great modernist film, **Das Cabinett des Doktors Caligari**, was to take issue with this problematic and hence with a large slice of the IMR.

Caligari grew out of the ideology and æsthetics of Expressionism, and we know how highly the proponents of the latter valued 'primitive' art forms (children's paintings and those of the insane, African art, folk prints). Thus it is not surprising that it reveals a kind of *self-conscious return* to the major features of the primitive cinema (and especially the autarchy and fixity of the primitive tableau in preference to the 'realism' of modern editing).[12] But as far as we are concerned here, it was not a matter either of a mere rejection of the new techniques, a 'backwardness', or even of a kind of mimicry, whether accidental or deliberate. Rather it was a matter of setting to work the parameters of a historical process that the film thereby enlisted in its textual system, in this instance an eminently singular textual system. What we have here is an early example of 'epistemological creation', which locates **Caligari** firmly as an example of absolutely deliberate modernism.

BUILDING A HAPTIC SPACE 183

Caligari's imagery plays constantly on a carefully sustained ambiguity. The film's notorious visual style presents each tableau as a flat, stylised rendering of a deep space, achieved by a design of dramatically oblique strokes so plainly graphic, producing effects of relief so artificial[13] that they immediately recall the tactile surface of the engraver's page. But at the same time the movement of the actors within these frames is always along the axis of the lens and perpendicular to the picture plane, in a style reminiscent of the staging in depth of Jasset or Perret, say. Thus, the same images seem to produce two historical types of spatial representation at once, two types which are as it were superimposed on one another.

This same problematic of surface and depth has of course been at work in a number of important films made in the last few decades—I am thinking of Godard, Snow, Dreyer's **Gertrud**, etc. (see Burch & Dana 1974). But what is striking about **Caligari** is that through its dialectical inscription of a historical process—depth and flatness being resolved into an 'average relief'—it provides an almost unexampled commentary on the constitution of the IMR as a pictorial system.

NOTES

1 'Photography ... destined to duplicate Hegelian closure, to produce mechanically the ideology of the perspective code, of its normality and its censorships' (Pleynet & Thibaudeau 1969, p.10).
2 One might wonder, on the other hand, why Méliès's imagery did not raise any doubts in the minds of these comminatory writers.
.3 Pathé films of this kind went so far as to alternate exterior shots and scenes in front of painted backdrops (cf. in particular **Un Drame en mer**, 'Tragedy at Sea', 1905).
4 The lateral chase in front of studio backdrops in **Tom, Tom, the Piper's Son** was anomalous by 1905, which adds weight to the suggestion that it might be a parody. If it is, however, its target may be theatrical rather than cinematic.
5 This suppression was, of course, not absolute. The primitive type of staging in depth persisted throughout the 1920's in Europe as a stylistic component more than as a primitive residue (Lang's **Doktor Mabuse der Spieler**, 'Dr. Mabuse the Gambler', Dreyer's **Präsidenten**, 'The President', L'Herbier's **Feu Mathias Pascal**, 'The Late Matthew Pascal').

6 The reduction in depth of field was encouraged by the introduction of lenses with wider apertures, making it possible to work at lower light levels, which was more comfortable for the actors. This reduced the optical depth of field, particularly in shots close to their subjects. The result was a kind of standardisation of the representation of deep space, utilising the relation between sharp and blurred, itself productive of relief.

7 While this film is emblematic of a contradiction common to primitive cinema as a whole, it does seem rather unusual in the context of early British films as we know them. In fact these were less spatially polarised than the French ones: the chases were often less stylised (less 'mechanical') and in a general way the use of space seems more 'modern' to us—especially in the exteriors, more commonly rural ones than French exteriors of the same period, the latter point helping to explain the former. I am thinking in particular of the chases and fights in **Desperate Poaching Affray**, also by Haggar, and those in Alf Collins's **The Eviction**.

8 An improvised lens hood is supposed to have encroached on the lens field.

9 It was the first important American film to deal with the well-to-do 'without moralising and from their point of view' (Jacobs 1939, p.337). But actually, its scabrous subject-matter, which so titillated the Parisian intelligentsia, drastically limited its audience in the USA.

10 Giovanni Pastrone in an interview in Turin in 1949, cit. Sadoul (1973), t.III, p.215.

11 Such was indeed the only depth clue in some primitive tableaux (which Münsterberg had perhaps not seen, at least as an adult: at the time he was writing, this cinema had already vanished), but it remained a purely 'theoretical' and unconvincing clue until joined by the others that had become commonplace by 1916.

12 These options may perhaps have been overdetermined by a relative ignorance in Germany in 1919 of what had been happening in the USA since 1914. True. But **Caligari**'s 'return' surely takes us as far back as 1908.

13 I cannot resist referring to an article published in *Photoplay* in 1921, in which the author, Willard Huntington Wright, 'one of the foremost authorities on painting and æsthetics', argued (Wright 1921) that the main characteristic of the modern movement in painting was the ability to produce 'the effect of a third dimension', and that **Caligari** was the first film to transfer this characteristic to the screen! But this critic's confusion is not incomprehensible: it demonstrates the lacunæ still possible in the practice of the plastic codes of the Institution in 1921 and the disturbance a film like **Caligari** could cause in this respect.

A Primitive Mode of Representation?

At this point in my examination, before turning to what is an essential aspect of the IMR, the unity-ubiquity of the spectator-subject, I must address the earliest period of cinema history from another direction. If it is true that after twenty or thirty years of cinema an Institutional Mode of Representation appeared, what then was the precise status of the period preceding its earliest manifestations? Was that 'simply' a transitional period whose peculiarities can be attributed to the contradictory forces pulling in various directions—the influence of popular spectacle and popular audiences on the one hand, bourgeois economic and symbolic aspirations on the other? Or was there a 'primitive mode of representation' in the same sense as there is an IMR, a stable system with its own inherent logic and durability?

My answer is clear. It was both these things at once.

There really was, I believe, a genuine PMR, detectable in very many films in certain characteristic features, capable of a certain development but unquestionably semantically poorer than the IMR. It is illustrated by some very remarkable films, from Zecca's **Histoire d'un crime** or Méliès's **Voyage dans la lune** to Gad's **Afgrunden** ('The Abyss' or 'Woman Always Pays', 1910) or Feuillade's **Fantômas** (1913-14). As early as 1906 it began to be slowly displaced, particularly under the influence of a conception of editing born in primitive films of a different, more 'experimental' sort which coexisted with the 'pure' system, often in the work of the same film-makers, often in the same film, and which was itself profoundly ambivalent. This was the case with a few rare French films,[1] several British ones, and above all a large number of Porter's films (**Life of an American Fireman, The Gay Shoe Clerk, The Great Train Robbery, A Subject for the Rogues' Gallery**, etc.) which upset the primitive equilibrium by introducing one or other procedure betraying characteristic aspirations to linearity, centring, etc. But these same films are still massively

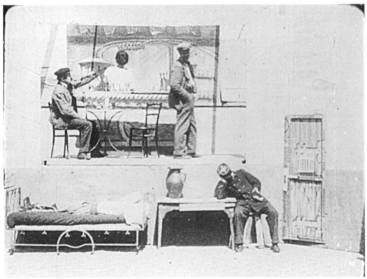

Fig. 22: **Histoire d'un crime**. This tableau showing the murder is an example of the influence of the illustrated tabloid front-page (e.g., *Le Petit Parisien*) on French films at the turn of the century. The tableau of the prisoner's dream is a curious early use of the 'balloon' technique to show the alcoholic antecedents of the crime. (The British would soon abandon this construction of the insert as a set in favour of a double-exposure technique—cf. **What the Curate Really Did**.)

implicated in the primitive system, a fact which often makes them seductive monsters, seductive, that is, when viewed from the standpoint of the institutional normality yet to be achieved, our normality.

What then constitutes this Primitive Mode of Representation? I have discussed some of its main features at length: autarchy of the tableau (even after the introduction of the syntagm of succession), horizontal and frontal camera placement, maintenance of long shot[2] and 'centrifugality'. These are features that can be detected in the text of a typical film, and they, the ambience of the theatres and the possible presence of a lecturer interact to produce what I have tried to define as the experience of *primitive externality*.

But there is another characteristic of the primitive film—really a whole cluster of characteristics—which I have hardly touched on as yet, although it will help us to understand an aspect of the IMR which has been so completely internalised that it is now very difficult to approach it directly. This is what I shall call *the non-closure of the PMR* (in contrast, in other words, to the closure of the IMR).

But I should make it clear that while this feature is found in various forms in a large number of films, many others, especially after 1900, already present a formal semblance of institutional closure. Hence insofar as this feature can be registered in certain films as narrative non-closure (in the sense defined below), it is not constitutive of the PMR in general. But if institutional closure is taken to be more than narrative self-sufficiency and a certain way of bringing the narrative to an end, if, on the contrary, it is treated as the sum of all the signifying systems that centre the subject and lay the basis for a full diegetic effect, including even the context of projection, then the primitive cinema is indeed non-closed as a whole.

However, the most acute manifestations of this non-closure do concern the narrative, its structure and its status.

Is the potential or actual presence of a lecturer alongside the primitive screen[3] the only explanation for the existence of films like Porter's **Uncle Tom's Cabin; or Slavery Days** (1903), a fifteen-minute, twenty-tableaux digest of a bulky novel? In any case, the extraordinary ellipses implied by such a procedure are hardly filled by the captions to the different tableaux ('Eliza's Escape Across the River on the Floating Ice', 'Eva and Tom in the Garden'). It is as if story and characters were assumed to be familiar to the audience, or this knowledge was to be provided for them during the projection.

Initiated with the Passion films, this setting aside of the narrative instance, this tacit affirmation that the narrative discourse is located outside the picture—in the spectator's mind or the lecturer's mouth—was to inform the cinema for twenty years and more. Vitagraph's early 'art films' (e.g., **Francesca da Rimini**, 1907, **Richelieu; or, The Conspiracy**, 1910, and the Vitagraph version of **Uncle Tom's Cabin**, 1910) still appealed to an external narrative instance. It is so self-evident today that a film must tell its own story[4] that we are often unable to read such narratives. To our eyes, **L'Assassinat du duc de Guise**, for example, is incomplete as a film without some knowledge of History, whereas **Intolerance**, eight years later, is 'self-sufficient'.

From the simple headings they started as, insert titles began to change around 1905 into summaries of the action preceding each tableau. But this did not make any basic difference; the externality of the narrative was now simply inscribed into the film. When in 1905 Bitzer made **The Kentucky Feud**, based on a celebrated feud between two subsequently famous families, the Hatfields and the McCoys,[5] he introduced each tableau with a long intertitle summarising in dry telegraphese all the bloody peripeteia of the shot that follows ('Home of the McCoys. The Auction. Buddy McCoy shoots at Jim Hatfield and kills Hatfield's mother'). Such intertitles, systematically anticipating the narrative content of the following shot and thus eliminating any possible suspense, were to constitute a major obstacle to the linearisation of narrative for a further ten years at least, and their traces can be detected right through the 1920's, though with connotations that were ironic (Sennett), cultural (Gance), or distancing (Vertov). There was clearly *no discontinuity* between this use of the intertitle and the lecturer's commentary. One more example of a 'step forward' that brought with it a retreat (until around 1914). One more example, too, of a primitive feature that was to be successfully integrated into 'cultural' cinema.

I should add that this externality of the narrative instance in

Fig. 23: **The Kentucky Feud** (Billy Bitzer, 1905).

the primitive cinema only existed for 'serious' subjects: Passion films, digests of famous plays or novels, melodramas, and, of course, scenics. It was hardly perceptible in trick films or burlesques, during which the bourgeois lecturer was at a loss for words.[6] Yet while these films with their very rudimentary stories, ritual rather than narrative, were sufficient unto themselves, it seems to me that they manifest the other, 'visible' face of what I call non-closure.

Let us therefore examine the history of *the ending* in the cinema, if only briefly and schematically.

The general rule in the Lumière films and in the subsequent 'Lumière school' was that the film (the shot) ended when there was no film left in the camera. Most of these films were actualities, which gave them the implicit signification that the action went on outside the film (before and after). But once we turn to Lumière's first entirely staged film we discover an initiatory feature.

Arroseur et arrosé concludes, more or less,[7] with a punishment: the mischievous boy is spanked by the angry gardener. Such *punitive endings* are legion throughout the primitive period: the voyeur in innumerable 'The Bride Retires' films is caught and beaten, or the bed canopy falls on him as he is about to substitute deeds for looks; as for the countless tramps and other outlaws of American and British films, they are invariably caught at the end of a spectacular chase and beaten black and blue, until the film runs out.[8] All sorts of variations are possible, from the umbrella blows a New York chaperone rains on the back of Porter's unlucky **Gay Shoe Clerk** (1903) to **The Ingenious Soubrette** in Zecca's film (1902) kicking off screen a cloddish valet. The symbolic import of these 'infantile', 'innocent' aggressions, these castratory endings (it is remarkable how often women have the punitive part, especially in the USA), is part of the overall symbolism of the primitive cinema that I must leave it to others to elucidate. But the extreme contrast between these endings and what we would recognise as an 'end' in the cinema today should draw our attention to the process whereby the 'satisfactory' endings of the institution were constructed. For the institutional ending was not self-evident, it was more than ten years before film-makers knew how to end their films in a way

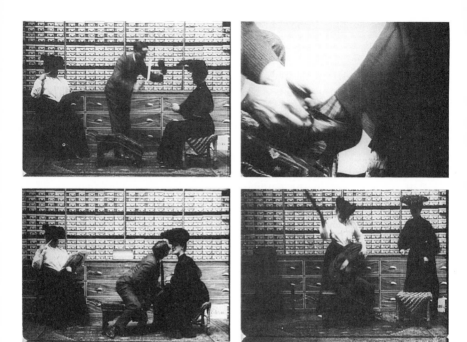

Fig. 24: **The Gay Shoe Clerk** (Porter, 1903). A classical punitive ending: the clerk is chastised for his kiss (and the spectator, perhaps, for his glimpse of a supposedly female ankle ... although the actor was probably a man!)

allowing the spectator to withdraw 'gently' from the diegetic experience, convinced that he or she had no more business in it and not feeling that the dream had been interrupted by a beating or by being kicked out of it.

The punitive ending came straight from the circus (the clown's closing kick in the behind) and from certain music-hall turns that themselves probably have the same source. The other main primitive ending was just as mechanical and arbitrary: the Méliès *apothéose*, adopted from the variety theatre and becoming almost obligatory in all French *féeries* and trick films[9] until the exhaustion of these genres around 1912. Punishment and *apothéose* have at least one thing in common: they are both open endings, associated with the primitive forms that were self-sufficient enough (popular enough?) to be able to dispense with either lecturers or intertitles—the chase and the *féerie*.

The next stage in the *history of the ending* had a life of its own and then an afterlife, both surprisingly long. It represented a decisive step towards closure—in particular because this new invention could involve both the end and the beginning of the film. This was the emblematic shot. The best known example today is surely the famous shot of the leader of the outlaws in **The Great Train Robbery** shooting at the audience to end (or begin) Porter's film (see p.197 below). Deriving directly from the autonomous genre of the primitive medium close-up—which died out between 1903 and 1906 as the emblematic shot became established—this kind of portrait could thus appear either at the beginning or at the end of a film, or both. As a general rule its semantic function was either to introduce the film's main concern (at the beginning of **Rescued by Rover** the baby is asleep, watched over by the dog) or to summarise the film's 'point', e.g., its moral (at the end of **How a British Bulldog Saved the Union Jack** the dog is filmed from close to with the flag between its teeth) or its 'joke' (at the end of **Le Bâilleur**, 'The Yawner', Pathé 1907, the protagonist's irrepressible yawning, the sole source of the film's humour, breaks a strap that has been fastened round his jaws, in close-up).

Emerging around 1903—and partly determined by the search for character presence and the establishment of eye contact between actors and spectators—emblematic shots continued to be

Fig. 25: In **The Great Train Robbery**, Porter sought perhaps to compensate for the impersonal quality of his stick-figures by providing an emblematic close-up which exhibitors could use to open or close the film *ad libidum.*

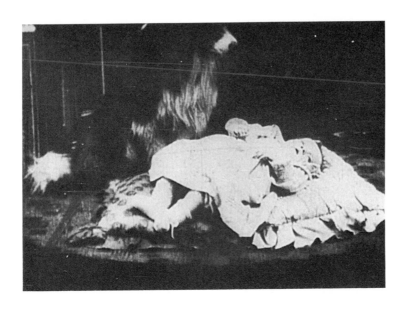

Fig. 26: The emblematic shot which opens **Rescued by Rover**.

used for six or seven years. After 1906 they often became a way to present, usually as an '*apothéose*', the smiling face of the heroine, at last seen from close to.[10] But at the same time more far-sighted spirits began to forge more consistent links between the emblematic shot and the main body of the narrative. One of these innovators was a notorious 'plagiarist', Siegmund Lubin. In his **Bold Bank Robbery** (1904), the initial presentation of the three gentlemen-crooks is made by a portrait shot which, although it is not matched with the succeeding action, is shot on the same set with the same characters dressed in the same costumes and in the same positions; they are simply 'posing' for the cameraman. The same is true of the final picture, in which the three pose once again, but this time in their convict's uniforms.

In its presentational and often extra-narrative dimension the emblematic shot was still a rejection of closure. At the beginning of the film it ultimately metamorphosed into a 'live' introduction of the characters (e.g. **The Cheat**), a practice that persisted throughout the silent cinema, in which it constituted a clear primitive survival. But the terminal emblematic shot, especially insofar as it was the repository of the 'point' of the film (for Lubin: 'Crime does not pay'), is particularly revealing about the future Institution.

The notion of an 'ideological point' (not always a particular 'message', sometimes just the reconfirmation of an institution like marriage) that each spectator should be able to take away at the end of a film seems to me to be an essential aspect of institutional centring. Linked to the notion of a central character anchoring diegetic production, this point was displayed in the last picture for a long time, like the primitive emblem: think of the handclasp of Labour and Capital at the end of **Metropolis**, or the corpse of **Little Cæsar** lying in the rubbish behind an enormous billboard. Think, too, of the final kiss in so many Hollywood happy ends. The Institution has become more sophisticated today, but this practice is still alive: consider the two workers, one white, the other black, attacking one another in a freeze frame at the end of Paul Schrader's pernicious **Blue Collar**.

One more characteristic of the primitive cinema taken as a whole:[11] the prodigious 'circulation of signs' that went on in it. At the time, of course, it was more common to speak of plagiarism or piracy. In the absence of appropriate legal provisions (an absence with its own history and its own lessons)[12] or international legal recourse, films could easily be copied in a laboratory and distributed without the producer-proprietor's agreement. But more interesting to us here is the fact that films could also be copied in their substance, their staging and their editing, by any other film-maker, whether a foreigner or a rival compatriot, and without any possible retaliation.[13] It seems even that, unlike the printing of pirated copies, the practice was hardly thought objectionable among film-makers. The first major trial involving the cinema in France that centred on artistic property occurred in 1908, when Georges Courteline sued Pathé for the unauthorised adaptation of his play *Boubourache*. Courteline's success established a precedent. For, in the primitive period, the notion of artistic property had not been felt to apply to the cinema: these pictures belonged more or less to everyone. Thus film-makers as important as Porter or Zecca could acquire subjects and conceptions of direction by unconcernedly stealing from each other and their English colleagues, who did not hesitate to repay them in kind.

Finally there is the characteristic of primitive cinema most obvious to modern eyes, a characteristic both of its peculiar forms of narrative and of the rules of direction then in force. I mean the absence of the *classical persona*.

In **The Great Train Robbery**, as in all narrative films up to that point (a few milestones as a reminder: Williamson's **Fire!**, Mottershaw's **A Daring Daylight Burglary**, Méliès's **L'Affaire Dreyfus**), although a certain linearisation is beginning to appear, the actors are still seen from very far away. Their faces are hardly visible, their presence on screen is only a bodily presence, they only have at their disposal a *language of gestures*. The essential supports of 'human presence'—the language of the face and above all of the voice—are still completely lacking. The addition to **The Great Train Robbery** by Porter and his collaborators at Edison of a mobile close-up—which could be shown at the beginning or at the end of the film, as the exhibitor chose[14]—was intended, among other things, to give the film this dimension, which they presumably felt it sadly lacked. I speak of an addition to the film rather than an insert because at this time the introduction of inserts was almost inconceivable.[15] That is why it wanders about the margins of the diegesis, with no fixed abode. And that was how the emblematic shot began. But much more was needed to make the cinema leave the field of a strictly external 'behaviourism' and embark for the continent of *psychology*.

One last word on the very notion of a Primitive Mode of Representation. Unlike some English and American writers, overinfluenced by modernist ideology, perhaps, I no longer really see the primitive cinema as a 'good object' on the grounds that it contains countless 'prefigurations' of modernism's rejection of classical readerly representation. These prefigurations are clearly no accident: it is not surprising that the obstacles that blocked the rise of the Institution in its 'prehistory' should appear as strategies in the works of creators seeking explicitly or implicitly to deconstruct classical vision. But to see the primitive cinema as a lost paradise and to fail to see the emergence of the IMR as an objective advance is to flirt with obscurantism.

Nevertheless, the primitive cinema did produce some films that strike us today as 'minor masterpieces', sometimes in a certain archaic perfection—as in Méliès's finest films, **Voyage dans la lune, Voyage à travers l'impossible, L'Affaire Dreyfus, Barbe Bleue, Le Royaume des fées**, and in certain films of Zecca's discussed in 'The Wrong Side of the Tracks' above. But there are other very different films in which primitive otherness produces a strange poetry all of its own, irreducible either to the codes of the popular arts of the period or to some anticipation of modernist strategies.

I have already discussed the magnificent British film **Charles Peace**, in which the combination of two systems of representation of space, of elements taken from the circus and from the serial novel, produce a poetry of this kind. **Tom, Tom, the Piper's Son** and **The Kentucky Feud**, two Biograph films Bitzer worked on, also seem to me to have this 'primitive originality'.

But I would like especially to evoke a little French film of 1905, of uncertain genre and only two minutes long, called **L'Envers du théâtre** ('Behind the Stage'), which is a condensation of primitive otherness. It consists of three shots, stencil-tinted in the version I have seen, which give a slight impression of having been taken from very different sources. (This is not completely impossible, what we would call collage having been a common technique at that time.)

1 A cab deposits some night owls in front of a theatre.
2 A tableau of a teeming crowd of people in a theatre dressing room; a flirtation, jealousy (all barely adumbrated).
3 The camera is at the back of the stage facing the auditorium (a painted backdrop glimpsed in the distance), the curtain is up. A prima donna is standing with her back to the camera. She finishes her song; flowers are tossed to her; the curtain falls; a fireman crosses the stage; the stage manager (?) comes and peeps through the spyhole in the curtain; a bit of the scenery falls on his head and breaks to pieces.

Whatever may have been thought when this film was 'rediscovered' at the FIAF Congress in Brighton in 1978, this really is a complete film: the *punitive ending*—punishing a voyeur into the bargain—so highly codified at the time, signifies without any shadow of doubt the end of a 'narrative' (which I see as a transposition of the gossip columnist's write-up), a narrative as open and non-centred as is conceivable, a kind of *haiku* produced in the Pathé factory, why and how we will probably never know.[16]

Here is a jewel buried in a 'heap of rubbish' that deserves to be dug into.

NOTES

1   For example, the astonishing **The Dialogue of Legs** (a French film of 1902?), an attempt to establish the cinematic equivalent of the 'synechdoche' (adumbrated in the same period by Porter in the close-up of the fire-alarm box in **Life of an American Fireman**). The film tells a 'dirty story' in several concatenated shots unashamedly showing an assignation with a prostitute in the grass of a Parisian wood. After a tableau presenting the situation in long shot (the streetwalker meets her client on a café terrace), we only see the characters' legs. But as this film was made at a time when the articulation of a series of close-ups was still inconceivable, the truncation of the bodies is achieved by a series of extraordinary off-centre long shots placing the legs at the very top

or bottom of the screen. The ambivalence of primitive 'advances' is admirably represented by this film, which was remade in 1914 in Italy, in accordance with the new codes of editing.

2 The genre (which in fact comprises several sub-genres) of the 'portrait' in medium close-up also seems to have been a stable form until its absorption into the emblematic shot (see below).

3 It is not impossible that there was a lecturer on hand for film projections in certain vaudeville houses in the USA, but I have no evidence of this.

4 To understand **All the President's Men** one does, it is true, have to have some general knowledge about the political situation in the USA in 1973 and 1974, for example. But the kind of cultural competence demanded by any modern film is one thing, the basically lacunary structure on the screen of these primitives is quite another.

5 There is a famous ballad about them.

6 'Comic films as a rule require no explanation, it is in dramatic and historical pictures that the need for some brief synopsis is most felt' (Anon. 1909b). By contrast, a 'comic' film that adopted the form of the political cartoon such as Porter's curious **Terrible Teddy, the Grizzly King** (1901) certainly needed a spoken 'caption'.

7 In fact the film ends a few seconds after the spanking with little going on (the gardener is about to return to work and the scapegrace is running off). But it is interesting that the series of 'popular' engravings of 1887 that is strikingly similar to Lumière's film (see Sadoul 1973, t.I, pp.296-7) ended with the actual punishment. The film goes on after this because the seventeen metres in the magazine had to be completely used up!

8 In other words, the film ends with a kind of 'closed groove' like a gramophone record, it does not terminate, it is arbitrarily stopped in a perpetual motion which is simply a condensation of the repetitive character of the chase as a whole.

9 It seems also to have been extended to more 'modern' genres in which the institutional narrative is already in gestation. At the end of the astonishing *composite* film **Tour du monde d'un policier** ('A Detective's Tour of the World', Pathé, 1906)—it alternates scenic shots and composed views—the end of the story strictly speaking (the pursued fraud settles his debt and sets up in business with the detective as his partner!) is followed in due form by an *apothéose*, a series of tableaux vivants evoking the different countries visited during the film, in the manner of a variety show.

10 1906 or thereabouts was also the time at which female parts ceased to be played by men: the world the cinema was entering was that of the close-up, in which such 'frauds' were no longer acceptable; but the world it was leaving was primarily that of the music-hall where this was a standard practice.

11 At this level I have already discussed the characteristic opposition between interiors and exteriors, flatness and depth (see p.173 above).

12 For a first, incomplete approach to this question, see Edelman (1979).

13 I need only mention the countless versions of **Arroseur et arrosé** and **Le Coucher de la mariée** ('The Bride Retires') or Porter's copy of **Rêve à la lune**

('Moon Lover' or 'Drunkard's Dream, or "Why You Should Sign the Pledge"') in **Dream of a Rarebit Fiend**, little more than the title of which was taken from McCay's cartoons.

14 Charles Musser (1981) sees this latitude conceded to the exhibitor as a vestige of the period when, in the USA especially, it seems, the film-maker's job consisted essentially of shooting raw material that he did not really know how to work up but preferred to hand over to the exhibitor to sort it, arrange it and establish its articulations. For example, **Execution of Czolgosz** (Porter, 1901) was sold both with and without the descriptive track along the outside of Auburn Prison (**Panorama of Auburn Prison**) that Porter also shot.

15 The situation shown in **The Gay Shoe Clerk** which permitted the insertion of the close-up, still quite exceptional in 1903, was itself rather exceptional: static, with few characters, a restricted set, etc. One has a feeling that this film, like other analogous ones (**A Subject for the Rogues Gallery**) was shot with the sole aim of introducing this close-up.

16 This description of the film is my decipherment after three viewings of it (projected, not on an editing table). Ben Brewster has pointed out to me that the Pathé Catalogue talks of an old stage-door Johnny snubbed by a dancing girl (?), obliged to give the bouquet intended for her to the stage fireman, and the butt of practical jokes from the stage hands. The example is, I believe, evidence both of the difficulties we often experience in deciphering the films of this remote period, and of the 'externality of the narrative instance', which, as is so often the case, is better articulated in the catalogues than it is on the screen. But however accidental, the poetry remains.

The Motionless Voyage:
Constitution of the Ubiquitous Subject

A pretty country road is seen, and in the distance a dog-cart travelling at a fair speed.... The cart ... passes, and as the dust which it raised clears away, a motor car is seen approaching very rapidly indeed.... The driver ... does not see the obstruction in the road until it is too late to steer past it.... The car dashes full into the spectator, who sees 'stars' as the picture comes to an end.

The film so described in Cecil Hepworth's catalogue (Anon. 1903b, p.26; cit. Low & Manvell 1948, p.83) is called **How it Feels to be Run Over**. 'Very rapidly indeed' means hardly more than seven miles an hour, but what is important here is that the 'obstruction in the road' is the camera.

What we have here is a remarkable 'epistemological' résumé of the formative phase of the IMR. Indeed, the beginning of the film—the empty road, the dog-cart passing in the distance— conforms perfectly to the Lumière model, a representation of space only including the spectator insofar as it reproduces monocular perspective, i.e., no more nor less than a Renaissance landscape.

As I have said, British film-makers were amazingly prescient of the essence of the IMR. And the precocity of the films made by these cultivated members of the middle class seems to stem from a kind of anxiety induced in them by 'primitive distance'. In this gag, a fast car—symbolic for us today of the industrialism of the turn of the century and the social status of its film-maker owner—comes flying out of the remote primitive tableau at the spectator/camera. Like the gags in **The Big Swallow** and **What Happened on 23rd Street, New York City**,[1] it is one of a series of battering rams beating on the 'invisible barrier' that maintains the spectator in a state of externality. Vain blows, moreover: it

Fig. 27: **How it Feels to be Run Over** (Hepworth, 1900).

was in fact to take more than fifteen years to *centre the spectator-subject*.

This film—like the famous movable shot of the outlaw firing on the audience in **The Great Train Robbery** three years later—is of course banking on the 'hallucinatory' effect the cinema produced in the very earliest period. Think of the spectators in the Salon Indien who, tradition claims, leapt up from their tables in terror at the train rushing towards them. But whereas for Lumière the hallucinatory effect was more or less accidental, an involuntary consequence of his 'scientistic' approach, for Hepworth and Porter it had become an intentional interpellation of the spectator, an explicit *invitation to the voyage*.

Another film of Porter's, made at the very end of 1902, reveals most clearly the *external position* occupied mentally by the primitive film spectator, a position which has become almost impossible for us even to conceive of today, except when our institutional expectations are radically frustrated by some strategy of the modernist cinema. Moreover, the historiography of **Life of an American Fireman** is in itself a fine demonstration of the *watertight barrier* between the institutional experience and what was possible in pre-1906 cinema.

After a first section showing in particular the up-to-date appointments of a fire station[2]—mostly actuality shots enlisted in the story by chase-type editing—the more important part of the film shows the firemen fighting a fire in a frame house. This second part consists of three set-ups, two exteriors, the third a studio interior. The first exterior shows the firemen arriving. Then Porter shot an interior and another exterior, each showing more or less the same action: In a first-floor room a woman and her small child are trapped by the flames. The woman at the window cries desperately for help, then faints on the bed. A fireman comes into the room, gets her through the window and down the ladder. Returning to the smoke-filled room he saves the child, then with a colleague he returns once again to the room to put out the fire, while in the street others are busy reviving the victims.

The film was long thought to be lost. But thanks to some stills and the 'script' given in an Edison catalogue, it was known that this film of Porter's evinced a precocious aspiration to camera ubiquity, to 'modern editing'. According to Lewis Jacobs (1939, p.41), for example, this section of the film was 'one of the earliest signs of a realisation that a scene need not be taken in one shot but can be built up by a number of shots. It was not until ten years later, however, that the shot as a single element in a scene of many elements was to be fully understood and used by film-makers.'

In the 1940's a copy of the film was at last rediscovered. And it seemed to confirm the 'evidence' of the Edison catalogue, that the film was an amazingly precocious example of cross-cutting, with the action of the mother and child being saved fragmented into a dozen shots, alternating exterior and interior. As late as 1980, this version was still distributed by the Museum of Modern Art.

Today, however, it is clear that, at some point in its history, some unknown distributor had felt the need to tamper with a film whose syntax was no longer acceptable. For in the original film, as copyrighted with the Library of Congress, the three tableaux were presented as follows: A pan follows a fire engine as it stops in front of a house from which smoke is pouring. Then follows the studio shot and all the action described above occurs once. Finally there is the longer shot of the same exterior in which *all the action is seen over again.*

Given the absolute hegemony of institutional structures by the end of the First World War, the unknown distributor had taken it upon himself to treat these shots as if they were rushes await-ing editing, needing to be fragmented into a multiplicity of shots capable of achieving the biunivocal concatenation that had become the only mode of temporal relation anyone could con-ceive in the cinema. The result was to articulate this scene into a perfect linear alternation such as Porter could never even have imagined in his day—but such as to make him seem a unique visionary.

A few years ago, American scholars found a distribution copy of the film in Maine, and it confirmed what all consistent histori-ans had suspected for twenty years:[3] that 1903 audiences (who, according to Jacobs again, gave this film an enthusiastic recep-tion) had indeed seen it in a version in which the two shots appeared integrally and the action was all repeated. In 1902, *no one would yet venture* ubiquitous editing, they preferred to rest

THE MOTIONLESS VOYAGE 205

content with a syntax which fundamentally contradicted the principle of temporal linearity even though this principle was strongly affirmed by the first section of the film, which adopted the codes of the chase.[4]

In a sense the whole thrust of this book[5] is to bring out the decisive gulf dividing a period in the cinema's history in which institutional oneness and continuity in all their aspects 'go without saying'—though by means of highly artificial constructions—from another in which what went without saying for both film-makers and audiences was *an awareness that one was sitting in a theatre watching pictures unfold on a screen in front of one.*

Porter, presumably in accord with the other people responsible for Edison productions, could not go 'beyond' this already in fact premonitory gesture, could not attempt the editing that could be so successfully achieved a decade or so later with the footage he shot in 1902, precisely because at the time an *external relation* to moving pictures still prevailed over a representation of time as linear. The film's enunciation can be translated as follows: 'Here is a scene shown from one viewpoint; now here it is seen from another.'[6] It thus reveals its roots in *primitive autarchy* (whose persistent survival in the chase film that was developed in the same period I have already pointed out). Here that autarchy still easily prevails over any impulse towards linearisation. Once one has noted how hard it was for Fritz Lang in **Metropolis** twenty years later and Julien Duvivier in **La Belle équipe** thirty years later to master the codes of spatial direction, one realises how deeply rooted that autarchy really was.

This film is perhaps the most spectacular example of this type of duplication signifying simultaneity, but it is entirely consistent with a film-making tradition often exemplified by Porter himself, but also by Méliès.

The beautiful film **Voyage à travers l'impossible** contains two pairs of shots supposed to be adjacent to one another in diegetic space and to succeed one another in diegetic time, but in both cases they are 'cut off' from one another by the principle of primitive autarchy. Georges Sadoul (1973, t.II, p.402) describes one example of this phenomenon and offers a commentary:

1 *Exterior of the Righi Inn*. The automabouloff crashes through the front and disappears inside.[7]

2 *Interior of the Inn*. Travellers are peacefully dining. The wall collapses. The automabouloff drives along the dining table.

Once again we have ... a style proper to the theatre, governed by changing sets. In the heat of the action the director is obliged to go back. He shows the beginning of an event the end of which we have already seen in a preceding tableau.

Sadoul goes on to contrast this 'blindness' of the Reactionary Méliès with Porter's method (modern shot-reverse-shot). In 1948, when this passage was published, Sadoul too believed that in **Life of an American Fireman** Porter had already mastered ubiquitous editing by 1902.

The passage is also characteristic of its time in automatically attributing the origins of this overlapping to the theatre in general. The external position that the overlap perpetuates is less that of the 'theatre'—i.e., a certain architectural combination of stage and auditorium, even if this syntax is a kind of mechanical translation of it—than that of the *caf'conc'*, the music-hall, the circus, the American vaudeville and all the forms of popular spectacle still in existence at the turn of the century and eventually more or less killed off by the cinema. For the bourgeois theatre, with its stage *à l'italienne*, its darkened house, its rapt, disciplined audience, already implied a centring, a ubiquity, a closure of its own.

There are many other examples of this kind of temporal overlap in films by Porter and his contemporaries (**How They Do Things on the Bowery, Off His Beat, Next!**). In all these cases, the temporal overlap is combined with an interior-exterior relation, more or less prefiguring the 180-degree match which was not to be generally mastered until the 1920's. By contrast, the editing figure adumbrated in the wish to have the automabouloff go through the wall of the Righi Inn was the very first classical figure to enter standard vocabulary. This is the figure I call the contiguity syntagm. I shall return to these two critical thresholds below.

Thus today we read in primitive films an effect of *distance* that seems inherent in their system. But we can only read this distance from where we are, within the Institution (but also, of course, from an experience of avant-garde practices explicitly directed *against* the Institution). This externality, this sense of non-involvement arises from a deficiency we feel as such. But did spectators feel any such thing at the time? Or did they establish the same relation with the minute characters, the action and the narrative of **The Great Train Robbery**, say, as a 1924 audience did with the diegesis of a film like **The Iron Horse**, or we do today with some James Bond film?[8] This is hard to believe. Most important, were they satisfied with the presumably distanced relations they had with films or, on the contrary, did they feel frustrated, as Maxim Gorky had with the Lumière Cinématographe? We have no sure way of telling.

However we interpret the internal evidence offered by the films themselves—and the evidence *a contrario* provided by the rise of the IMR—it should never be forgotten that the preconditions of this externality were also inscribed in *the conditions in which these films were exhibited*. Whether fairground booths in France or Wales, or nickelodeons in America, the places in which early films were presented were smoke-filled and noisy.[9] People came and went almost non-stop in the nickelodeons, and the fairground booths were hardly soundproofed at all. And in both venues a more or less gifted lecturer might retail a more or less facetious patter. The picture palaces of the 1920's, muffled, dark and isolating, with huge organs and usherettes to help 'discipline' the popular sections of the audience—and the children—were qualitatively more conducive to the 'voyage'.

****

Ignoring the major ellipses of 'indefinite scope' that articulated filmed boxing matches and Passion plays, the first editing figures to be generalised, though unevenly, were the axial match and direction match or, more generally, contiguity syntagm, already discussed.

The contribution made by the axial match to the *centring of the spectator*, our primary concern here, seems to be of the same nature as that of all the other figures of ubiquity. As it also happens to be the simplest of them in form, especially given the exceptional persistence of frontality, it historically preceded all the other direct matches. It has remained the same until today, only developing to the extent that it has been allowed to combine more and more discrepant shot scales as dramaturgy and stylistics have progressed.

The contiguity syntagm has a richer development: we have traced its emergence in the chase film, its change into a direction match with Hepworth's animals, then Griffith's communicating doors. The culmination of a process I believe to have been a homogeneous one was its transformation into shot-reverse-shot, as a mastery of eyeline directions was achieved equivalent to that of the directions of the movement of bodies and vehicles.

This all constitutes a single privileged lineage. For the direction match brought with it the first explicit consideration of the *psycho-physiological orientation of the spectator*.

As is well known, the basic principle underlying the whole series of orientation matches (of direction, eyeline and position) is a rigorous respect within a certain syntactic unit on the screen for the spectator's left-right orientation. The semiotic status of this principle which I long found fairly perplexing seems to me today to be describable in terms of Peirce's categories.[10] In fact we are here dealing with a signification system which is enormously variable in its substances of expression, but is manifestly *indexical* if we consider the 'existential' relation (in Peirce's sense) between this system and the left-right 'binarism' of the spectator's own body. This homology between directions on the surface of the screen—occasionally contradicting those of pro-filmic space (see p.211 below)—and those of the spectator-subject was the starting-point for the cinema's *centring* of the spectator by making him or her the reference point 'around which' was constituted the *oneness and continuity* of a spectacle destined to become more and more fragmented.[11]

The French makers of chase films seem to have been aware of a rule for entrances and exits, in other words of direction matching, from very early on. Like Cecil Hepworth and Lewin Fitz-

Fig. 28: **Rescued by Rover**.

hamon in **Rescued by Rover** they managed to produce the sense of a continuous and consistent trajectory by repeating movements towards the camera to signify 'outward journey' and movements away from the camera to signify 'return journey'. But Griffith was one of the very first film-makers to have been aware of the 'illusionistic' nature of the direction match and the need to use it *even against the logic of profilmic topography*. This distinction lies at the heart of the whole *practology* of the IMR.

In **The Lonely Villa**—made at the end of April and the beginning of May 1909, i.e., less than a year after **The Adventures of Dolly**—we twice see the following sequence: long shot with the villa in the distance and to left of frame with the three ne'er-do-wells in the foreground also to the left making ready for their crime (to get the paterfamilias called away so that the mother and children will be at their mercy). On the first occasion, when one of them, having disguised himself as a tramp to deliver a bogus telegram, goes towards the house, he exits frame right[12] to enter frame left in the next shot which shows the villa's porch and steps from closer to. The same sequence occurs a second time to bring the whole trio to the villa door. In both cases the rule is (already) respected: the character(s) exit(s) right and enter(s) left. And yet the slightest examination of the topography presented in the first of the two shots shows that the entrance on the left is totally aberrant: in the first shot the camera is manifestly placed far 'to the right' of the villa (in the pro-filmic space, assuming we are facing the front of the house), so an entrance on the left in the second shot is unlikely, to say the least. The bogus tramp and then the whole trio would have had to make a weird detour to approach the steps from the left, all the weirder in the second case insofar as the path they would have to have taken passes in front of the villa whereas the criminals are supposed to be trying to keep hidden.

The fact that in 1909 Griffith chose a pro-filmically 'false' solution to achieve a correct match shows a remarkable insight into the nature of the historical strategy of the integration-centring of the spectator. However, an awareness that eyeline 'sutures' work in the same way took a lot longer to develop. In his famous 1911 film **The Lonedale Operator**, Griffith does manage one correct eyeline match. The girl waves goodbye to her boyfriend who responds in a second shot in what is an early form of shot-reverse-shot. But a few minutes later, when the girl and the villains are supposed to see each other through the station window, there is a crude mismatch. For the early Griffith, room equals tableau, which links his cinema to the primitive universe until at least 1913. Communicating doors having enabled him to achieve a perfectly rigorous continuity from room to room,[13] he was able to extend this articulation to the exterior, too, so long as the guarantee was always the movement on foot of a human body.[14] In **The Lonedale Operator** again, the mismatched directions of the train (in the closer shots the driver looks off left whereas in the long shots the train is travelling right) show that with this type of mechanical motion as with eyelines, there was as yet no question of matching for Griffith. Could this be because, the basis of the left-right relationship being the spectator's body (i.e., the director's body), it was more directly translatable into the body of an actor or an actress?

Without pretending to trace these subtle and diversified developments (the Danes were possibly ahead of Griffith in this respect, too), it can be postulated that the next stage on the semantic level was represented by a film like **The Cheat** (1915). Here the main set (Sessue Hayakawa's 'oriental' salon) is fragmented laterally by the cutting: when Fannie Ward faints at the news of her ruin, for example, Hayakawa drags her off screen (right) and reappears in another shot (entering left) without having left the room. Even in moving from one room to another, characters are rarely seen going through doors: simply leaving the frame has become the pivot of topographic articulation.[15]

But the very earliest articulating figures—direction matches, eyeline matches (and of course axial matches)—first developed under the ægis of frontality. In the films of DeMille, Barker and Ralph Ince, the eyeline directions in the few reverse shots attempted from around 1913 are still a long way from the lens axis; similarly, entrances and exits close to the camera are almost unknown. And, most important, the camera stayed constantly 'in front' of the action, contemplating it always from one and the same side. Only very gradually did the actors' looks get close to the lens axis or the camera 'insinuate itself' between interlocutors, positing the portions of space containing them as set against one another, and eventually, around the mid 1920's, leading to the topographic encirclement of the spectator-subject.

But before carrying forward my examination of this development, I should return once again to the 'origins' and take up the story of a certain *exchange of looks.*

****

On the one hand there is the look towards camera (or rather two looks of this kind: one that sees the camera and one that does not). On the other hand there is the look of the spectator *constituted as a voyeur.*

Well before the full IMR implicitly constituted the spectator as a voyeur, the primitive cinema in its first hesitant steps did so explicitly. Indeed, one of the first archetypes of cinematic narrative, appearing at the same time as the Passion film and well before the chase film, was the film of voyeurism in the strongest sense: a woman undresses under the gaze of a man (normally concealed from the woman, if only by a convention of the 'Bride Retires' kind).

In 1896, the collaboration of three men, the photographer Pirou as producer, the cameraman Joly, a refugee from Pathé, and one of Pirou's employees, Kirchner alias Lear, who directed, resulted in the appearance on Parisian screens of the very first version of **Le Coucher de la mariée** ('The Bride Retires'), with such success that two other projection points had to be opened to satisfy the demand.

How many versions of this scene were to be produced, mostly copied from this 'master stroke', right up until about 1905? I cannot say, and unfortunately an examination of the producing firms' catalogues is unreliable given the fact that the film's countless remakes either have the same title as the original or one of the three or four substitute titles invented for it. I have personally seen about ten films on the subject.

This inscription of the man's gaze as a gaze-that-stages is so obviously crucial for the future of the Institution that I need hardly insist on it. The American scholar Lucy Fischer has already demonstrated in her excellent article 'The Lady Vanishes' (1979) that, before 1900, especially in Méliès's films, it was the male magician who could make the woman's body he gazed at vanish at will. The primitive cinema often said out loud what the IMR would contrive to say *sotto voce*.

Note also that in many of the versions of **Le Coucher de la mariée**, the bride looks into the lens of the camera filming her as if to summon the spectators to bear witness, like the stage stripper; occasionally the voyeur-'husband' also appeals *via the lens* to his 'brothers' watching him.[16]

Are these winks and nods historically the earliest kind of *deliberate* look at the camera, as opposed to the accidental glances of the Lyon Congress delegates at Lumière's camera?[17]

At any rate, these looks derive from the popular theatre, be it the variety stage with its direct address, or melodrama and farce with their as it were parenthetic address. Such procedures, outlawed by the naturalistic codes then in force in bourgeois drama, relegated to the boulevard comedy and the operetta, were already, as we have seen (p.83 above), the *bête noire* of the managers of British music-halls, anxious for a better policed audience.

The cinematic aside was by no means restricted to striptease films, it was a standard practice throughout the primitive period until 1915 at least in France (Feuillade's **Les Vampires**)[18] whereas the Selig Polyscope Company was to prohibit it officially in 1909 in the USA (see below). Moreover, the note it published on this occasion suggests also that actors had the bad habit of looking towards the camera for suggestions or encouragement from the director. In addition, in the absence of paid extras—or assistants to marshall them—the unpaid 'extras' in early street scenes often look at the camera, like the Lyon Congress delegates. It is thus hardly surprising that looks into the lens remained very common for fifteen years.

Around 1908, however, it began to be realised that in the nascent new conception these looks into the lens had a quite different effect from that of glances at the audience from a theatrical stage. For a living actor who turns his gaze on an audience with whom he is really co-present addresses a collectivity which submerges each individual into what is both a solidarity and a

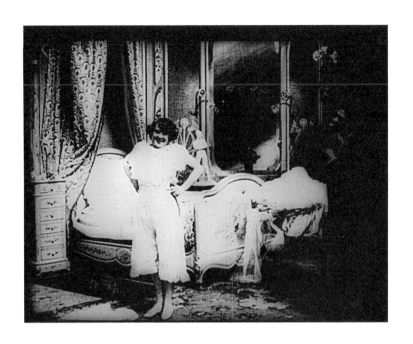

Fig. 29: **Le Coucher de la mariée** (Pathé, 1904?).

THE MOTIONLESS VOYAGE 215

concealment from a look which 'sees me no more than it does anyone else'. In the very long shot of the primitive tableau, the effect is still more or less the same, given especially that it is hard to tell the difference between a look *towards* the camera and a look *at* the camera. By contrast, as characters came closer in the American cinema after 1908 (with the introduction of the famous '*plan américain*', the medium long shot cutting the figure off at the knees), a look directed at the centre of the lens became a look into the eyes of each spectator individually, wherever he or she might be sitting in the auditorium.[19]

From a mechanistic standpoint it might be imagined that strategies of ubiquity such as the nascent *contiguity syntagm* which would soon harmonise the set of orientation matches were moving towards a perfect convergence with the cinematic aside, which 'also' tended to produce the spectator as a single individual in front of 'his' or 'her' peephole (the Kinetoscope effect, in other words). But this is to consider only one aspect of the phenomenon. The solitary and ubiquitous voyeurism of the Institution demanded as its indispensible complement the spectator's *invulnerability*: the actors spied on[20] must never return the spectator's look, must never seem aware of the spectator's presence *in this auditorium*, their looks must never pin the spectator down to that particular seat.

And this is why the Selig company included in the set of rules it issued for the actors in its employ an explicit prohibition of looking towards the camera (Anon. 1973). Most other firms in the USA seem to have adopted the same rule about this time, and hence the aside disappears from the American cinema (except in the slapstick genre which maintained its connections with the primitive cinema in a whole variety of ways until its disappearance in the 1930's).

But it is one thing not to look at the camera, quite another to turn one's back on it while acting.

Many actors and directors will contend that it is necessary to get the facial expressions over to the spectators and this continual and monotonous facing front is therefore unavoidable. How weak this contention is must be apparent after a moment's thought. When the movement or attitude of the player is obviously unnatural in turning his face toward the camera he betrays by the act the fact that he is acting—and there is someone in front unseen by the spectators to whom the actor is addressing himself. Immediately the sense of reality is destroyed and the hypnotic illusion that has taken possession of the spectator's mind, holding him by the power of visual suggestion, is gone (Woods 1910).

The problem pointed out here by this amazingly perspicacious critic—who was to become a Hollywood producer!—is that of the actor's feigned unawareness of the camera; that of the need to make the place of the spectator-subject completely 'invulnerable', not only by avoiding the actors directly 'looking at them', but also by preventing them even facing them if it was not possible to establish that in doing so they were not looking *towards them*.

Uncertainty about this matter lasted a long time. Maurice Tourneur, whose comedy about film-makers and film-making, **A Girl's Folly** (1917), shows a considerable mastery of the new editing techniques, shot a version of Maeterlinck's **The Blue Bird** in 1918. Perhaps the theatrical character of the sets and pictures in this film explains why shot-reverse-shot scenes are almost always staged in profile (whereas in the 1917 film there were a number filmed full face). But when one of the children in **The Blue Bird** is supposed to address the audience, the direction of his gaze is at least thirty degrees away from the lens axis. There can be no doubt that what is involved here is the survival of a veritable taboo that had come to surround the issue of looking into the lens as a result of the emergence of an awareness of the question around 1909.

A codification in this matter was established only during the 1920's when, as Frank Woods had wished in 1909, it became normal practice for actors to turn their backs to the camera—the over-the-shoulder shot—and a look towards camera no longer risked being perceived as a look towards the spectator but was seen as a look off screen to a space somewhere 'behind'.

DeMille's important and very modern film **The Cheat** (1915) seems to evoke all the parameters of this issue. When Fannie Ward, whom Hayakawa has induced to visit his house, is informed that the money she 'borrowed' from the charity for which she was treasurer has disappeared thanks to a friend's incompetent speculations, the appearance of this friend as the bringer of bad tidings in a doorway is the object of a *cutaway* which is in fact a rather 'modern' reverse shot (the angle of his eyeline is less than thirty degrees off the lens axis). By contrast, when he enters a repeat of the previous master shot to join Hayakawa and Ward, he arrives from directly right, the angle of this entrance not matching at all with that of the previous eyeline. The most remarkable thing about this third shot, however, is that his companions' eyelines, which corresponded fairly well with his while he was still off screen, move away from the camera as he approaches until they meet his as he enters at the back of the set. In DeMille's mind (and presumably in the minds of his spectators), the camera was still an obstacle to be avoided, unless his principal anxiety was not to show the back view of an actor. At any rate, in the end frontality re-establishes its full regime, just as it is entirely dominant in the scenes in Ward's boudoir, for example.

By contrast, in the great trial scene, Ward addresses the court—seen full face in a reverse shot—'over the top' of the camera, with an eyeline which is already that of the institutional conversation scene. Presumably this is facilitated here by the fact that the profilmic situation reproduces a 'theatrical' one and it was possible to revive the look embracing the whole audience—even from close to, now—without fearing that the spectators would feel themselves to be individually addressed.

These are the same conditions that had made possible the earliest 'shot-reverse-shots'; it is not at all surprising that they occurred to render theatrical situations. An audience before 1910 could hardly have been expected to accept the ubiquity of the camera to the point that the latter might 'turn back on itself' in any situation whatsoever (the problem of **Life of an American Fireman**). But when the action is located *in a show place*, real audacities became possible: having inscribed the spectators reflexively in the film, they could be asked to imagine they are 'on stage' being looked at.[21]

In **A Drunkard's Reformation** (Griffith, 1909), the shot-reverse-shot alternates between a theatrical action depicting the ravages of alcohol and the reactions of a drunkard to that representation

Fig. 30: **A Drunkard's Reformation** (Griffith, 1909).

which for him is one of his own story. In **Rosalie et Léontine vont au théâtre** (1911), the main action consists of showing fragments of some kind of melodrama taking place on the stage of a theatre and the outrageous and mirth-provoking reactions of two women seated in the balcony.

But such experiments only had a limited effect; only a particular case was resolved here. By contrast, at the very beginning of the century a film-maker from the 'Brighton school' had posed this relationship between spectator's look and actor's look in far more complex and probably more conscious terms:

> 'I won't! I won't! I'll eat the camera first.' Gentleman reading,[22] finds a camera fiend with his head under a cloth, focussing him up. He orders him off, approaching nearer and nearer, gesticulating and ordering the photographer off, until his head fills the picture, and finally his mouth only occupies the screen. He opens it, and first the camera, then the operator disappears inside. He retires munching him up and expressing his great satisfaction.

What this catalogue summary of **The Big Swallow** (Anon. 1903a, p.115; cit. Low & Manvell 1948, p.75), presumably written by Williamson himself, does not tell us, however, is that when this 'gentleman' gets near the camera, his look and hence his gesticulations seem to be addressed to someone at least thirty degrees away from the camera. The modern spectator even finds it quite difficult to grasp that this look is directed at the 'camerafiend', who, we are told, has his head under a black cloth, so that his look coincides with that of the camera. However, after the mouth has 'swallowed' camera and cameraman—by a childish trick: against a 'matched' black background they fall over an 'invisible parapet'—the swallower retreats looking *straight into the lens.*

Is this not a kind of presentiment of the critical distinction the Institution was to sanction between 1910 and 1920, i.e., that a look into the lens implies the *disappearance* of the camera—as

---

Facing Page: *Fig. 31:* **The Big Swallow** (Williamson, 1901).

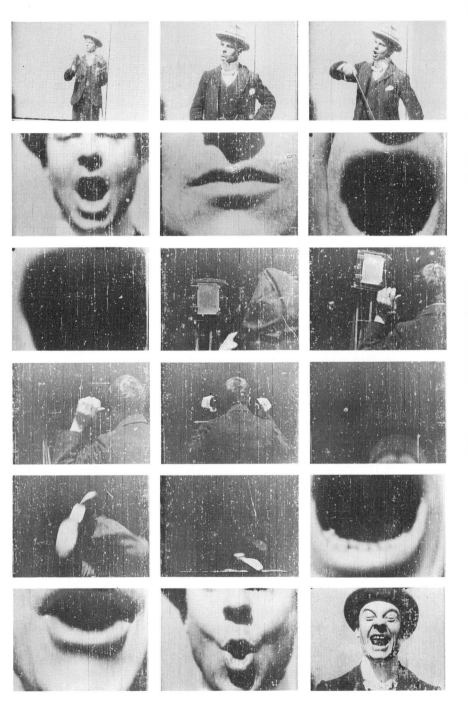

vehicle of the spectator's identification, as invulnerable and invisible 'bathyscaphe' transporting us to the universe of the stars—whereas the look (of shot-reverse-shot) that 'sutures' should skim past the camera but not see it?[23]

This film was no doubt a unique experiment.

But there is a much more generalised feature of the primitive cinema, more so even than 'theatrical' shot-reverse-shot, yet one that just as explicitly prefigures the voyeuristic presence/absence of the institutional spectator.

For the 'Bride Retires' films were only the first avatars of an explicitly voyeuristic thematic that recurs all through the early history of the cinema. From 1901 to about 1906, a 'through-the-keyhole' genre appeared alongside the former's 'laying out' of boudoir voyeurism, taking a step towards the identification of the spectator with the camera.

In its most typical form this film genre showed a man (but occasionally a woman) looking through a keyhole (long shot, usually from behind) followed by the picture of what he (or she) is seeing. This basic syntagm can be repeated several times, generally in a non-evolving system. **La Fille de bain indiscrète** ('The Indiscreet Bathroom Maid') is characteristic of the genre except insofar as the voyeur is a woman and the object of her look on every occasion a man. Climbing one by one up to the fanlights of a series of three bathroom cubicles, she sees three unconnected comic scenes.[24]

The genre reached a 'peak' with the 1903 Biograph film **A Search for Evidence**, in which a deceived wife accompanied by a private detective bends down to the keyholes of a whole row of hotel rooms, allowing the showing of a series of scenes some of which are comic, some banal. The last room is the 'right' one, and the point-of-view shot is linked—in a way quite unusual for the period—to a shot showing the same set from a different angle (the wife and the detective burst in on the right to catch the husband *in flagrante delicto*).

A contemporaneous variant of this genre, starting apparently with such films as Smith's **As Seen through a Telescope** (1900) and Zecca's **Ce que je vois de mon sixième** ('Scenes from my Balcony', 1901), showed gentlemen, usually of a certain age, looking through a telescope at the feminine objects of their scopic drive.

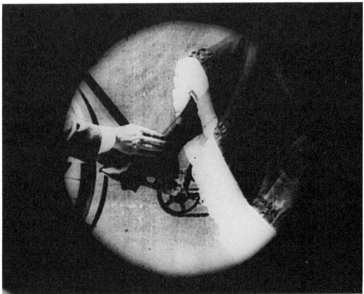

Fig. 32: **As Seen through a Telescope** (Smith, 1900).

Tom Gunning has suggested (in the discussion included in Musser 1982, p.57) that the vogue for films of this type in which the spectator is explicitly led to adopt the cinematic protagonist's place via the intermediary of the lens was encouraged by the actual situation of many spectators who still watched these films through the 'peephole' of the Edison Kinetoscope and of the Mutoscope[25] that the Biograph Company perfected to evade their rival's patents. However, not only does this voyeuristic genre seem to have started in Britain and France where this method of presentation had all but disappeared, but I believe that even if this factor had some influence on American versions of the genre, it was not the most important such influence.

Nor should we be detained here by the 'invention' of the 'point-of-view shot' or 'subjective camera', a figure which, as such (x looks out of the window/what x sees) never came to occupy a key position in the edifice of the IMR. In particular, this was by no means the way the cinema constituted anything equivalent to the first person in the novel (see pp.250ff. below).

On the contrary, this type of film should be seen as a 'natural' extension of the first voyeuristic films of the 'Bride Retires' type, and this 'voyeuristic syndrome' overall as one of the main ways the primitive cinema exploited, 'up front', as it were, what was to be buried in the very facture of the institutional film, i.e., the voyeuristic position of the spectator, the invulnerability/invisibility, the absence/presence that would eventually constitute the 'secret' of the cinematic subject.

I am aware that there is something 'metaphysical' about the notion that the primitive cinema manifestly revealed attitudes that were subsequently to be concealed in the very tissue of the institutional 'language'. For the moment I am unable to explain it. And yet.... The chase film is surely a naive affirmation of the basic linearity that the Institution would continue to deploy, but in vastly more subtle forms. The literal fragmentation of bodies that occurs in so many trick films of the first fifteen years of the cinema is surely an infantile version of the fragmentation to be carried out by the editing of the IMR (see p.269 below).

****

To complete this examination of the modes of ubiquity as they are revealed through figures of editing (for figures of movement, see pp.180f.), I have still to speak of 180-degree and 90-degree matches (the latter in fact comprising a whole range of angles from 30 degrees to 90 and more).

What first strikes the historian is that these two figures do not seem to have become commonplace until the very end of the historical process I am trying to describe here. Frontal shot-reverse-shot does become a figure available to all Western directors by 1920 and its first adumbrations date from around 1910. But, axial matches apart, *direct matches* (in which a second shot reveals a recognisable new aspect of the previous field of vision) were mastered even later.

The earliest attempt at a 180-degree match in a homogeneous pro-filmic space[26] that I know appears in a naive form but one which it is difficult to avoid reading today as demonstrating an (unconscious) *pedagogic irony*. It occurs in a British film preserved in the National Film Archive in London under the descriptive title **Ladies' Skirts Nailed to a Fence**. Made by the Bamforth company, long-time specialists in the production of lantern slides, it dates from around 1900. It shows a kind of fragment of a fence in front of which two women (clearly men in drag) are gossiping. Two boys creep up behind the fence. Shot change: but this 'new shot' is in fact identical to the first in pro-filmic space—the characters have simply changed sides, the boys are now in front of the fence, the gossips behind it. The boys nail the ladies' skirts to the fence with the obvious results in a return to the 'first shot'.

What are we to make of this curious film? I do not think it is pertinent to an understanding of what was done here that the bushes visible behind the fence might have made it impossible to place the camera on the other side. If this solution had occurred to the makers of this film, they would have looked for another location. To my mind this film confirms in particular that ubiquity could at this date be expressed *on the terrain of frontality*, i.e., the terrain of the fixed viewpoint: in front and behind are presented to us one after the other and in the same frame, as the IMR would require, but also in the same pro-filmic space, a typically theatrical, or lantern-slide, device. The film-makers relied on the acceptance of a crude convention rather than risking the invitation to the voyage which was eventually to characterise the institution.

But it has to be said that it was also Britain that produced what is generally reckoned today to be one of the most precocious examples of a 180-degree match. This is another of those 'experimental gags' like **How it Feels to be Run Over, The Big Swallow** and **A Subject for the Rogues Gallery**.

In **The Other Side of the Hedge** (Fitzhamon for Hepworth, 1905), two young lovers outsmart the vigilance of their chaperone by placing their hats on sticks behind a hedge so that they seem to be sitting a decent distance apart, whereas in reality (the shot on the other side of the hedge) they are making love between them. The precocious audacity of the film is inscribed in its very title, which prepares the spectator for the unaccustomed change in viewpoint and designates the change as the film's raison d'être.

But if one set out to trace the detailed history of the direct match with a change in axis, one would find that, despite such aphoristic films, and despite a few other British examples as remarkable for their precocity as for their off-handedness (Haggar's **Desperate Poaching Affray** of 1903, Alf Collins's **When Extremes Meet** of 1905), such figures were not to spread elsewhere for another twenty years.

And if one needed an extra proof of the fact that the match with angle change was still unthinkable in the USA in 1905, there is an admirable one in the remarkable **The Story the Biograph Told** ('Biograph' here referring to the camera produced by that firm). A reporter-cameraman shows an office boy how to work the camera he then leaves 'lying about' on a table at the back of the set. Taking advantage of the fact that his boss and the latter's secretary are busy kissing, the boy films them without their knowing it. In a second tableau, the boss and his wife are in the audience at a vaudeville show during which a 'Biograph film' shows on the screen the same scene as the preceding one, but taken from a quite different angle and from much closer. It is clear that the whole arrangement thus put in place by means of an archetypal narrative of domestic jealousy[27] only had one purpose: to bring about, via the detour of an inscription of the production process itself, a 'direct match' with angle change. We are

Fig. 33: **The Story the Biograph Told** (1905): the close shot that tells all, the 'point' of the film.

dealing in fact with a narrative linearisation which ultimately repeats but also rationalises the aberrant duplication of **Life of an American Fireman**.

Let us finally consider another limit situation, one which offers an additional indication as to spectator 'psychology' before 1906. Two Pathé films made in 1902 and 1904(?) respectively present a 'trick' that is very instructive in this respect. In **The Ingenious Soubrette** or **Magic Picture Hanging**, a young woman in eighteenth-century costume hangs a series of four paintings on a wall by walking up it like a fly. The trick is 'obvious' to the modern eye,[28] and depends on the use of two camera positions, one horizontal, the other vertical.[29] The effectiveness of the trick at the time undoubtedly lay in the fact that the clues to downward verticality were absolutely unrecognisable—it was an unthinkable angle never seen in a system whose basic reference point was a flat screen unfailingly perpendicular to the gaze of a spectator seated in a theatre. This hypothesis is confirmed by **La Danse du Diable**, a film which seems completely pointless today until it is realised that the dancer in the gaudy imp's costume rolling about on the ground and *filmed in a vertical downward tilt* is supposed to be performing these 'magical' acrobatic feats *in a vertical plane*. It was a kind of optical illusion made possible at the time by the absence in the culture of reference points abundantly available to us today, so commonplace did this dimension of camera ubiquity become only twenty years after this film.

Do I have too simplistic a view of what constitutes the ubiquity of the spectator subject, of what is thus the first cause of the 'primary identification' the spectator unconsciously makes with the camera—or rather with the latter's viewpoint—within the institutional apparatus? I do not think so. Of course, the diegetic process as a whole is not the mere sum of such procedures. But the logic that emerges from a historical examination of the real gestation of the procedures that every film-maker had to master in order for his work to find a place in the institutional economy, that every spectator had to master as an indispensable competence in modern social life, this logic is indeed that of the 'motionless voyage' so often evoked in this book. Unless all the conditions necessary for this voyage to be set into motion are met, a film becomes inaccessible to the vast majority of today's

Fig. 34: **The Ingenious Soubrette** (Zecca, 1902).

audiences—as is amply proved by the few avant-garde films that reject these conditions, whenever they happen to leave their cultural ghetto and confront 'unsuspecting' audiences.

NOTES

1   A remarkable film of Porter's (1901) which simultaneously *centres* the spectator's gaze and the unveiled female body. From the depths of a broad and long-held tableau of a busy street, a couple, apparently ordinary passersby, appear and advance towards the camera with others until the draught from a subway ventilation grating blows up the skirts of the girl, who feigns fright, then laughs.

2   The 'balloon' showing the fire chief's dream is a typically primitive device used frequently until about 1909. There are examples in **Histoire d'un crime** and a British film called **What the Curate Really Did** (Fitzhamon for Hepworth, 1905). In her memoirs (Gish & Pinchot 1969, p.59), Lillian Gish speaks of it as still a possibility (though an outdated one) when she made her debut with Griffith. By contrast, the *synecdochic close-up* of the fire alarm being set off by a hand in **Life of an American Fireman**, which condenses a whole action (the fire starts/someone sees it/someone gives the alarm), is undoubtedly one of Porter's most prescient insights, insofar as it anticipates the explicit extension of narrative time into the gaps between the shots, and hence ellipsis.

3   I.e., since the discovery of the 'copyright version' preserved as a paper print in the Library of Congress, which presents the two tableaux integrally in the order indicated.

4   It should be emphasised that the Edison catalogue tells the story of the film as if it unfolded 'normally' with a move to the interior, then another to the exterior. This reassured historians. I think it is clear that the mastered code (writing) was spontaneously expressing a linearity that could as yet only be rendered by a kind of non-linear hieroglyphics in moving pictures.

5   And of my film **Correction Please, or, How We Got into Pictures** (Arts Council of Great Britain, 1979), that derives from it.

6   An American scholar, Robert Gessner (1962), got to know the copyright version in the early 1960's and naively compared its primitive non-linearity with that of a modernist film, **L'Année dernière à Marienbad**. Here is a further pointer to the difficulties we have today in realising that the cinema before 1908 or 1909 was still on another planet, and that the anomalies which we meet in it and which appeal to our modernism derive from the fact that the contradiction between the PMR and the emergent IMR will seem by its very nature to be 'deconstructive *ante diem*'.

7 The effect intended. In fact, the fantastic vehicle knocks down the wall and stops; then there is a dissolve.

8 For television, however, see pp.260ff. below.

9 There is in France a striking correlation between the large-scale entry of the middle classes into the cinemas (at the beginnings of sound) and the *prohibition of smoking* in them. Remember the words of Brecht (1964, pp.8-9), who dreamt of a smokers' theatre (*Rauchentheater*) where the audience's relation to the stage would be like that of ringside spectators at a boxing match. 'I even think that in a Shakespearian production one man in the stalls with a cigar would bring about the downfall of Western art. He might as well light a bomb as light his cigar.' The fact that smoking has never been prohibited in British cinemas is a tribute to the British obsession with individual freedom (the London Underground was still afflicted with indescribably filthy cars for smokers until 1983). I believe the French prohibition is more characteristic. 'Respectable' people interviewed by a journalist for *Comœdia* in 1927 said they never went to the cinema because of the smoke—smoking was all right at a circus but not a theatre. Medical science has proved them right about the smoke, but this by no means invalidates the heuristic content of the observation for our understanding of class attitudes to the cinema.

10 Which I may well be using differently from Peter Wollen, although it was he who suggested their use to me (see Wollen 1969).

11 Do we refer so much more frequently to left-right binarism than to up-down binarism just because the former is more often *active* on the screen than the latter? In theory, of course, the spectator's 'bodily' centring is a homogeneous whole, and modern practice attaches equal importance to all its axes. But historically the problem was always the left-right relationship, partly because high- and low-angle shots developed belatedly, but mostly, I think, because of the way in which the distinctions between left hand and right hand in the human body are bound up in a whole education process, whereas the up-down relation is an immediately perceivable geophysical datum (gravity).

12 To have avoided his exit by catching him in an axial match would have been to resort to a very rare strategy everywhere at this time, action matching being still in its earliest infancy.

13 The 1913 Biograph film **The Switchtower**, not directed by Griffith, shows that even within a single production company this awareness grew unevenly. The transitions from the interior to the exterior of the hut in which the villains have imprisoned the signalman and his wife are systematically mismatched.

14 Note that, as early as 1909, Griffith did the same thing *within a single room*, but as far as I know this is an isolated case in his work at this time. This kind of editing only began to become at all widespread in 1913-14.

15 In **The Cheat** we also find the elimination of all those countless corridors, lobbies and staircases in Griffith's films, intended to support the concatenation of an editing trajectory according to the same repetitive (pedagogic) principle as that which presided over his 'cross cutting'. DeMille's film often seems to be returning to the primitive principle of one set = one shot, but in doing so it is in fact making a 'progressive' gesture. Now that the diegetic process is solidly

entrenched in the vast off-screen space represented by all possible other shots—this is what was achieved by Griffith and his contemporaries—more respect can be paid to narrative economy: simultaneity can be signified by one shot change only, transitions from one place to another by ellipses.

16 The sexual composition of early European cinema audiences does not seem to be well established. Did lower-class women go into fairground booths in France and Britain in the fairground era? Did nurses and grandmothers take middle-class children to films before the opening of the first permanent cinemas around 1906? There is no question that the content of French films of all genres almost always suggests a crudely patriarchal viewpoint (this is much less true in the USA where it is well known that vaudeville had mixed audiences), and even when this was no longer literally present as it was in films of the 'Bride Retires' type, there was often an implicit 'man-to-man' wink or nudge. In Britain and America, one should add, 'The Bride Retires' and other striptease films were seen in men-only 'smoking concerts' where the woman's body, as yet undraped in the veil of narrativity, was consumed with cigars, as in Brecht's favoured boxing matches.

17 **Arrivée des Congressistes à Neuville-sur-Saône** (1895). But Lumière carefully concealed his camera when filming his workers leaving the factory, so as to avoid attracting their attention (see p.15 above).

18 In which not only the comic Marcel Lévesque but also the reporter-detective Edouard Mathé and the anti-heroine Musidora glance complicitly or interrogatively towards the camera.

19 This phenomenon—a daily occurrence in advertising films or television news—is, of course, an effect of the laws of the optical construction of perspective which in some sense it *unveils*.

20 The problem as to whether the voyeuristic position constructed by the IMR can ever be analysed independently of the historical masculinity of voyeurism, cinematic or otherwise, is one currently the subject of considerable debate. I refer to the excellent article by Mary Ann Doane (1982).

21 If the Lacanian concept of the 'mirror stage' is of any relevance to the theory of the cinema, it is perhaps here that its principle lies, for the threshold crossed with this crude reflexiveness does indeed resemble that crossed by the small child perceiving for the first time that it is both 'in' the looking glass and in front of it.

22 The fact that it is a member of the middle classes who resists being photographed already suggests his class relationship with the photographic image in 1900 (see p.71 above). But the fact that this man is *reading* also clearly suggests the reluctance of a class to be 'importuned' by a means of expression (the cinema) that it saw as 'backward' in comparison with the printed word.

23 The historical and theoretical importance of Fritz Lang's great diptych **Doktor Mabuse der Spieler** (1922) lies in part in the demonstration that the spectator could now ultimately receive an actor's look full in the eyes without believing that he or she (the spectator) is intended, but experiencing the thrill of the fictional recipient nonetheless (see Burch 1981b). The relations between hypnotism and classical cinema have been studied by Raymond Bellour (in

unpublished pieces) and Jorge Dana asked me once if it could really be an accident that the cinema began just as Freud was abandoning hypnosis and initiating a technique of *blind dialogue*.

24   A Pathé film in the same genre made in 1904, **Un Coup d'œil par étage** ('Scenes at Every Floor'), is peculiar in that it uses 'stock shots': the scenes witnessed by a concierge who takes advantage of his delivery of the mail to look through the keyholes on each floor, are in fact single-shot films to be found in Pathé's catalogues of earlier years.

25   Film frames were glued onto small sheets like postcards which were fastened round a drum. The pictures were made to move by turning the drum with a handle. Mutoscope advertisements boasted of the spectator's ability to slow down, speed up or stop the picture—a perfect example of a primitive trait!

26   One can speak of a 180-degree match in **Life of an American Fireman**, but in **Next!** or **Off His Beat** the attempts of this kind are inscribed in a 'cellular' conception of editing; the sets change completely 'as in the theatre', as Sadoul would have put it. These are thus one more manifestation of the autarchy of the primitive tableau, 'axial' equivalents of the lateral matches through interposed doors so dear to Griffith.

27   When the house lights go up, the wife beats her husband. In the last tableau, which returns to the office, she forces him to sack his female secretary and take on a male one. This anecdote is a precocious example of a basic ambiguity which continues to inform American cinema. The female audience can see in this film a woman legitimately defending 'her rights', the male audience a confirmation of the stereotype of the shrewish repressive wife.

28   Although I have been surprised to find that some lay spectators are still mystified by it even today.

29   To judge by the picture itself, a studio set seems to have been painted to match very precisely with the glass roof of the studio on which the vertical shot was made, the link between the two locations being achieved by skillful action matches.

Beyond the Peephole, the Logos

The distinction established in French between *cinéma muet* and *cinéma parlant*, i.e., literally 'dumb cinema' and 'talking cinema', correctly locates what was at issue in the 'revolution' of 1926-9 (but without conveying all its historical complexity, for there was a time when that dumb cinema was quite loquacious); by contrast the English opposition between *silent* and *sound* is utterly inappropriate, the first term of it having always been incorrect.

Indeed, it is generally accepted today that cinematic pictures were only very exceptionally shown 'in silence', i.e., only accompanied by the ordinary ambient noises. The projections at the Salon Indien were accompanied by a piano. And I have already evoked the Kinetophonograph desired by Edison and constructed by Dickson: evocative music from a wax cylinder came over headphones while the film showed a mimed or danced scene in the eye-piece (but for Edison, wholly committed to the dream of singing shadows, this was only a second best).

What is the reason for this need for a musical accompaniment, felt from the very beginning? Is it of the same kind as the need for synchronised speech which by 1900 had generated much less confidential manifestations than the Kinetophonograph, despite the technological obstacles?

As far as I know, the first presentations of the Lumière Cinématographe to scientific audiences (Pinel 1974, pp.411-12 & 418) took place without musical accompaniment, unlike what was to be the case in the Salon Indien. I will be told that there is nothing remarkable about this: in a show music would be *de rigeur*, just as it would have been otiose in a scientific demonstration. But the fact that this musical option was *self-evident* is far from absolving us of the task of questioning it. For it is deeply ambiguous from the point of view of our genealogy: in one respect it is an anti-naturalistic choice. Music was not what Gorky missed, and anyway he presumably had his ears filled with it—he was at a cabaret after all. Yet he does not mention this music: it was simply part of the artificial atmosphere of that den of vice 'Aumont's'. Nevertheless, this 'low-musical' aspect of film, linking it to balancing acts with orchestral accompaniment, for example, was to remain an integral part of the cinema throughout the silent period, an obstinate hangover from its origin in popular and presentational spectacle.

But confronted with moving photographic pictures, music also did something it did not do in the circus, say. It created a 'higher' space embracing both the space of the auditorium and the space pictured on the screen, and formed a kind of sound barrier around each spectator. Thus from the beginning music served to isolate the spectator from projector noise, coughing, whispered commentaries, etc. In this respect, the introduction of music at projection points was the first deliberate step towards what was to become the institution's interpellation of the film spectator as an individual. With the enclosure of the projector in a box and the development of the fairground cinema in Europe, then the nickelodeon in the USA, the function of music became to combat the contamination of diegetic 'silence' by accidental noises from outside, by the audience's comings and goings in the auditorium, their conversations, etc., replacing them with an organised sound space, a kind of 'red line between the film and the spectator' in Marcel L'Herbier's phrase (1968, p.33).

Hence the silence of silent cinema was always an *artificial silence* consisting of music. But the need for musical accompaniment was not a matter of pure contingency, not just a mechanical response to the 'accident' of external disturbance. On the contrary, it was part of the global process of the 'naturalisation' of the film show, just as much as the later close-up and ultimately synchronised speech.

The first film music, it seems, was only vaguely related to the pictures as an 'ambience'. Pieces from the standard repertory were simply performed *in extenso*, as for the magic lantern. There were apparently often long silent intervals. Only gradually did the profession of the 'picture pianist' emerge, requiring a certain improvisatory talent, soon supported by collections of musical fragments classified according to their 'meanings' (fear, pathos, passion, etc.). The desire to subject the musical discourse strictly to the visual narrative resulted eventually in specially composed scores, but the one Saint-Saëns put together in 1908 for **L'Assassinat du duc de Guise** remained fairly isolated until the end of the War, it seems. And up to the end of the silent period, more or less skillful collages of classical fragments were more common.

In seeking to have the music cleave as closely as possible to the pictures, to action, expressions, sentiments, etc., the aim, long before the introduction of the optical track, was already the mechanistic subordination of sound to picture. The vulgar naturalism of the Institution was more or less consciously anticipated: a sound should never be anything but a consequence of the movement of a picture, just as a real sound is never anything but the consequence of a mechanical movement (a vibrating oboe reed, a slamming door).

But this was not just a deliberate development.

The reason why it was so self-evident to strive in this direction, and why such strivings were in some sense inevitably successful, is that music, because of the great ambiguity of its 'signifiers', is so easily *captioned*—I nearly wrote 'violated'—by almost any moving picture. This is a phenomenon anyone can observe today simply by turning down the sound on a television and putting almost any disc on the record player, so long as the music is sufficiently familiar (in language) but also sufficiently unknown (free of specific connotations). There will invariably be effects of visual and psychological 'synchronisation', and sometimes sound and picture will 'match' for minutes at a time.

During the 1920's and at the beginning of the 1930's in France, Germany and the USSR,[1] film-makers and musicians looked for alternatives to this simplistic internalisation, this mechanistic subordination of music to the 'states of mind' of the narrative. However, this approach survived the arrival of talking pictures by only a few years.

But let us return to the beginnings.

****

I have already evoked the lecturer on several occasions and I shall return to him shortly. But first we must examine the other primitive avatar of speech, the 'right' one, i.e., speech intended to be synchronised with the movements of the lips.

Georges Demenÿ and his Living Portrait that so well illustrates the ideological significance then attached to the representation/reproduction of speech, have already been mentioned above (see p.26). And I have noted that it was through his contact with Demenÿ that Léon Gaumont became interested in talking cinema in 1900.

Historians (especially American ones, because of the system's failure in the country of Edison) often fail to realise that the Gaumont Chronophone in its various versions was very present in Parisian cinemas for at least five years. Alice Guy shot more than 100 Phonoscènes for the firm: songs, comic monologues and operatic scenes.[2] Not to forget that Pathé—originally a company specialising in phonographs—had its own system, about whose exhibition I know absolutely nothing. But it is clear that in Paris between about 1904 and 1912, 'singing and talking' cinema was more or less as familiar as films in colour in the USA in the 1940's. How about the other French cities and fairgrounds or the other European capitals, some of which had autochthonous systems, Oskar Messter's in Germany,[3] Will Barker's in Britain?

If the very existence of these talking films is all but forgotten today, it is not just because their synchronisation left something to be desired or their amplification was deficient. The historians who repeat these things *ad nauseam* also tell us that the second Kinetophonograph[4] was completely satisfactory in both these respects in 1913—and was used to produce nineteen films, of which at least two have survived in the Library of Congress—a demonstration film called **The Edison Kinetophone**, and a playlet called **The Politician**.

It is, of course, demonstrable that the economics of the cinema at the time was not such as to be able to sustain the costly effort of the transformation of cinemas and other equipment that was to be implied, when the time came, by the transition to synchronised sound.[5] In France Pathé was in the doldrums, in the USA the long years it was going to take to build the picture palaces had only just begun, and the German industry was still in its cradle. But is it ridiculous to argue that in 1913 speech had arrived too early for superstructural reasons, too? That the mode of representation and its narrative systems had first to be completed—as they were to be around 1925, with the exception of the ever fluctuating 'punctuation' codes of temporal articulation?

It would take a good ten years for audiences and professionals to complete the process positively initiated hardly five years earlier, to make the visual system a stable, flexible, viable instrument—capable, in fact, of putting up a stiff resistance to the new technology when the time came? Surely it was only once this work had been completed that the kind of general shift of the whole edifice produced by synchronised sound could be made.[6]

And it does seem that when Edison presented his new system to the public, the 'thirst' for the Word had considerably declined: houses specialising in 'living synchronisation'[7] were going bankrupt, lecturers could no longer find work in cinemas. A historical phase had begun in which the externality I have posited as an essential feature of the primitive cinema had started to lose its hegemony nearly everywhere, not just at isolated points, the odd shot or exceptional match, as in Griffith's Biograph films. In 1914 a film as modern as **The Bank Burglar's Fate** (see p.136 above) could be produced in the USA, Ralph Ince, Barker and DeMille had come to the fore. And in Denmark advances were being made, on different fronts but sometimes even more quickly.

Faced with the distant, 'external' pictures of the primitive cinema, the aspiration to the Word was a response, for those who felt it—perhaps entrepreneurs and publicists more than their popular audiences who were accustomed to less logocentric forms of spectacle—to a certain *frustration of presence*. But once this presence began to be established by visual signifiers alone (which was hardly more than a dream in 1905-8 when agitation for synchronised sound seems to have reached its peak), then this frustration began to be relieved by purely visual procedures which in combination at least were novel: a new flexibility in editing, the gradual introduction of titles indicating the key bits of dialogue at the moment spoken, the beginnings of the institutional balance between detail shots and long shots. In this context the nasal

Chronophone—condemned by its technology to the primitive single-shot film—had no place at all. Any more than bad actors behind the screen doing their best to match their voices with the movements of the players. And above all, there was no longer any need for a lecturer to tell the story.

Deriving in the main from (religious or secular) magic-lantern shows in Britain or the USA, from the fairground parade and its barkers in France, lecturing, which declined in the USA between 1900 and 1906, persisted in France, until 1909 at least, as a 'normal feature' of the cinema show.[8]

A scientific history of lecturing remains to be written—and the project is highly problematic, as we lack one essential source, the texts of the lectures! What exactly did they say, these people whose training and backgrounds were so different? In the USA, for example, the function could be carried out by educated men and women, professional public speakers, or by humble cinema staff, endowed with a certain glibness and employed primarily to spin a line to the crowd of idlers outside the nickelodeon.

In the USA, as in Britain, quite long scene-by-scene summaries of the films began to be published around 1909, supposedly for the use of lecturers (they sometimes even contain direct allusions to the pictures)[9] and the supporters of lecturing greeted this as a great reform.[10] But did these texts provide the lecturers with more than an aide-mémoire?

I have already examined the lecturer's role in the advance of linearisation and the role it was hoped, in the USA but also in Britain, he would have in the embourgeoisement of the cinema show.

However, there is another reading of the lecturer, one that does indeed involve his social role, but also casts a special light on the future status of sound in the institution.

Take any dramatic or historic picture: in fact, almost any picture, barring the magic and comic subjects [cf. p.200 n.6 above]. Stand among the audience and what do you observe? As the story progresses, and even at its very beginning, those gifted with a little imagination and the power of speech will begin to comment, to talk more or less excitedly and try to explain and tell their friends or neighbours. This current of mental electricity will run up and down, wild, irregular, uncontrollable. The gifted lecturer will gather up and harness this current of expressed thought. He has seen the picture before, and convincing his audience from the very start that he has the subject well in hand, all these errant sparks will fly toward him, the buzz and idle comment will cease, and he finds himself without an effort the spokesman for the particular crowd of human beings that make up his audience.

This frank passage (Bush 1909) enables us to see the lecturer as a kind of general inspector with the job of silencing the 'bad boys and girls' of a popular audience. Bourgeois paternalism is plainly visible here. But is it not also a formulation that could be applied to the function of film music from the very beginning, i.e., the function of imposing an order, in the auditorium and on the screen, until the day when that order could at last be guaranteed by social mixing and huge organs in the former, and by the IMR on the latter?

****

In 1929, the rush to sound, no doubt urged on by the Great Crash (is this an echo of the way the minor recession of 1907 hastened efforts at the recruitment of a broader audience?), was to mark the apotheosis of the push towards analogical representation fantasised by Edison and Villiers, each in his own way sacrificing to what I have called the Frankenstein syndrome. The cinema had a 'soul' at last, its body was no longer voiceless, the internalisation process was complete. One last survival of the primitive system, the intertitle, had finally been suppressed. Music could at last be interrupted, sometimes for long periods, and hand over a significant part of its role to the noble Word, detaching the cinema once and for all from both the plebeian circus and the aristocratic ballet.

Obviously there is no point in imagining one might put the clock back: the silent cinema is quite 'dead'. Obviously, too, synchronised sound represented a gain in means of expression for the cinema in its cultural role; in its social role it also represented a gain in its means of control ... or mobilisation.

But there were also losses. For the economic interests that caused the sudden emergence of the talky abruptly terminated as well a 'silent language' which was barely entering on its maturity and which we have no reason to believe was exhausted after a mere decade.

There was also a loss insofar as the logocentrism of the early 1930's profoundly disorientated and discouraged a whole generation of exceptional creators—especially the whole French avant-garde, Dulac, Epstein, L'Herbier, Gance, but also Von Stroheim—condemning them either to silence or to triviality.

With the death of the silent cinema, there disappeared, no doubt, the last great Western narrative art that was at once both popular and, to a large degree, *presentational*, that is, morphologically closer to the plebeian circus and the artistocratic ballet than to the theatre of the middle classes, that *representational* art par excellence. With the appearance of the uninterrupted musical score, the silent film in its hey-day—1914-29—is a kind of lyric theatre, wherein the voice figures as gestus and the word as graphy. These displacements, moreover, call to mind those peculiar to opera, where the word dissolves into song, silence becomes orchestral sound and the plot is read ... in the programme notes. Today, in fact, it is the popular opera of Italy that is probably the only form of entertainment still alive in the West that can be compared with the silent cinema.

NOTES

1   Léger-Antheil (**Ballet mécanique**), Clair-Satie (**Entr'acte**), Richter-Hindemith (**Vormittagsspuk**) in the avant-garde, but also Vertov-Timofeiev (**Entuziazm**), and Ivens-Eisler (**Regen**, 'Rain', **Nieuwe Gronden**, 'The New Earth') in documentary. The same was occasionally attempted in fiction, especially in France with L'Herbier-Milhaud (**L'Inhumaine**), Gance-Honegger (**La Roue**) and in the USSR with the collaboration of Prokoviev, Tynyanov and Faintsimmer, for example, in that inexplicably neglected masterpiece, **Poruchik Kizhe** ('Lieutenant Kizhé').

2　Including twelve tableaux for **Carmen** amounting to 700 metres and 22 tableaux for **Faust** amounting to 1,275 metres, more than an hour's projection time: potentially the first 'talking' feature!

3　This great pioneer, at once inventor, producer and director, left us a film revealing an extraordinary prescience about the role of sound effects in the extension of off-screen diegetic space, even within the regime of the autarchic primitive tableau. In a 1904 (?) film called **Auf der Radrennbahn in Friedenau** ('At the Friedenau Cycle Race Track'), preserved in the Stiftung Deutsche Kinemathek, Berlin, he presents a group of people standing behind the barrier beside a race track; facing the camera they watch bicycles passing whose presence *behind the camera*—and presumably that of the crowd—was represented at the time by the sound from a phonograph. The same anticipatory function was performed by the thunderclaps and other noises off (deriving from a certain theatrical naturalism) sometimes produced by effects personnel or noise organs in nickelodeons and European fairground booths.

4　With a precise mechanical connection between phonograph and projector and mechanical amplification.

5　The slowness of the transition in the USSR and Japan at the beginning of the 1930's, leading to the production of silent films until 1934 and 1936 respectively, was due in the main to problems of this kind.

6　However, there is no doubt that post-1909 films would 'work' for us as post-synchronised films if anyone was perverse enough to undertake anything so absurd (by contrast, I doubt if the same is true of **The Great Train Robbery**, say, because the contradiction between the presence contributed by speech and the distance of its pictures would be too great).

7　Synchronised dialogue was provided more or less successfully by actors concealed behind the screen, often in combination with sound-effects systems which also failed to survive beyond this period.

8　According to a columnist of *Le Cinéma* in 1910.

9　However conservative they may have been, the defenders of lecturing in the trade press had been quick to realise that a certain internalisation was incumbent on the lecturer, too, if primitive distance was to be reduced at the same time as primitive chaos was organised: 'The art of lecturing to pictures, then, consists in assisting the minds of an audience to a voluntary state of illusion regarding the pictures.... It is essential that the lecturer ... on no account whatsoever say or do anything disturbing to the illusionary condition of his hearers' (Lawrence 1909).

10　Here, too, we cannot for the present be certain whether this is a sign of the growth of the phenomenon or of its decline, which some people were trying to resist by this means among others.

Narrative, Diegesis: Thresholds, Limits

Having come thus far, I must stand back from the early cinema to come to grips with a theoretical question that arises directly from all the previous chapters. The reader may judge—perhaps rightly—that this is an issue that smacks of a specious essentialism, but I regard it as absolutely unavoidable.

I must confess, however, that I find myself hard pressed to define this issue in rigorous terms. For a start, I might say that what I see at stake is the status of the general[1] experience of classical narrative film. The problem is, perhaps, to situate theoretically the historical, social and æsthetic space which we call classical narrative film—the meaning-production/consumption cycle of the institution—in terms of what is essential to that space, of what determines its oneness, its specificity, within the larger sphere of cultural production. In short, I wish to define, for us today, the status of that 'motionless voyage' whose parameters I have just laid bare.

****

There is no reason to doubt the reports that some spectators started up from their seats when first they saw Lumière's train rushing at them where they sat, comfortably esconced at their tables in the Salon Indien. However, I question fundamentally the notion, so often and so glibly bandied about, that this was the first manifestation of the *cinematic illusion*. As Christian Metz reminded us a few years ago (1982, p.101), 'belief' in the cinematic image as an analogue of real phenomena, if it was ever a hallucination (such as might be induced by drugs or psychosis, for example), has long ceased to be one; it is indeed a 'willing suspension of disbelief', in Coleridge's words, an emotional involvement which may certainly attain great depths of anguish or compassion, but which is always grounded in the awareness that the subject is 'only watching a film'. It is in this repect, Metz further suggests, that the filmic experience resembles that of the fantasy rather than the dream.

The first spectators of **Arrivée d'un train à La Ciotat**, reacting with their whole bodies to what they fleetingly perceived as an external manifestation, were indeed in a brief hallucinatory state, their unfamiliarity with the messages they were receiving having induced a state of mild sensorial confusion.

Even such a sophisticated viewer as Maxim Gorky, understanding no doubt how the Cinématographe worked, and prepared in any event for what he was going to see, seems to have experienced similar 'hallucinations': 'Carriages ... moving straight at you, into the darkness where you sit.... A train appears on the screen. It speeds straight at you—watch out! .... You imagine the spray will reach you, and you want to shield yourself.' But even if these are not simply hyperbolæ—feigned hallucinations whose true experience is implicitly attributed to others—Gorky takes significant care to distinguish between these hallucinatory effects of moving photographs and the illusion of full presence which he equated with a 'true' representation of reality, and linked with synchronised sound: 'No rattle of the wheels is heard.... This, too, is but a train of shadows.... Nor can you hear the gurgle of the water' (1960, pp.407-8).

This text, with its call for sound, colour, and the presence afforded by the close-up, thus sets forth, over three decades before its accomplishment, the parameters of what gradually became the hegemonic principle of the institution: the achievement of the full diegetic effect.

This achievement, which I situate at the dawn of synchronised sound, constitutes a major threshold. In the USA and Europe, classical cinema had reached full growth since at least 1917 as a visual system.[2] Yet is it not verifiable in many ways that lip-synch sound immediately became an essential component of a fuller diegetic process, qualitatively different from anything that the silent cinema had ever known? This, I suggest, is the chief reason why involvement in silent-film narrative requires a certain apprenticeship today; it is the relative weakness of its diegetic effect which perturbs the uninitiated viewer as much as the difficulty of assimilating some of the standard narrative codes of the 1920's. I take this as a preliminary indication of the relative autonomy of the narrative and diegetic principles.

Conversely, it is undeniable that the reproduction, with this new substance of expression (film), of structures analogous to those of classical narrative *in general*, contributed historically to the gradual enrichment of the diegetic process—shot-reverse-shot, for example, developed as an essentially narrative procedure— between 1906 and 1929. I nonetheless maintain that even before the advent of synch sound, that relative autonomy is demonstrable. In fact, I believe that if there is any useful answer to the perennial question of cinema's specificity, a hobby horse in France in the 1920's, it seems reasonable to suggest that within the broad spectrum of classical narrative in general, it is the singular strength of its diegetic production that sets cinema apart, that has made it a uniquely powerful tool, not merely of social control but of social and even revolutionary mobilisation as well.

The term *diegesis* was revived and appropriated by Etienne Souriau to account for a phenomenon which most scholars have associated peculiarly with cinema—and this in itself points to a privileged status among the other signifying practices. However, there is no doubt whatsoever that novelistic reading and writing, for example, involve a diegetic process, not only in dialogue and descriptions of the action but also in the adjunction of not directly narrative passages describing places, people, clothing, sounds, odours, etc. Moreover, one can easily imagine (and in fact find, among the productions of the *nouveau roman*) non-narrative fictional writing, consisting, possibly at book length, solely of descriptions and excluding any manifest narrative action, which would nonetheless conjure up that imaginary presence which we call the diegetic effect in the cinema. However, the almost inevitable *unreadability* of non-narrative literary fictions, in contrast with the eminent readability of, say, those impressionistic documentaries or sequences of nature scenes with musical sound tracks used to fill gaps in TV programming, does suggest that the diegetic effect in literature is more closely intertwined with the narrative process, no doubt because of the symbolic, discontinuous nature of the typographic sign—as opposed to the iconic, continuous nature of the sign of animated photography. Hence, perhaps, in literature the weakening of diegetic process and the foregrounding of writing as such attendant on the 'withdrawal' of narrative.

Literature also makes it clear that the diegetic effect can be manifested with varying degrees of intensity: do not those sparse narratives imagined by Borgès often seem closer to Propp's bare résumés of Russian folktales than to, say, a Balzac *conte*, precisely because they are more weakly diegetic than a text like *La Fille aux yeux d'or*?

Before proceeding further, I must deal with a question of terminology: is the diegetic effect equivalent to the 'illusion of reality' so generally ascribed to film? Though experientially the phenomenon may be the same, from a theoretical point of view a distinction between these two concepts appears crucial. For what we are talking about is, of course, no illusion at all in any rigorous sense; whatever-it-is does not resemble reality, as any of us actually experiences it (a comparison with holograms is edifying in this respect). The historical maximisation of the diegetic effect has in fact resulted from the accumulation of only a limited number of pertinent indices of phenomenal reality. The colour threshold itself was diegetically trivial in comparison with that of lip-synch sound. And the apparent non-pertinence here of the lack of any indices other than audio-visual ones (the sporadic careers of Smellorama, Sensurround, etc., are tangible signs of this), as well as the continuing audience preference for the imaginary three-dimensionality of institutional screen-space over the illusionistic three-dimensionality of stereoscopic films, incline one to believe that the term 'illusion of reality' is a malapropism masking the existence of *a rationally selective system of symbolic exchange*.

This is not to say, however, that the peculiar impact of the cinematic diegesis does not derive, as has often been stressed, from the fact that it involves almost exclusively iconic signification—and the replacement of the printed intertitle by the synchronised voice was a decisive step in the establishment of an 'iconic hegemony' (over the indexical codes as well, of course—see pp.150f. above—for they need iconic support). After 1930, nearly all the main narrative signifiers (with the important exception of music, and the occasional off-screen commentary or title) are diegetic as well, whereas in the classical novel there is usually a great deal of extra-diegetic 'voice-over' (explicit commentary from the author, psychological observations, descriptions, etc.). But of course the diegetic effect in literature is always mediated in a way in which it is not in the cinema, where the narrative and diegetic processes tend to fuse,[3] causing, of course, the frequent heuristic confusion between them.

The illusion of fusion is also to some extent a construct, with a history of its own. The development of the syntagmata of simultaneity, successiveness and contiguity is, as we have seen, coextensive with the emergence of the spectator-subject's identification with the camera, that linchpin of the full-blown diegetic effect in film.

****

Is it meaningful to assign a single 'threshold of emergence' to the diegetic process which we today associate with moving photographic pictures and lip-synch sound? No doubt such a threshold was crossed when people began seeing *in motion* complete photographic images (as opposed to Muybridge's silhouettes, anyway only projected to a few elite audiences). Gorky realised this at Aumont's cabaret: 'You anticipate nothing new in this too familiar scene, for you have seen pictures of the Paris streets more than once. But suddenly a strange flicker passes through the screen and the picture stirs to life' (1960, p.407).

And surely the coming of synchronised sound was a decisive threshold as well.

I am tempted to see 1895 and 1927 as the confines of a period of elaboration of the diegetic process which began at the Salon Indien and came to completion with **The Jazz Singer**.

Can we, however, *qualitatively* exclude from this historical space the experience of the viewers of British magic-lantern shows, with their dissolving views and Life Models? The latter, after all, prefigure certain aspects of film editing, their pictures are more or less realistically tinted, and the shows included voice, music and sound effects. Or, for that matter, the spectators of Daguerre's dioramas or Robertson's *Fantasmagories*?[4] Or of Reynaud's Praxinoscope? And what of the stereoscope? What of photography itself?

It seems self-evident today that the introduction of the analogical replication of movement adds a decisive element to the production of photographic meaning. True, the enlargement to screen-size of the lantern show had already considerably enhanced the analogical power of the photograph, and sequencing, also practised in lantern shows, had introduced a 'semantic equivalent' of movement by the concatenation of the iconic signifiers of photography. But it was the seamless concatenation of film frames which could make this semiosis as continuous and 'natural' as iconic signification itself. Similarly, thirty odd years later, a technology born of the vacuum tube made it possible to naturalise the Word, integrating it into the iconic continuum in a way neither the lecturer nor the intertitle could achieve.

****

Ben Brewster has stressed (1982) the centrality to the novelistic text of strategies of *point of view* and demonstrated how Griffith was at pains to introduce them early in the films he made for Biograph. In the exemplary **Gold is not All** (1910), audience identification with the poor-but-happy couple is effortlessly achieved through a *mise en scène* which produces the rich-but-wretched family as scene, *viewed from the place of the poor couple*, perpetually shown peeping in at the rich from the outide, a situation of comfortable, 'ring-side omniscience', *paralleling that of the cine-spectator*. And indeed, it is from the films of Griffith and his contemporaries that we may date the origin of a narrative system symbiotic with the system of spatio-temporal representation which makes it possible to privilege the viewpoint of the character(s) with whom spectators are 'programmed' to identify. In **Gold is not All** it is the Others, the rich, who appear most often on the screen; but it is established from the beginning of the film that 'our' gaze has become the gaze of the 'happy poor',

Fig. 35: **Gold is Not All** (Griffith, 1910): 'The poor gazing with wonder and envy upon the rich.'

even in their absence. It is this strategy of narrative viewpoint, most often asserted without the recourse to 'subjective camera'—still extremely rare in Griffith's films in 1910—which would henceforth perennially serve to naturalise precisely such assertions as 'the poor are happier than the rich'.

Undeniably, identification with *the gaze that tells* is essential to the power of classical narrative—both on the screen and in the novel. I would argue, however, that the specific experience defined by the cinema institution involves, as Jean-Louis Baudry (1974-5) and Christian Metz (1982, esp. pp.49-51) have argued, a 'primal identification' with *the gaze that sees*, the gaze that *is-there*, with the gaze of the camera 'before' the formation of the narrative meaning of any particular pro-filmic gaze. In the continuing debate around these issues, I would argue resolutely in Baudry's and Metz's favour because my own examination of the genealogy of classical cinema seems to me to support their thesis.

I have analysed one by one each of the successive acquisitions of the mode of spatio-temporal representation of the institution: the re-creation on the screen of the perspectival box of the Renaissance, the mastery of the moving camera, and the refinement of all the other strategies whose signified is summed up in the shot-reverse-shot: the absence/presence of the spectator at the very centre of the diegetic process. For all of these factors clearly converge upon a single effect, embarking the spectator on that 'motionless voyage' which is the essence of the institutional experience. Through this constant identification with the camera's viewpoint, the experience of the classical film interpellates us solely as *incorporeal individuals.*

One of the critical thresholds crossed in the course of this historical movement was the ban, by certain American companies around 1910, against actors looking at the camera (see p.216 above).

Yet, curiously enough, forty years after the Selig Polyscope Company had included in a list of do's and don't's for actors an explicit ban on looking at the camera, a Hollywood actor turned director shot a film which deliberately and systematically violated that time-honoured taboo. The 1940's and the beginning of the 1950's were Hollywood's 'experimental' years. But this experiment, at least, has remained absolutely unique in Hollywood's history for the very good reason that it was a resounding commercial failure.

And yet the subject, the script, the dialogue and the acting were no worse than those of such great successes of the period as **Murder, My Sweet** and **The Big Sleep**. And yet Robert Montgomery's gimmick for his adaptation of Raymond Chandler's novel *Lady in the Lake* was in fact a very reasonable one: he would simply transfer directly to the screen the first-person narrative technique that had long been successful in the crime novel and in the hard-boiled detective novel in particular.

However, the establishment of a constant homology between the *narratively subjective camera* (the institutional camera is *always* diegetically subjective) and the novelistic first person, re-introduced effects that were profoundly disruptive of the diegetic process. On the one hand, the long takes and elaborate, not to say pedantic, camera movements tended towards a denaturalisation, a mechanisation of the process of meaning production: the camera, so long concealed, invisible (notably because it followed the characters discreetly rather than panning abruptly from one to another as it does here) suddenly interposed itself again between audience and 'diegetic world'. Above all, however, the fact of these characters constantly looking straight into the lens simply gave the whole game away! The secret of the maximisation of the diegetic process is always the spectator's invisibility/invulnerability. Attempting to squeeze the subject of narrative identification into the same point in the mental space of the film experience as that already occupied, as it were, by the subject of the 'primal identification', was to pit the pot of clay against the pot of iron, as the French proverb goes. The spectator finds him/herself thrust into the line of fire, while the character Phillip Marlowe finds himself relegated to somewhere 'behind' the spectator. The choice of a rather distant, as it were over-projected tone for the detective's voice-off seems to have been determined unconsciously by the inevitable outcome of that unequal contest between the two modes of identification. From the subject's point of view the conflict can be summed up as follows: how is it possible for 'me' to occupy 'my' place if 'I' am no longer invisible, if all those people keep looking at 'me'?[5]

The 'first person' of the institution involves a *split*, isomorphic but not identical with the split in spectatorial consciousness between the 'I know full well' and the 'but all the same' by which Octave Mannoni, in a seminal text (1969), has compared the conditions of the theatrical illusion with the mechanism of *Verleugnung* or disavowal as it is encountered in analytic practice. There is the tacit, unconscious 'I' of camera identification, the 'I' that experiences the diegetic process as a dream. And then there is the 'I' of narrative identification, that experiences the story as a daydream. This latter identification is non-specific to cinema and only incidentally ensured, within the institutional framework, by point-of-view shots. The point-of-view shot—if we do not simply mean one member of the shot-reverse-shot, which more properly belongs to the subjectivity of 'primal', diegetic identification—is essentially contingent upon the *action of the film*, upon narrative incident. A film can easily contain no scenes in which the central character looks out of the window at something going on in the street or any action of the kind, susceptible to point-of-view treatment. And yet it is perfectly possible for that film to be in 'the first person' by the constant presence of the central figure on the screen, or by the use of voice over, etc. It is even possible to achieve this by the mere arrangement of the narrative, as Griffith did in 1910. For in a sense, these are simply avatars of a well-known and coded literary device, the 'disguised' first person. In fact the fundamental opposition between character-identification and camera-identification is that the former operates at the level of the (novelistic) signified of the classical film text, while the latter operates on the side of the signifier.

Lady in the Lake, then, seeking to collapse the one into the other, could only succeed in expelling the subject from the film in a certain sense, and seriously compromising the full development of the diegetic process. A lesson learnt pragmatically some forty years before was now at last demonstrated—theory in a practical state—for all to see.

Several such limit instances were produced in immediate post-War Hollywood. Not surprisingly, all were carried out in conjunction with the telling of heavily coded crime-stories. But whereas Montgomery's abolition of the impunity of the spectatorial subject may be said to introduce a major diegetic disruption, Hitchcock's quasi-abolition of shot change in **Rope**, Russell

Rouse's abolition of dialogue in **The Thief** both demonstrate that neither major vehicle of narrative meaning is essential to the production of the diegetic effect demanded by the institution.[6]

For although Hitchcock derives some truly surreal effects from the viscous flow of real time induced by the suppression of ellipsis, **Rope** is in fact simply a rigorous demonstration of Eisenstein's thesis (Nizhny 1962, pp.94-139) that one can recreate classical editing within the confines of the single take through strategies of framing, blocking and camera movement alone. Hitchcock's constantly roving camera, always seeking the 'true' centre of the narrative (e.g., remaining focussed on the maid clearing the chest that conceals the cadaver rather than concerning itself with the after-dinner talk round the table), perfectly capable of placing the spectator 'with' James Stewart in his role of honest-intellectual-turned-judge, ensures also identification with the ubiquitous camera as surely as classical editing.[7]

However mediocre artistically (and odious ideologically), **The Thief** is just as interesting from a heuristic point of view. It shows that the suppression not only of dialogue but of the act of speech itself (as opposed to what happened in the period when silence was a 'convention') does not necessarily produce a 'throwback' to the diegetic level of the titleless films of the late silent era.[8] It shows that the presence of *synch sound effects*—even just background reverberation—is quite enough to raise the diegetic level to perfect fullness: we keep expecting these characters to talk, they obviously have that capacity, we constantly see consequences of their speaking, we are just never there to hear it happen, but the synch sound effects are the guarantee of that potentially manifest presence.

We also encounter here (and complementarily) a demonstration of the essentially narrative role, within the institution, of the music which accompanies the diegesis. Incidental music in the sound film remains an extra-diegetic narrative signifier, just as it was in the 'silent' film. In **The Thief** it can be said, among other things, to replace dialogue which normally it would complement or reduplicate. But, like the textless picture narrative itself, it can only 'speak' in clichés, it can exclude ambiguity—and for the Institution manifest ambiguity must be excluded at all costs—only at the cost of having recourse to a broad, heavily coded

symbolism. This film lays bare the role of dialogue in the constitution of 'singularity' in the classical film. For the uncaptioned
photoplay, like photographs, can *make legible* only the most
highly coded narratives, peopled by stereotypes. In the USA of
1952, this was almost bound to be an archetypical Cold War
fiction—an unmarried scientist (his bachelorhood sustains the
bias and contributes to the character's unreliability) who Betrays
His Country for some twisted, unknowable motive, is soon forced
to Go Underground when Something Goes Wrong and finally,
after a protracted, graphic Bout With His Conscience, finally
decides to Turn Himself In.

If the diegetic effect can be said to be weakened here at all, it is
insofar as one is aware of the artificiality of the gimmick. But this
weakening exists only as a cumulative effect: any single sequence,
taken by itself, seems endowed with full diegetic presence, unlike
most sequences in **Lady in the Lake** which seem 'bizarre'. If **The
Thief**'s gimmick seems intrusively gratuitous today—unlike those
of **Rope** and **Lady in the Lake**—it may have seemed less so to an
American audience in 1952: the rejection of speech must have
seemed highly appropriate to the treatment of a subject so
shameful, in every sense, at the time of the murder of the Rosen-
bergs.

Is a major lapse such as that instanced in **Lady in the Lake** of
greater or lesser impact upon the integrity of the diegetic process
than, say, the sophisticated return to an 'archaic' frontality and
the quasi-elimination of shot-reverse-shot in Dreyer's **Gertrud** and
Chantal Akerman's **Jeanne Dielman**?

Wary, henceforth, of the pitfalls of quantification, I hesitate to
answer such questions. One thing is sure, however: for an audience culturally able to cope with the idiosyncracies of Dreyer or
Akerman, their readings of these works are bound to be very
different from those they would make of the 'diegetic deficiency'
of **Lady in the Lake**. To a mass audience, however, the two
'inadequacies' might be somewhat similar, both films still being
readable (unlike Snow's), but never comfortably so.

Indeed, there are a relatively large number of films on the
edges of the Institution which, while adhering in the main to the
norms of its system of representation, occasionally introduce concerted, positive strategies which tend to weaken the diegetic

process in one way or another. Jean-Pierre Lefebvre in **Le Vieux pays où Rimbaud est mort**, had his characters look at the camera directly as a distancing strategy. The films of Ozu, as I have sought to demonstrate elsewhere (1979, pp.160-172), involve temporary suspensions of diegetic presence (relative, that is, to a specific context: there are no 'non-diegetic' images in Ozu). These suspensions are in the form of what I have called 'pillow shots', which punctuate all of his films after 1932. They are characterised by the temporary removal from the screen of the human figure, of synch sound (after Ozu's adoption of the latter in 1936) and of movement, and these last two, as we have seen, are directly associated with the two fundamental thresholds in the history of diegesis in film, while the human figure, the character, is the very centre of the diegesis. Nor, it should be noted, are we dealing with a procedure such as the freeze-frame which permanently suspends the diegesis at the end of many a classical film, and which constitutes a facilitation of the painful withdrawal from the thrall of the institution. The pillow shots very definitely stand for a narrative duration, but this duration is one which they measure from outside the narrative properly so-called, and from the outer fringes of the diegetic space-time which may be said to contain it.

Chris Marker's fine film **La Jetée**, making a knowing return to the magic-lantern lecture, undertakes to extend a comparable weakening to the entirety of a film made almost exclusively of fixed frames, conveying, with the help of the voice of a 'lecturer', a complex narrative. And yet, the full diegetic effect is alluded to only once and fleetingly: a close-up shot of the young woman protagonist opening her eyes.

However, the outer limits of diegetic production have seldom been systematically tested. They have, of course, been crossed, at least since Viking Eggeling's animated abstractions (1920 to 1925), many, many times. But it struck me some years ago that there was perhaps only one body of work in the mass of modernist film-making which may be seen as systematically exploring the limits of diegesis. I am referring to the work of Michael Snow.

The film which called my attention to this aspect of Snow's work was **La Région Centrale**. Here, it seemed evident, was a film that had achieved at last a self-reflexive utopia: the diegetic continuum was reduced wholly to the state of 'immanent' referent—it was what we saw and heard, no more nor less—as opposed to ordinary fictional and documentary films whose diegetic space-time fills the gaps created by ellipsis and extends far beyond the frame. Diegesis became exactly coextensive, not with narrative—there was none—but with the process of filmic production itself. Of course, this process was *represented*—the bleeps 'controlling' the camera at the end of its universally articulated crane were fictional, after-the-fact creations. But bleeps and movements were located on the same plane in diegetic space-time, both were forcefully present, through the cause-and-effect relation seemingly linking the two tracks. Thus, besides establishing what may be one minimal threshold of diegetic production, the film indicated, by the very strength of its diegetic effect in the absence of any animate beings or of any natural sound, that the production of that effect depends neither on direct sound (an apparently 'natural' sound produced 'by the image') nor even on pro-filmic movement—the landscape is completely static—but can be generated by the camera alone and a 'non-figurative' sound, a simple digital translation of the camera's movements. So long as the image is readable (at a certain speed the blurring of the image suspends the diegetic process, as had already happened in ↔ —see p.258 below) and so long as camera-identification is ensured through movement, then there will be diegetic production. It is interesting to note that in this context, the appearance on the screen of the camera shadow impinges not at all upon the diegetic process; in fact, I would hazard that it actually reinforces the 'I-but-not-I' and the 'there-but-not-there' aspects of the identification process: 'I am the camera, but its shadow is not mine.'

Subsequently, as I looked back over Snow's previous films, it became apparent that all of them, in one way or another, dealt explicitly with these issues.

The most comprehensive in this respect is Snow's best-known work, **Wavelength**. During the forty-odd minutes which it takes for the 'camera-I' to 'cross' the Manhattan loft, the diegetic effect, the sense of camera identification indeed, is repeatedly lost and found again owing to various departures from and returns to the norms of conventional cinematography (as regards exposure, colour temperature, negative-positive relations, etc.). At the same time, the threshold between the domain of classical diegetic process and other possible modes of writing/reading of moving images and sounds is continually manifested in the contrast between inside and outside: even when the image has been almost entirely washed out by over-exposure, even when it is tinted a deep shade of pink or appears in negative, such depredations—profoundly disruptive of diegetic production, linked as it is to photographic realism—are perceived as taking place 'inside' (due in particular to the room's general emptiness of people and of pro-filmic movement) while 'outside', in the street, life goes on. It is remarkable that this decisive difference persists in spite of the fact that the departures from 'technological' image norms affect that part of the frame as much as the rest. Here we have a further indication that movement constitutes one of the minimal conditions for diegetic production.

Wavelength also engages with the issue of the relations between narrative and diegetic process. Do the increasingly narrative moments of human activity strung out across the film—from the bringing in by movers of a 'casing shelved' (see below) to the discovery of a dead body by a young woman—determine actual intensifications of the diegetic effect? In my view, what we experience here is the *centring* of the diegesis which is invariably brought about by the installation of narrative (and by the constitution of character). As soon as this loft appears on the screen, with the roofs of trucks passing by outside those windows—generating what appears, at least, to be loud synch background sound—institutionally determined expectations are such that it can only be perceived as *waiting for* something to happen, for *someone* to come in, such is the anthropocentric bias of the classical film.[9] But the diegetic process as such is already fully engaged. Subsequently, someone does come in, the diegesis appears centred, in preparation for the appearance of recognisable narrative structures, and characters. Clearly we are dealing with a perfectly coded succession, considerably more protracted than is usual, but that is all. Of course, as the film proceeds and as such expectations are only met at long intervals—and the expectation of characters, never—these 'normal' images, when they reappear now and then, may have lost some of their credibility. Comparisons are difficult, since an acoustic sine wave soon begins to blot out the live sound—but perhaps this disruptive wail merely manifests our 'disenchantment', our inevitable loss of faith through repeated depredations. Nonetheless, when the woman finds the dead body—at the climax of the film's abortive narrative (the telephone conversation)—full diegetic strength returns 'behind' the sine wave, in much the same way that it seems to have hitherto been maintained through thick and thin 'out there', beyond the windows.

Consequently, it would seem, generally, that even in the absence of any narrativity, even in the absence of any representation of a living being, and with sound and picture highly parasitised, pro-filmic movement and synch sound are amply sufficient for diegetic production to take place.[10] What part is played here by the advance of the camera, so slow as to be imperceptible as movement? There can be no doubt that we have here a *figuration* of camera movement as bearer of the primal identification. It is of course a self-reflexive kind of figuration, foregrounding the process of identification itself, although in the long run this does not deny it a certain diegetic effectivity. Be that as it may, it is clear nonetheless that the diegetic effect could in this case easily do without this movement.

The film whose non-verbal title ↔ is rendered as 'Back and Forth', shows exactly how much obliteration the picture can take before the diegetic process is seriously affected. It is not until the camera, swinging back and forth across that occasionally peopled classroom, attains a speed so high that the picture is no longer recognisably representational at all, and until the sound of the swinging camera-boom has become a mechanical screech that blots out all ambient sound, that we can speak of a momentary suspension of diegetic process.

Another limit-instance in the relations between narrative and diegetic process is revealed in **A Casing Shelved**, a single-slide and tape piece designed to be presented and attended to in conditions so similar to those of the motion picture that it can, as Annette Michelson has pointed out (1971), be legitimately assimilated to Snow's work as a film-maker. A single still is projected on a screen for nearly an hour. It shows a set of home-made shelves lined with dozens of objects belonging to the artist. The work's 'narrative' is carried solely by Snow's own voice on tape, telling the story behind each of these objects in turn (but not in the order of their arrangement on the shelves). It is hard not to be reminded of the primitive lecturer 'deciphering' an image which it was no doubt often hard for the spectator to read. But the tenuousness of the visual guarantees, and in particular the absence of movement—even that of the dust particles can set off diegetic production—as well as the lack of causal connections between picture and sound (following from the first absence, of course) make it impossible to speak of any diegetic process in connection with this piece, nonetheless *saturated with narrativity*.

As can be seen, Snow's work tests certain outer limits of diegesis and narrativity, but in *marked* contexts, resolutely outside the institution. By contrast, there is a short British film that makes it possible to isolate these two dimensions of cinematic representation, even inside institutional practice. The Scottish physician-cum-poet-cum-film-maker Margaret Tait, among other attractive works, has made a remarkable and beautiful film, **Place of Work**, which can be said to constitute a laboratory experiment in the maximisation of the diegetic process in the almost total absence of narrativity. The film is an exploration/meditation in and around a house which, as the author announces briefly at the outset, she and her family are about to leave after many years spent living and working there. But although a ditch-digger may be glimpsed out on the road beyond the hedge, people are largely absent from the screen, as pans and fixed shots of the house and its garden follow one another in 'impressionistic' order. The sound track, though not actually recorded synch, it appears, was edited and mixed to produce a perfect illusion of the live. The result, then, of these camera movements and of this sound track, is a perfectly full sense of *being there*: the stage is set, once again, for characters to make their entrance and a story to begin. But with two brief exceptions neither occurs.

The single moment of narrative emergence—an abortive emergence at that—involves not humans but animals, almost the only other possible support for a story (though generally with a more or less disguised anthropomorphism). During a series of garden views, a shot of a cat is followed by one of a bird. Nothing actually transpires, except for this imaginary transmission of a 'gaze': Tait's camera (and scissors) move on to other views. And yet any attentive audience, with the appropriate cultural reference points (cats are dangerous to birds) will grasp that this shot-change is potentially the first articulation in a tri-partite narrative sequence: *cat* (possessing a particular potential as a predator)/*stalks bird*/*eats bird.*

It is also interesting to note that the only centred appearance of a human being in the film (the ditch-digger is part of the scenery), although it too introduces a kind of micro-narrative, a more complete one this time, at the same time challenges the very identificational system upon which diegetic production rests. At one point, as the camera explores the ground floor, it focusses on the open front door. A postman steps into view, withdraws again quickly when he sees the camera pointed at him. Tait's voice calls to him, telling him to come ahead, that it's all right, and he reappears to exchange a few words with the woman behind the camera. The postman's reflex response, his knowledge that he oughtn't to 'be in the picture', shows how far the institutional codes have been internalised by all of us along with our competence as spectators. But this momentary impingement upon the conditions of diegetic production as they have been established in this film throws them into disarray. For at the point when Tait's voice calls out, we suddenly find that our position at the camera keyhole has been occupied—or rather that it was 'always already' occupied by someone who had hitherto remained silent and invisible but now seems to be urging us out of the way. The situation in **Lady in the Lake** momentarily recurs.

In these two moments, then, the film seems to illustrate two crucial boundaries, first, the boundary between diegesis and narrativity, and, second, that between an 'illusionistic' diegesis and one which acknowledges its process of production.

****

It has occasionally been argued, in rebuttal of my attempts to define an Institutional Mode of Representation, essentially unchanged, I claim, since the coming of sound, that 'television has changed all that'. Before a recent stay in the USA and the massive exposure to TV in the North American style that I received there, I had seen no evidence of any fundamental differences between 'ordinary' television and 'ordinary' cinema in this respect. Today, having observed the way in which Americans relate to a television which runs 24 hours a day (a quantitative change—as compared with continental Europe, of course—with qualitative consequences) and whose chief function may be said to be *the trivialisation of everything*, having observed the converging strategies of disengagement which have been built into the new medium as they have been into North American society as a whole, I have to admit that I was wrong. In the USA at least, television really has 'changed all that'.[11]

It is strange to see the many ways in which United States network television constitutes a 'return' to the days of the nickelodeon: a continuous showing cut up into brief segments of from one to ten minutes, with an audience that drifts in and out as their everyday activities and the control knobs will allow, the incredible mixture of genres, and especially perhaps the confusions between reality and fiction to which television audiences seem so prone.[12] Even découpage seems to have regressed in the sit-coms—recorded with an audience and broadcast in the evenings—with a prevalence of three-walled frontality and the medium shot and medium long shot. The apparently obligatory use of off-screen laughter in these same shows seems to be a way of situating the audience in a noisy theatre; but vicariously so, as it were: other people laugh for me. Moreover, the use of the word *'theatre'* here is tantamount to implying 'unreal', not to be taken seriously. For this indeed is what is universally signified by United States television today: none of it matters, not the news with its litany of violence and complacent lies, any more than the soap operas aimed at women, not the election campaigns any more than the ads, which often have built-in elements of self-derision that seem to say 'even these', presumably the true raison d'être of commercial TV, are not to be taken seriously! There has even been one astounding return to an 'undercutting' lecture in the true spirit of the primitive period: the adventures of the stunt-driving **Dukes of Hazzard** are punctuated by an ironic, chortling, home-spun narration which unerringly dedramatises every situation.

For years certain Marxist critics and film-makers—in Great Britain, especially, but also on the continent and in the USA—have assumed that the 'alienation' effect was inevitably illuminating and liberating, that anything which undercut the 'empathetic' power of the diegetic process was progressive. To be reminded that the scenes unfolding on stage and screen were artifice, to experience any mode of 'distantiation' was for an audience to be made able to think the textuality, to read the dialectics of the production of meaning, etc. I believed this, and still do so in the appropriate, slightly elitist context to which the idea is still pertinent. But it is beginning to appear to me today that United States television—more 'advanced' in this respect than any other, save perhaps that of Japan and Latin America, and now Italy, alas!—mobilises a number of strategies whose cumulative effect is to induce a certain disengagement, a certain feeling that what we see—no matter what it is—does not really count. Distancing, in short, has been co-opted; it has found a place among the panoply of weapons available to the ruling class of the USA to depoliticise, demobilise the working masses (ethnic and racial divisions, geographic distance, overconsumption, etc.).

There is a striking contrast between this kind of distantiation, this deliberate weakening of the diegetic process and the relative engagement elicited by the classical cinema of the 1930's and 1940's and indeed by most Hollywood films today (though not all: the Burt Reynolds type of CB film, with the bouncy music that trivialises all those car-wrecks—as it does the bloody slaughter in the Eastwood Dirty Harry films—and with their completely imaginary narrative topography, maximally electronic and MacLuhanite,[13] eliminating any centring, 'involving' reference to the spectator's body, these films are the clearest examples of a feed-back effect from TV to classical film).[14]

However, the primary strategy of undercutting the diegetic process on US commercial television is the constant interruption through commercials, a kind of pro-filmic pendant of the plethora of apparently accepted live interruptions peculiar to the 'average' North American household's relation to their TV set. (It is extremely rare, for example, that callers will be asked to ring back, even if the person receiving the call is watching TV: 'it isn't that important'.) And there is good reason to believe that the sluggish pace and pedantic repetitiveness of the day-time soaps is designed to mesh with the rhythm of housework.

In contradistinction to this experience of chopped-up audio-visual discourse one is tempted to feel that the uninterrupted duration of diegetic production over a period of an hour or more might well be an essential element in that maximisation of the diegetic effect which we associate with the classical film—and with European public television. Perhaps this too is the crucial importance of the shift in programme format between 1908 and 1914, from a series of six-to-ten-minute shorts with songs or lantern slides between each, to one centred around a film well over an hour long.

The 'cool', disjunctive format of United States television may be seen as a veritable turning back of the clock, which is anything but innocent. Audio-visual expression returns to a quasi pre-discursive state, in which pure sensation overwhelms meaning. It has abandoned the absorbing presence of the full diegetic process—which after all did elicit some kind of mental involvement, the motionless voyage cannot be made all alone—in favour of a sort of bland detachment (clinically observed to be close to a state of narcosis or hypnosis—see Mander 1978, pp.192-215). The repression in El Salvador is no more or less 'involving' than **The Price is Right**, and even the most outspoken (fictional) denunciation of, say, migrant workers' camps in Florida, will be taken with the same mixture of cynicism and incredulity as the para-psychological exploits of **That's Incredible!** I suggest that any European reader still inclined to equate the strongly diegetic film with 'manipulation' take a look at the manipulation that is going on across the Atlantic on an unprecedented scale and to which the key is precisely a certain undercutting of the classical diegetic effect whose genealogy has been the major subject of this book.

NOTES

1 General within its main sphere of relevance: the mass audience of developed Western nations—although even in our cities a Black audience will tend to turn a Harlem-style kung fu movie into an 'epic' ceremony, and children will do the same to almost any film. And then there is the strange cult of **The Rocky Horror Picture Show**. Still, the experience I refer to, an experience which is observable for a James Bond film in the West End or a screening at the National Film Theatre, remains by far the majority experience in the industrialised West.

2 The earliest film I know which seems to display a complete mastery of the institutional découpage is Maurice Tourneur's **A Girl's Folly** (1917) in which the principle of camera ubiquity (in the film-studio sequence) is displayed with a skill still absent from such milestones as Barker/Ince's **The Italian** or DeMille's **The Cheat** (both of 1915). Whatever the case, it is during these crucial years that the decisive threshold is crossed.

3 Roland Barthes speaks of the apparent fusion between the connotative and denotative levels in the still photograph. In the talking cinema the (con)fusion between these two levels is far more complete, not only because of the syntagmatic extension (in time) of the denotative level but also because of the material integration at the iconic level of the specifying text, the Word, which, with the photograph, is always writing, i.e., symbolic, non-analogical (the system of the silent cinema is much closer to the advertising poster than to that of the talkies).

4 'Robertson, a physicist and illusionist, had, during the Revolution, drawn all Paris to his presentations of *fantasmagories* ... produced by means of a *Fantascope*, a lantern mounted on wheels and able to move silently on rails .... Sounds of rain, thunder and funeral bells accompanied these apparitions. Occasionally a lightning-streaked sky was glimpsed; a point of light emerged and grew, and enormous phantoms seemed to approach from the distance, rush up to the spectators, and vanish just as they were about to reach them' (Sadoul 1973, t.I, p.226).

5 Maxim Gorky, so prompt to denounce the lack of presence that detracted from the Lumière films as far as he was concerned, elsewhere revealed a precocious insight into the ideological implications of institutional voyeurism. At the beginning of his fine novel *The Spy* (published in 1908), he attributes a significant fantasy to his young anti-hero, soon to be enrolled as a Tsarist police spy: 'There were many other good things about the church. Besides the quiet and tender twilight, Yevsey liked the singing. When he sang without notes, he closed his eyes firmly, and letting his clear, plaintive soprano blend with the general chorus in order that it should not be heard above the others, he hid himself deliciously somewhere, as if overcome by a sweet sleep. In this drowsy state it seemed to him that he was drifting away from life, approaching another gentle, peaceful existence. A thought took shape in his mind, which he once expressed to his uncle in these words: "Can a person live so that he can go everywhere and see everything, but be seen by nobody?"

"Invisibly?" asked the blacksmith and thought a while. "I should suppose it would be impossible"' (1908, pp.5-6).

6   True, neither of these films was a box-office success, which might argue against the idea that the transgression that characterises **Lady in the Lake** has any privileged status. But the analyses provided here encourage me to think, considering the generally recognised mediocrity of **The Thief** (and the commercial failure of nearly all the 'counter-subversive' films of the McCarthy era), given the intellectualism and homosexual undertones of **Rope**, that there is indeed a qualitative difference between the reasons for their failures and that of a film otherwise as honourably conventional as **Lady in the Lake**.

7   By contrast, the decentring procedures used by Paulino Viota in **Contactos** (1970)—scenes taking place 'too far away' from the camera or in off-screen space—provide an example of a deliberate destabilisation of the 'primal process'.

8   I am convinced that the ultimate rationale behind the elimination (or near-elimination) of titles from such films as **Hintertreppe, Der letzte Mann** ('The Last Laugh'), **The Wind** or **Ménilmontant** was indeed the heightening of diegetic homogeneity and hence of characterisation and narrative presence. By contrast, a genuinely speechless, silent and also titleless film like Philippe Garrel's **Le Révélateur** was indeed such a 'throwback', but with modernist intentions.

9   Characters are the centre of the diegetic and narrative worlds, as well as the privileged link between them. No doubt it is they that most effectively mask the relative autonomy of these two levels. It may be objected that there are audiences which have different expectations when they watch films by Michael Snow, which is obviously true. It is also obviously true that it is statistically most unlikely that someone lacking the socio-cultural formation permitting him or her such 'alternative' expectations will attend such a screening, although it is true that on certain American campuses today this has become more possible. But I would claim that even for avant-garde aficionados—those of them that go to the cinema from time to time or watched television until they were fifteen (i.e., almost everyone in industrialised societies)—the expectation here that *someone will enter the stage* is inscribed in their awareness as *non-marked*, whereas the persistence of this empty frame beyond a 'reasonable' length of time is *marked*. And the fact that after three or four minutes the film does satisfy this expectation can only reinforce the marked quality of that emptiness.

10   Is either of these elements alone enough today? **Le Révélateur**—but also the experience of silent films with musical accompaniment—would seem to suggest that the answer is no for movement, but a limit case like Ken Jacobs's film **Blonde Cobra** might imply that it is yes for sound alone. When the story-teller Jack Smith's face gives way to a black screen but we continue to hear his voice, our expectation of the return of the picture gives this sound a presence quite unlike that of a voice on the radio, closer to the situation of a picture breakdown on television.

11 Of course, television in itself permits a 'divided attention', and this is no longer found only in the USA. But certain safeguards—restricted viewing periods, a rejection of constant interruptions from advertisements, and especially the cultural vocation of state television networks—continue to maintain a strong connection between the diegetic production of European television and that of cinema.

12 The actor who played a doctor in a very popular serial received more than a quarter of a million letters in one year, most of them requesting medical advice (see Mander 1978, p.255).

13 There is a more sophisticated example of the same kind of thing at the beginning of **Alien**.

14 I find it very significant that 'cinéma-vérité' codes, so present in American fiction films in the late 1960's and early 1970's, have almost entirely disappeared from US cinema screens as well as TV (a 'discussion' on American television, political or otherwise, is about as spontaneous as a sit-com), so that even their most consistent proponent, John Cassavetes, was forced to abandon them almost completely in **Gloria**.

Conclusion

I have left a number of blank spaces in the picture, consciously if not exactly voluntarily. There are, I think, three of them.

I have noted in passing that some parameters—shot-reverse-shot in particular—took much longer to become generalised than others—the axial match, for example. But I have not ventured any interpretation of this phenomenon. I have devoted pages to the claim that there was nothing natural about the route taken by the constitution of the IMR, and yet I have only examined its socio-economic and socio-ideological determinations, ignoring the role of the symbolic system presiding over psychical formation in the West (the Œdipal instance, etc.). Finally, I have located *character* at the centre of diegesis, I have even made it the relay between diegesis and narrativity, but I have offered no theory of the formation of the *institutional persona* equivalent to those of the centring of the subject, the constitution of a haptic space, etc. The reason is that all these questions relate to disciplines in which I do not feel myself to be competent. However, here are a few pointers.

The constitution of the *persona* is in part subsumed under the narrative instance, of course. Elsewhere (1979, pp.64-5), I have outlined what I believe to be the narrative model of the central character, the object of narrative identification, locatable insofar as he or she is *endowed with contradictions* and as there is a galaxy of characters whose 'distance from the centre' is defined by their degree of stereotypicality revolving around and thereby defining him or her.

But it is clear that there are other dimensions to the constitution of the *persona*. Historically, it is linked to the development of the insert close-up and of the star system, and the transition to the latter is linked to the move from the artisanal to the industrial stage. When, even before the generalisation of the close-up, the studios began to receive mail addressed to certain characters in certain films, the producers concealed it from the actors they still employed on an 'egalitarian and anonymous' basis. Only once the massification of the American audience was envisaged did the star system begin to emerge with the rise of the Vitagraph Girl and the Biograph Girl, something which happened well before credit titles appeared.

As for the deeper symbolism of the star system, it is surely a subtle extension of the Frankensteinian ideology of the exorcism of death (the film character dies—if only because the film ends—but the star will be reborn in the next film). This helped to take the edge off the traumatism of the Institutional ending and make it ultimately acceptable. Perhaps that is why the death of a star while still young, i.e., still a star (Valentino, Dean, Monroe) is experienced as such a great tragedy.[1]

As for the order in which the achievements I have analysed were made, I have to admit that the only insight that has occurred to me is based on studies often rejected on principle by modern Freudianism and as unscientific by some psychologists. Nevertheless, the observations reported by Piaget and Inhelder that I find illuminating here do seem to be relatively well established.[2] In their book *The Child's Conception of Space* (1956),[3] the two Swiss scientists propose a model of the child's perceptual development: in a first stage the child can only conceive of its environment in a 'frontal' way; it takes several years of training before it can imagine any but its own immediate viewpoint.[4] Now we have seen that the axial match is the first change of viewpoint 'discovered' by film-makers, whereas the 90-degree cut is one of the last, becoming common even later than shot-reverse-shot. It would be rash to derive from this fact the hypothesis that the 'phylogeny' of cinematic representation recapitulated the ontogeny of human perception, and much more research is required before it could be envisaged. And even were such a hypothesis to be confirmed, it might be asked how far this would help us understand the nature of the IMR? And in particular, what would be the connection between determinations of this kind and those of a symbolic kind, which have so manifest a place in the formation of the IMR?

I have already suggested the hypothesis that the 'infantile' voyeurism of primitive cinema was an 'acting out' prefiguring another voyeurism, the 'repressed' voyeurism of the institutional spectator caught in the toils of shot-reverse-shot and the other manifestations of ubiquity (see p.224 above). Could there be other prefigurations of the same kind?

For several years now, I—and not I alone—have felt interpellated by the dialectic established from around 1912 between the close-up of the face or some other part of the body and shots showing the body complete.

Among the 'infantile' themes of the early cinema (see pp.61f. above), the frequency of the occurrence of that of the 'fragmented body' can, of course, socio-historically speaking, be attributed to the influence of popular spectacle. The villain of melodrama or Grand Guignol, like the circus conjurer, cut women in half (see Fischer 1979). But the mechanical and optical tricks invented by the cinema almost from its birth gave extraordinary impetus to this theme which was manically pursued for the first ten years. And it is also undeniable that it disappeared as soon as a *dissecting editing* appeared. Think, for example, how rare it is even in the most manic slapstick films of the American golden age: Keaton or Chaplin would have rejected as childish the violent acrobatics of the male and female wrestlers who change sex and tear off each others limbs in **Nouvelles luttes extravagantes** (Méliès, 1900). And of course, they were childish: a kind of acting out of the fantasies of infantile aggression Melanie Klein (1975, p.70) associated with the 'paranoid-schizoid position': 'Fritz ... had phantasied about a woman in the circus who was sawn in pieces and then nevertheless comes to life again, and now he asked me whether this is possible. He then related ... that actually every child wants to have a bit of his mother, who is to be cut into four pieces; he depicted quite exactly how she screamed and had paper stuffed in her mouth so she could not scream and what kind of faces she made, etc.'

How can one fail to compare this quotation with an anecdote from the beginnings of cinema (but whose source I can no longer trace) according to which a woman who went to see a film shortly after the introduction of close-ups emerged completely traumatised by what she thought of as a horror film: 'All those severed hands and heads!'

So what are we to make of the transition from a period

characterised by the pro-filmic presentation of infantile amputations and dismemberings to what was eventually to be the institutional balance between detail and full shot of the body via editing? Can it be seen as isomorphous with the stage in psychical development Klein locates at the age of four months: 'With his growing integration, the child begins to perceive the mother as a whole person .... This change [is] the beginning of the *depressive position* .... The mother is now felt to be a whole object ... in contrast to the part objects of the previous state.... The shift from the paranoid-schizoid to the depressive position is a fundamental change from psychotic to sane functioning' (Segal 1979, pp.78-9 & 132).

Is it licit to think that the phenomenon remained anchored in the Institution 'in a synchronous state'? Is the institutional 'fragmentation of the body', the kind of 'respiratory' oscillation between close shots and long shots an endless repetition of a 'transition' that Klein herself came to see as 'endless', beginning over and over again, towards the mature integration of the human personality. Stephen Heath seems to be suggesting this in an important essay. Discussing an anecdote reported by Lillian Gish about the producers' and technicians' 'neurotic' resistance to the *loss of the body* produced by the closeness of the camera demanded by Griffith and others, he writes (1976, pp.36-7):

> Cinema can and does fragment the body (the hands over the piano in **Letter from an Unknown Woman**, the movement up over the body of Lina—Joan Fontaine, from feet to face, at the beginning of **Suspicion**) but the human figure, the total image of the body seen, is always the pay-off (as the examples indicate: the hands express the pianist; the movement up is the appraising sweep of the male gaze, fixing the woman for the film). Within limits, those of narrative again, film plays on the passage between fragmented body and the image possession of the body whole, making identifications, remaking identity.

I believe that in order to be convinced that this is a neuralgic point of cinematic representation one need only think of the anxiety that grips us as institutional spectators—and there is an institutional spectator in all of us—at a film (whether primitive or

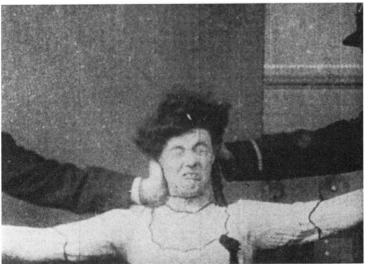

Fig. 36: **A Subject for the Rogues Gallery** (Biograph, 1904). An early experiment with the moving camera which also seems to inscribe an essential gesture of the future institution: the violation of the female face. The prostitute tries to avert her gaze but the men force her to confront the oncoming camera; still struggling to *withold her image* she contorts her features; but finally, in close-up, she breaks down and cries.

avant-garde) which only offers us long-shot silhouettes *beyond our reach*, and the anxiety that suffocates us by contrast when we see some 'experimental' or merely mannerist piece that only offers us the intimacy of the close-up (Dreyer built a masterpiece out of this 'suffocation' in **La Passion de Jeanne d'Arc**, but the young George Lucas could only get bogged down in it with his **THX1138**).

The final question and the most recent—raised by others, but challenging the conclusions of this book: does the cinema spectator's 'primary identification' conform to a patriarchal model, are women alienating themselves from themselves in identifying with ... the camera?

To my mind there is no doubt, as Laura Mulvey (1975), Mary Ann Doane (1982) and others (Kaplan, ed., 1980) have shown, that a certain 'look' of the classical cinema is constituted along such lines. But this is either the pro-filmic look or the look of the camera *constituted as a pro-filmic look* (the close-up of Barbara Stanwyck's anklet in **Double Indemnity**). What about the *neutral look* of the camera, that summum of the looks available to it in the IMR? Is it really possible to think that for three-quarters of a century women have experienced the cinema less completely than men? Nothing suggests such a thing. Besides, it is even conceivable that the possibility for women to enter a masculine skin to achieve the narrative identification necessary to obtaining pleasure from a Howard Hawks Western, say, is explained precisely by the power of the primary identification.

This is why I cannot follow certain British and American women critics and film-makers, seemingly convinced of the fundamentally patriarchal character of the IMR itself, who see in the 'deconstructive' strategies of the avant-garde the way to a 'language' that will belong to them as women. This seems to me an attitude too close to the Stalinist distinction between proletarian science and bourgeois science.

These are arguments others will take up or have already taken up. As for me, given my conviction that no 'fatal necessity' presided over the constitution of the IMR, I cannot speak of any 'conspiracy', even an objective one. This is clearly an overdetermined history, in which the symbolic order does intervene as some kind of 'cultural fatality', and which, in the last instance, is rooted, via the whole history of the West, in Græco-Roman civilisation. I have examined several socio-ideological and economic aspects of this determination. I have hardly touched on the symbolic aspects, but not because I think they are secondary. On the contrary, it seems clear that the extraordinary success of the cinema both as an industry of pleasure and as an instrument of manipulation (or mobilisation) arises precisely from what was eventually to declare itself as the perfect harmony of the system of representation set up between 1895 and 1929 and structures inherent in the Western psyche as they are formulated by psychoanalytic theory and practice.

Certain studies demonstrating the correlations between dream mechanisms and the devices of cinematic narrativity (Kuntzel 1978, Metz 1982) and some intuitions I cherish as to the homology between the archetypical structures of fantasy and those whose history I have traced—the object of a future work, perhaps—lead me to think even that this research programme is the least futile of all today.

Paris-Columbus-London-Paris, 1977-85.

NOTES

1   There are two noteworthy monographs on this question: Morin (1960) and Dyer (1979).
2   Even though I am inclined to agree with those scholars who reject the extrapolation these authors make from their discovery to a *natural ego-centrism* of the small child.
3   I should like here to record my debt to the late Anna Ambrose, who drew these studies to my attention.
4   American scholars maintain that a repetition of the experiment in the 1960's with American children did not give such conclusive results. If this is true, I think it might well constitute not so much an invalidation of the Piaget-Inhelder results as a commentary on the pedagogic power of the orientation codes of cinema and television, which Swiss children in the 1920's were clearly not exposed to to anything like the same extent.

Bibliography

Robert C. Allen (1980): *Vaudeville and Film 1895-1915: A Study in Media Interaction*, Arno Press, New York

Anon. (1903a): *Charles Urban Trading Company Catalogue*, London, November 1903

Anon. (1903b): *'Hepwix' Films for the Cinematograph, Edison Gauge*, Hepworth Manufacturing Company, London

Anon. (1908): 'Editorial .... Our Visits', *The Moving Picture World* v 2 n 5, February 1st 1908, p.71

Anon. (1909a): 'Editorial .... The Factor of Uniformity', *The Moving Picture World* v 5 n 4, July 24th 1909, pp.115-16

Anon. (1909b): 'Explaining the Pictures', *The Bioscope* no. 124, February 25th 1909, p.3

Anon. (1910a): 'The Lecturer and the Picture', *The Moving Picture World* v 7 n 14, October 1st 1910, p.750

Anon. (1910b): 'Lora Bona, the Celebrated Dramatic Reciter', *The Moving Picture World* v 7 n 20, November 12th 1910, pp.1 & 113

Anon. (1911): 'Too Near the Camera', *The Moving Picture World* v 8 n 12, March 25th 1911, pp.633-4

Anon. (1973): 'Pointers on Picture Acting' issued by the Selig Polyscope Company, in Kalton S. Lahue, ed.: *Motion Picture Pioneer*, A.S. Barnes & Co., South Brunswick & New York, pp.63-4

Roy Armes (1978): *A Critical History of the British Cinema*, Secker & Warburg, London

Jacques Arnault (1972): *Les Ouvriers américains*, Editions Sociales, Paris

Jacques Arnault (1976): *La Démocratie à Sacramento (USA)*, Editions Sociales, Paris

Linda Arvidson (Mrs. D.W. Griffith) (1925): *When the Movies Were Young*, E.P. Dutton & Co., New York

Peter Bailey (1978): *Leisure and Class in Victorian England—*

Rational Recreation and the Contest for Control 1830-85,
Routledge & Kegan Paul, London

Fred Balshofer & Arthur C. Miller (1967): *One Reel a Week*,
University of California Press, Berkeley & Los Angeles

Charles Baudelaire (1965): 'The Salon of 1859, II: The Modern
Public and Photography' in *Art in Paris 1845-62*, trans.
Jonathan Mayne, Phaidon Press, London, pp.149-55

Jean Baudrillard (1976): *L'Echange symbolique et la mort*, Gal-
limard, Paris

Jean-Louis Baudry (1974-5): 'Ideological Effects of the Basic
Cinematographic Apparatus', *Film Quarterly* v XXVIII n 2,
pp.39-47

André Bazin (1967): 'The Ontology of the Photographic Image'
in *What is Cinema?*, trans. Hugh Gray, University of California
Press, Berkeley & Los Angeles, Vol.I, pp.9-16

François Bédarida (1979): *A Social History of England 1851-1975*,
trans. A.S. Forster, Methuen, London

Bebe Bergsten (1973): *The Great Dane and the Great Northern
Film Company*, Locare Research Group, Los Angeles

Maurice Bessy & G.M. Lo Duca (1948): *Lumière l'inventeur*, Editions Prisma, Paris

Gottfried Wilhelm Bitzer (1973): *Billy Bitzer His Story*, Farrar,
Straus & Giroux, New York

Bertolt Brecht (1964): 'Über das Theater der grossen Städte' in
John Willet, ed. & trans.: *Brecht on Theatre, the Development
of an Æsthetic*, Methuen, London, pp.8-9

Ben Brewster (1982): 'A Scene at the "Movies"', *Screen* v 23 n 2,
July-August 1982, pp.4-15

Noël Burch (1973): *Theory of Film Practice*, Secker & Warburg,
London

Noël Burch (1979): *To the Distant Observer, Form and Meaning in
the Japanese Cinema*, Scolar Press, London

Noël Burch (1981a): 'Charles Baudelaire versus Doctor Frankenstein', *Afterimage* nos. 8-9, Spring 1981, pp.4-21

Noël Burch (1981b): 'Notes on Fritz Lang's First **Mabuse**', *Cine-
Tracts* no. 13, v 4 n 1, Spring 1981, pp.1-13

Noël Burch (1982): 'Narrative/Diegesis: Thresholds, Limits',
Screen v 23 n 2, July-August 1982, pp.16-33

Noël Burch (1983): 'Passion, poursuite: la linéarisation',

Communications no. 38, pp.30-50

Noël Burch & Jorge Dana (1974): 'Propositions', *Afterimage* no. 5, Spring 1974, pp.40-67

W. Stephen Bush (1908a): 'The Coming Ten and Twenty Cent Moving Picture Theatre', *The Moving Picture World* v 3 n 9, August 29th 1908, pp.152-3

W. Stephen Bush (1908b): 'Shakespeare in Moving Pictures', *The Moving Picture World* v 3 n 23, December 5th 1908, pp.446-7

W. Stephen Bush (1909): 'The Human Voice as a Factor in the Moving Picture Show', *The Moving Picture World* v 4 n 4, January 23rd 1909, p.86

W. Stephen Bush (1911): 'The Added Attraction, Article II', *The Moving Picture World* v 10 n 8, November 25th 1911, p.617

C.W. Ceram (1965): *The Archæology of the Cinema*, Thames & Hudson, London

Leonora Corbett (n.d.): Reminiscences once held by the British Film Institute Library, London

John Corbin (1898): 'How the Other Half Laughs', *Harper's New Monthly Magazine* Vol.XCVIII, December 1898, pp.30-48

Alain Cottereau (n.d.): 'Les Cultures ouvrières contre le fonctionnement d'une force de travail en France (1848-1900)', unpublished paper

Georges Demenÿ (1892): 'Les Photographies parlantes', *La Nature*, 20ème année no. 985, April 16th 1892, pp.311-15

Jacques Deslandes (1966): *Histoire comparée du cinéma*, t.I, Casterman, Paris

Jacques Deslandes & Jacques Richard (1968): *Histoire comparée du cinéma*, t.II, Casterman, Paris

Henri Diamant Berger (1977): *Il était une fois le cinéma*, Jean Claude Simoën, Paris

Mary Ann Doane (1982): 'Film and the Masquerade—Theorising the Female Spectator', *Screen* v 23 nn 3-4, September-October 1982, pp.74-87

Richard Dyer (1979): *Stars*, British Film Institute, London

Bernard Edelman (1979): *The Ownership of the Image: Elements for a Marxist Theory of Law*, trans. Elizabeth Kingdom, Routledge & Kegan Paul, London

Thomas Alva Edison (1895): Preface to W.K.L. Dickson & Antonia Dickson: *History of the Kinetograph Kinetoscope and*

Kineto-Phonograph, published by W.K.L. Dickson, New York

Jean Epstein (1946): *L'Intelligence d'une machine*, Editions Jacques Melot, Paris

Elizabeth Ewen (1980): 'City Lights: Immigrant Women and the Rise of the Movies', *Signs*, Supplement to v 5 n 3, Spring 1980, pp.S45-S65

Henri Fescourt (1959): *La Foi et les montagnes, ou le septième art au passé*, Paul Montel, Paris

Audrey Field (1974): *Picture Palace, A Social History of the Cinema*, Gentry Books, London

Raymond Fielding (1973): 'Hale's Tours, Ultra-Realism in the pre-1910 Motion Picture' in Donald E. Staples, ed.: *The American Cinema*, Voice of America Forum Series, USIA, Washington D.C. 1973, pp.12-24; and in a slightly different version in John L. Fell, ed.: *Film before Griffith*, University of California Press, Berkeley & Los Angeles 1983, pp.116-31

Lucy Fischer (1979): 'The Lady Vanishes', *Film Quarterly* v XXXIII n 1, Fall 1979, pp.30-40; and in John L. Fell, ed.: *Film before Griffith*, University of California Press, Berkeley & Los Angeles 1983, pp.339-54

Françoise Foster-Hahn (1973): *Eadweard Muybridge, the Stanford Years*, Stanford University Department of Art, Stanford, California

Pierre Francastel (1977): *Peinture et société* in *Œuvres* t.I, Denoël/Gonthier, Paris

Robert Gessner (1962): 'Porter and the Creation of Cinematic Motion; An Analysis of **The Life of an American Fireman**', *Journal of the Society of Cinematologists (= Cinema Journal)* vol.2, pp.1-13

Lillian Gish & Ann Pinchot (1969): *The Movies, Mr. Griffith and Me*, Prentice-Hall, Englewood Cliffs N.J.

Douglas Gomery (1978): 'The Picture Palace: Economic Sense or Hollywood Nonsense?', *Quarterly Review of Film Studies* v 3 n 1, Winter 1978, pp.23-36

Maxim Gorky (1908): *The Spy*, Duckworth & Co., London

Maxim Gorky (1960): Review of the Lumière programme at the Nizhny-Novgorod Fair as printed in the *Nizhegorodsky Listok* newspaper, July 4th 1896 and signed I.M. Pacatus, translated by Leda Swan in Jay Leyda: *Kino, A History of the Russian and Soviet Film*, George Allen & Unwin, London, pp.407-9

Tom Gunning (1981): 'Weaving a Narrative: Style and Economic Background in Griffith's Biograph Films', *Quarterly Review of Film Studies* v 6 n 1, Winter 1981, pp.11-26

Alice Guy (1976): *Autobiographie d'une pionnière du cinéma*, Denoël/Gonthier, Paris

Louis Reeves Harrison (1910): 'A Great Motion Picture [**Ramona**] and its Lesson', *The Moving Picture World* v 6 n 22, June 4th 1910, p.933; reprinted in Stanley Kauffmann & Bruce Henstell, eds.: *American Film Criticism from the Beginnings to 'Citizen Kane'*, Liveright, New York 1972, p.45

Stephen Heath (1976): 'Screen Images, Film Memory', *Edinburgh '76 Magazine*, Edinburgh International Film Festival, pp.33-42

Gordon Hendricks (1961): *The Edison Motion Picture Myth*, University of California Press, Berkeley & Los Angeles

Gordon Hendricks (1966): *The Kinetoscope*, The Beginnings of the American Film, New York

Cecil M. Hepworth (1951): *Came the Dawn, Memoirs of a Film Pioneer*, Phœnix House, London

Eric Hobsbawm (1968): *Industry and Empire, An Economic History of Britain since 1750*, Weidenfeld & Nicolson, London

H.F. Hoffman (1912): 'Cutting off the Feet', *The Moving Picture World* v 12 n 1, April 6th 1912, p.53

Lewis Jacobs (1939): *The Rise of the American Film, A Critical History*, Teacher's College Press, New York

E. Ann Kaplan, ed. (1980): *Women in Film Noir*, British Film Institute, London

Melanie Klein (1975): 'The Rôle of the School in the Libidinal Development of the Child (1923)' in *The Writings of Melanie Klein*, Vol.I: *Love, Guilt and Reparation and Other Works 1921-1945*, Hogarth Press, London, pp.59-76

Thierry Kuntzel (1978): 'The Film Work', *enclitic* v 2 n 1, Spring 1978, pp.38-62

Francis Lacassin (1964): *Louis Feuillade*, Editions Seghers, Paris

Brian Lawrence (1909): 'Lecturing to Pictures', *The Bioscope* no. 142, July 1st 1909, p.3

Jean-Patrick Lebel (1971): *Cinéma et idéologie*, Editions Sociales, Paris

Marcel L'Herbier (1968): 'Autour du cinématographe', interview by Jean-André Fieschi & Jacques Siclier, *Cahiers du Cinéma* no. 202, June-July 1968, pp.26-43; reprinted with supplementary material in Noël Burch: *Marcel L'Herbier*, Editions Seghers, Paris 1971, pp. 34-128

Albert Londe (1896): *La Photographie moderne, traité pratique de la photographie et de ses applications à l'industrie et à la science*, 2nd ed., G. Masson, Paris

Rachel Low (1948): *The History of the British Film*, Vol.II: *1906-1914*, George Allen & Unwin, London

Rachel Low & Roger Manvell (1948): *The History of the British Film*, Vol. I: *1896-1906*, George Allen & Unwin, London

Albert McLean (1965): *American Vaudeville as Ritual*, University of Kentucky Press, Lexington

Jerry Mander (1978): *Four Arguments for the Elimination of Television*, Willis Morrow & Co., New York

Antonio Mangano (1917): *Sons of Italy*, New York Missionary Education Movement, New York

Octave Mannoni (1969): 'Je sais bien, mais quand même ...' in *Clefs pour l'imaginaire, ou l'Autre scène*, Editions du Seuil, Paris, pp.9-93

Etienne Jules Marey (1874): *Animal Mechanism: A Treatise on Terrestrial and Aerial Locomotion*, Henry S. King & Co., London

Etienne Jules Marey (1895): *Movement*, trans. Eric Pritchard, Heinemann, London

Etienne Jules Marey (1898): *La Chronophotographie appliquée à l'étude des actes musculaires dans la locomotion*, Gonthier-Villars et Cie., Paris

Etienne Jules Marey (1899): 'Préface' in Eugène Trutat: *La Photographie animée*, Gonthier-Villars et Cie., Paris

Jean-Marie Mayeur & Madeleine Rébérioux (1984): *The Third Republic from its Origins to the Great War, 1871-1914*, Cambridge University Press

Russell Merritt (1976): 'Nickelodeon Theatres 1905-14: Building an Audience for the Movies' in Tino Balio, ed.: *The American Film Industry*, University of Wisconsin Press, Madison, pp.59-79

Félix Mesguich (1933): *Tours de manivelle, souvenirs d'un chasseur d'images*, Bernard Grasset, Paris

Christian Metz (1966): 'La Grande syntagmatique du film narratif', *Communications* no. 8, pp.120-4

Christian Metz (1972): *Essais sur la signification au cinéma*, t.II, Editions Klincksieck, Paris

Christian Metz (1974): *Film Language*, trans. Michael Taylor, Oxford University Press, London & New York

Christian Metz (1982): *Psychoanalysis and Cinema, The Imaginary Signifier*, trans. Celia Britton, Annwyl Williams, Ben Brewster & Alfred Guzzetti, Macmillan Press, London

Annette Michelson (1971): 'Towards Snow, Part One', *Artforum* v 9 n 10, June 1971, pp.30-37

Jean Mitry (1967): *Histoire du cinéma, art et industrie*, t.I: *1895-1914*, Editions Universitaires, Paris

François Napoléon Marie Moigno (1852): 'Centre photographique ... 1: Le Stéréoscope', *Cosmos, Revue encyclopédique hebdomadaire des progrès des sciences*, t.I no. 1, May 2nd 1852, pp.4-10

Duncan Moore (1894): 'Size or Realism', *The Optical Lantern and Cinematograph Journal and Photographic Enlarger* v 5 n 58, March 1st 1894, pp.55-7

Edgar Morin (1960): *The Stars*, trans. Richard Howard, Grove Press, New York

Laura Mulvey (1975): 'Visual Pleasure and Narrative Cinema', *Screen* v 16 n 3, Autumn 1975, pp.6-18

Hugo Münsterberg (1970): *The Film, A Psychological Study, The Silent Photoplay in 1916*, Dover Publications, New York

Charles Musser (1981): 'The Eden Musée in 1898: The Exhibitor as Creator', *Film and History* v XI n 4, December 1981, pp.73-83 & 96

Charles Musser (1982): 'Symposium: Cinema 1900-1906 Session 3' in Roger Holman, ed.: *Cinema 1900/1906 An Analytical Study*, Fédération Internationale des Archives de Film, Brussels, Vol.I, pp.53-60

Charles Musser (1983): 'The Nickelodeon Era Begins: Establishing the Framework for Hollywood's Mode of Representation', *Framework* n 22/23, Autumn 1983, pp.4-11

Charles Musser (1984): 'Another Look at the "Chaser Theory"', *Studies in Visual Communication* v 10 n 4, Fall 1984, pp.24-44

Vladimir Nizhny (1962): *Lessons with Eisenstein*, ed. & trans. Ivor

Montagu & Jay Leyda, George Allen & Unwin, London

Charles Nodier (1841): 'Introduction' in Charles Guilbert de Pixérécourt: *Théâtre choisi*, t.I, Paris & Nancy, pp.i-xvi

Maurice Noverre (1930): 'Le Gala Méliès', *Le Nouvel art cinématographique*, Brest, 2nd series no. 5, January 1930, pp.71-90

Erwin Panofsky (1953): 'Artist, Scientist, Genius: Notes on the "Renaissance-Dämmerung"' in *The Renaissance, A Symposium*, Metropolitan Museum of Art, New York, pp.77-93

John Ayrton Paris (1827): *Philosophy in Sport Made Science in Earnest; being an Attempt to Illustrate the First Principles of Natural Philosophy by the Aid of Popular Toys and Sports* in three volumes, Longman, Rees, Orme, Brown & Green, London (published anonymously)

Jean Piaget & Bärbel Inhelder (1956): *The Child's Conception of Space*, Routledge & Kegan Paul, London

Vincent Pinel (1974): *Lumière, Anthologie du Cinéma* no. 78, Supplement to *L'Avant-Scène Cinéma* no. 147, May 1974

Marcelin Pleynet & Jean Thibaudeau (1970): 'Economique, idéologique, formel', interview by Gérard Leblanc, *Cinéthique* no. 3, pp.7-14

Terry Ramsaye (1926): *A Million and One Nights, A History of the Motion Picture*, Simon & Schuster, New York

Lily May Richards (n.d.): 'Biography of William Haggar, Actor, Showman and Pioneer of the Industry', unpublished document preserved in the British Film Institute Library

Robert Roberts (1973): *The Classic Slum: Salford Life in the First Quarter of the Century*, Penguin Books, Harmondsworth

Auguste Rodin (1912): *Art*, compiled by Paul Gsell, trans. Mrs. Romilly Fedden, Hodder & Stoughton, London

Georges Sadoul (1964): *Louis Lumière*, Editions Seghers, Paris

Georges Sadoul (1973): *Histoire générale du cinéma*, revised and expanded edition with the participation of Bernard Eisenschitz, Denoël, Paris: t.I: *L'Invention du cinéma 1832-1897*; t.II: *Les Pionniers du cinéma (de Méliès à Pathé) 1897-1909*; t.III: *Le Cinéma devient un art 1909-1920*

Barry Salt (1982): 'Symposium: Cinema 1900-1906 Session 1' in Roger Holman, ed.: *Cinema 1900/1906, An Analytical Study*, Fédération Internationale des Archives de Film, Brussels, Vol.I, pp.31-44

Jean-Paul Sartre (1964): *Words*, trans. Irene Clephane, Hamish Hamilton, London

Marcel Schneider (1963): *Richard Wagner*, Editions du Seuil, Paris

Hanna Segal (1979): *Klein*, Fontana Modern Masters, London

Zdeněk Štabla (1971): *Queries Concerning the Hořice Passion Film*, The Film Institute, Prague

Simon Stampfer (1833): *Die stroboscopischen Scheiben*, Vienna

Rollin Summers (1908): 'The Moving Picture Drama and the Acted Drama. Some Points of Comparison as to Technique', *The Moving Picture World* v 3 n 12, September 19th 1908, pp.211-13

Robert C. Toll (1976): *On with the Show: The First Century of Show Business in America*, Oxford University Press, London & New York

Anne Ubersfeld (1972): 'Le Mélodrame' in Pierre Abraham & Roland Desné, eds.: *Manuel d'histoire littéraire de la France*, t.4: *1789-1848*, Part 1, Editions Sociales, Paris, pp.669-75

Jules Verne (1893): *Castle in the Carpathians*, Sampson Low & Co., London

Dziga Vertov (1984): 'The Council of Three' in *Kino-Eye: The Writings of Dziga Vertov*, ed. & intro. Annette Michelson, trans. Kevin O'Brien, Pluto Press, London, pp.14-21

Philippe Auguste comte de Villiers de l'Isle-Adam (1977): *L'Eve future*, José Corti, Paris

Peter Wollen (1969): *Signs and Meaning in the Cinema*, Secker & Warburg, London

Frank Woods (1909a): 'Reviews of Licensed Films', *The New York Dramatic Mirror* v LXI n 1574, February 20th 1909, p.16 (pseudonymously as 'The Spectator')

Frank Woods (1909b): 'Reviews of Licensed Films', *The New York Dramatic Mirror* v LXI n 1588, May 29th 1909, p.15 (pseudonymously as 'The Spectator')

Frank Woods (1910): 'Spectator's Comments', *The New York Dramatic Mirror* v LXIII n 1638, May 14th 1910, p.18 (pseudonymously)

William Huntington Wright (1921): 'The Romance of the Third Dimension', *Photoplay Magazine* v 20 n 4, September 1921, pp.41-2 & 105; reprinted in George Pratt, ed.: *Spellbound in Darkness, A History of the Silent Film*, 2nd ed., New York Graphic Society, Greenwich Conn. 1973, pp.360-2

Adolph Zukor (1927): 'Origin and Growth of the Industry' in Joseph P. Kennedy, ed.: *The Story of the Films*, A.W. Shaw Company, Chicago & New York, pp.55-76

Adolph Zukor (1930): 'Comment je me suis lancé dans le cinéma', *La Revue du Cinéma*, année 2 n 7, February 1st 1930, pp.37-45; reprinted in Marcel Lapierre, ed.: *Anthologie du cinéma, textes réunis et présentés*, La Nouvelle Edition, Paris 1946, pp.108-116

Filmography

This filmography gives minimal information on the films and television programmes mentioned in the text. Each entry has one or more titles, and, to the extent the information was available, the country of production, the production company (p.c.), the 'director' (d.), the release date in the country of production (r.d.), and the original release length. The main name is the one used in the text; if it is in bold, it is the name under which the film was first released in its country of production, or, if that name cannot be traced, the original release title in the United Kingdom or the United States of America, or the title assigned by the archive in which the print discussed is preserved. The exceptions to this are those prints which I know have been assigned descriptive titles by the archive preserving them as no contemporary title is known; such titles are enclosed in square brackets and not printed in bold. In brackets after non-English titles, one or more English titles are given. If these are in inverted commas they are original release titles in the UK, the USA or both; if the brackets are square they are my translations of the original title. The country given is that in which the company producing the film was registered, the occasional co-production thus being assigned to more than one country. The production company or companies' names are those registered at the time the film was released. The name given for the 'director' is that of the individual judged most directly responsible for the film. 'Director' is anachronistic for many of the earlier films, where the individual in question was rather a factotum (e.g., George Albert Smith or Georges Méliès). In the case of Biograph and Edison, internal company records indicate that until about 1908 the cameraman was this key individual, and in these cases he is indicated as 'ph.' (for 'photographer'). The date is the release date of the film in its country of production as accurately as I can determine it; for a few titles for which this information was not available some other date such as a date of production, a copyright date, or the date of the film's first known screening or première is given instead. For silent films, lengths are in feet for 35mm prints, and are those given in contemporary catalogues or the trade press; in a few cases the length is that of an extant print in a (named) archive. For sound films, lengths are in minutes. Dubious entries are accompanied by a query. The final figures in brackets are page references to this book.

The Adventures of Dolly, USA, p.c. American Mutoscope & Biograph Company, d. D.W. Griffith, r.d. July 14th 1908, 713 feet (pp.153, 211)

L'Affaire Dreyfus ('Dreyfus Court Martial'), France, Star Film, d. Georges Méliès, Autumn 1899, ten parts, 650 feet (pp.66, 197-8)

L'Affaire Dreyfus [The Dreyfus Affair], France, p.c. Pathé Frères, 1899 (p.66)

Afgrunden (UK: 'The Abyss'; USA: 'Woman Always Pays'), Denmark, p.c. Kosmorama, d. Urban Gad, r.d. September 12th 1910, 2,460 feet (p.186)

Alien, UK, p.c. Brandywine-Ronald Shusett Productions for Twentieth-Century-Fox (London), d. Ridley Scott, US r.d. May 25th 1979, 117 minutes (p.266 n.13)

The Aliens' Invasion, UK, p.c. Hepworth Manufacturing Company, d. Lewin Fitzhamon, r.d. October 1905, 450 feet (p.107 n.9)

All the President's Men, USA, p.c. Wildwood Enterprises/Warner Brothers, d. Alan J. Pakula, r.d. April 7th 1976, 138 minutes (p.200 n.4)

Amor pedestre [Pedestrian Love], Italy, p.c. Arturo Ambrosio e C., d. Marcel Fabre (?), 1914, 340 feet (Museum of Modern Art print) (p.199 n.1)

And the Villain Still Pursued Her; or, The Author's Dream, USA, p.c. Vitagraph Company of America, r.d. December 5th 1906, 800 feet (p.129)

L'Année dernière à Marienbad, France/Italy, p.c. Terra Films/ Cormoran/Percitel/Como Films/Argos Films/Films Tamara/

Cinetel/Cineriz, d. Alain Resnais, 1961, 100 minutes (p.230 n.6)

Another Job for the Undertaker, USA, p.c. Thomas A. Edison, ph. Edwin S. Porter, US copyright May 15th 1901, 85 feet (pp.116, 144, 157)

Are You There?, UK, p.c. Williamson's Kinematographic Company, d. James Williamson, r.d. October 1901, 75 feet (p.157)

L'Argent ('Money'), France, p.c. Ciné Mondial/Cinégraphic, d. Marcel L'Herbier, r.d. January 11th 1929, 12,140 feet (pp.74-5, 181)

Arrivée des congressistes à Neuville-sur-Saône [Photographic Congress Delegates Disembark at Neuville-sur-Saône], France, p.c. Société Lumière, ph. Louis Lumière, screened at the Congress in Lyon June 12th 1895, 56 feet (pp.19, 214, 232 n.17)

Arrivée d'un train à La Ciotat ('Arrival of a Train at La Ciotat'), France, p.c. Société Lumière, ph. Louis Lumière, 1895 or 1896, 56 feet (pp.17, 19, 35-6, 172-3, 244)

Arroseur et arrosé ('The Gardener, the Bad Boy and the Hose', often known as 'Watering the Gardener'), France, p.c. Société Lumière, ph. Louis Lumière, screened at the Congress of French Photography Clubs, Lyon, June 10th 1895, 56 feet (Vincent Pinel argues that the film normally known by this name or as **L'Arroseur arrosé** and photographed by Louis Lumière in the Summer of 1895 is not the film issued by the Société Lumière under this title, but an uncatalogued film entitled **Le Jardinier et le petit espiègle**) (pp.22 n.8, 33, 149, 159 n.1, 191, 200 n.7, 200 n.13)

L'Assassinat du duc de Guise ('Assassination of the Duke of Guise'), France, p.c. Le Film d'Art, d. Charles Le Bargy/André Calmette, première November 17th 1908, 1640 feet (pp.56, 57 Fig.4, 156, 189, 236)

As Seen through a Telescope, UK, p.c. GAS Films, d. George Albert Smith, r.d. September 1900, 75 feet (pp.222, 223 Fig.32)

Attack on a China Mission—Blue Jackets to the Rescue, UK, p.c. Williamson's Kinematographic Company, d. James Williamson, r.d. November 1900, 230 feet (pp.92, 93 Fig.9, 107 n.8, 158)

Au bagne ('Scenes of Convict Life'), France, p.c. Pathé Frères, d. Ferdinand Zecca, 1905, 705 feet (pp.72, 100, 102, 140 n.10,

170)

Auf der Radrennbahn in Friedenau [At the Friedenau Cycle Race Track], Germany, p.c. Messters Projektion (?), d. Oskar Messter (?), 1904 (?), preserved Stiftung Deutsche Kinemathek, Berlin (p.242 n.3)

Au pays noir (USA: 'Mining District'; UK: 'Tragedy in a Coal Mine'), France, p.c. Pathé Frères, d. Lucien Nonguet/Ferdinand Zecca, r.d. May 1905, 820 feet, preserved Cinémathèque Royale de Belgique, Brussels, as 'Le Mineur' (pp.71-2, 140 n.10, 170)

Le Baîlleur ('The Yawner'), France, p.c. Pathé Frères, 1907 (p.193)

Ballet mécanique, France, Fernand Léger/Dudley Murphey, 1924, 900 feet (p.241 n.1)

The Bank Burglar's Fate (UK: 'Detective Burton's Triumph'), USA, p.c. Reliance, d. John G. Adolfi, r.d. August 8th 1914, 2 reels (c. 2,000 feet) (pp.136, 137 Fig.17, 238)

Barbe Bleue ('Blue Beard'), France, p.c. Star Film, d. Georges Méliès, 1901, 690 feet (pp.167, 198)

Barber Shop, USA, p.c. Thomas A. Edison, ph. W.K.L. Dickson, first public showing April 14th 1894, 50 feet (pp.30 Fig.2, 113)

The Bargain Fiend; or, Shopping à la mode, USA, p.c. Vitagraph Company of America, r.d. August 10th 1907, 500 feet (p.130 Fig.15)

Bathing Not Allowed, UK, p.c. Haggar & Sons, d. William Haggar, r.d. October 1905, 145 feet (p.102)

La Belle équipe, France, p.c. Ciné Arys Productions, d. Julien Duvivier, 1936, 101 minutes (pp.74, 206)

La Bête humaine ('The Human Beast'), France, p.c. Paris Film/Productions Robert Hakim, d. Jean Renoir, r.d. December 29th 1938, 87 minutes (p.35)

The Big Sleep, USA, p.c. Warner Brothers/First National, d. Howard Hawks, r.d. August 31st 1946, 114 minutes (p.251)

The Big Swallow, UK, p.c. Williamson's Kinematographic Company, d. James Williamson, r.d. October 1901, 60 feet (pp.95-6, 202, 220, 221 Fig.31, 222, 226, 232 n.22)

The Birth of a Nation, USA, p.c. Epoch Producing Corporation, d. D.W. Griffith, première February 8th 1915, 12 reels (c. 12,000 feet) (pp.77 n.9, 128, 158)

Black and White Washing, UK, p.c. Walturdaw Company, 1900(?), 57 feet (National Film Archive print) (p.159 n.4)

Black Beauty, UK, p.c. Hepworth Manufacturing Company, d. Lewin Fitzhamon, r.d. August 1906, 475 feet (pp.107 n.9, 160 n.14)

Blonde Cobra, USA, Ken Jacobs, 1963, 28 minutes (p.265 n.10)

The Blue Bird, USA, p.c. Artcraft Productions, d. Maurice Tourneur, r.d. March 31st 1918, 5 reels (c. 5,000 feet) (p.217)

Blue Collar, USA, p.c. TAT Productions, d. Paul Schrader, r.d. February 12th 1978, 114 minutes (p.196)

The Bobby's Downfall, UK, p.c. Sheffield Photo Company, d. Frank Mottershaw, r.d. July 1904, 150 feet (p.103)

Bold Bank Robbery, USA, p.c. Lubin Manufacturing Company, US copyright July 25th 1904, 600 feet (p.196)

Le Brigandage moderne ('Modern Brigandage'), France, p.c. Pathé Frères, d. Ferdinand Zecca, 1905, 525 feet (pp.173, 174 Fig.20)

[Brown's Duel] (National Film Archive descriptive title), France, p.c. Pathé Frères, 1906 (?), 344 feet (National Film Archive print) (possibly US: 'What a Razor Can Do', r.d. February 29th 1908, 426 feet) (p.64)

Brutality Rewarded, UK, p.c. Haggar & Sons, d. William Haggar, r.d. October 1904, 75 feet (p.102)

The Burglar, USA, p.c. American Mutoscope & Biograph Company, ph. A.E. Weed, r.d. September 21st 1903, 101 feet (p.117)

Buy Your Own Cherries, UK, p.c. Paul's Animatograph Works, d. R.W. Paul, r.d. June 1904, 300 feet (p.107 n.11)

Das Cabinett des Doktors Caligari ('The Cabinet of Doctor Caligari'), Germany, p.c. Decla-Bioscop, d. Robert Wiene, première February 27th 1920, 5,600 feet (pp.75, 164, 170, 183-4, 185 n.12, 185 n.13)

Cabiria—visione storica del terzo secolo A. C., Italy, p.c. Itala Film, d. Piero Fosco (= Giovanni Pastrone), r.d. April 18th 1914, c. 9,850 feet (pp.135, 181)

A Career in Crime, USA, p.c. American Mutoscope & Biograph Company, ph. Arthur Marvin, US copyright November 11th 1902, 823 feet (p.113)

Carmen (Phonoscène), France, p.c. Léon Gaumont & Compagnie,

d. Alice Guy, r.d. August 1906, 12 parts, c. 2,200 feet (p.242 n.2)

A Casing Shelved (slide and tape), USA, Michael Snow, 1970, 40 minutes (pp.258-9)

Ce que je vois de mon sixième ('Scenes from My Balcony'), France, p.c. Pathé Frères, d. Ferdinand Zecca, 1901, 132 feet (p.222)

Charles Peace, UK, p.c. Haggar & Sons, d. William Haggar, r.d. September 1905, 770 feet (pp.99-100, 101 Fig.11, 173, 175 Fig.21, 176, 182, 185 n.7, 198)

The Cheat, USA, p.c. Jessie Lasky Feature Plays, d. Cecil B. DeMille, r.d. December 12th 1915, 5 reels (c. 5,000 feet) (pp.50, 59, 74-5, 179-80, 185 n.9, 196, 212, 217-18, 231 n.15, 264 n.2)

A Chess Dispute, UK, p.c. Paul's Animatograph Works, d. R.W. Paul, r.d. August 1903, 80 feet (p.25 Fig.1)

Les Chiens contrebandiers ('Dogs Used as Smugglers'), France, p.c. Pathé Frères, d. Lucien Nonguet, 1906, 607 feet (pp.67, 78 n.20, 158)

La Chute de la maison Usher ('The Fall of the House of Usher'), France, p.c. Films Jean Epstein, d. Jean Epstein, r.d. October 5th 1928, 4,290 feet (p.74-5)

La Civilisation à travers les ages ('Humanity Through the Ages'), France, p.c. Star Film, d. Georges Méliès, r.d. February 1908, 1,000 feet (p.167-8)

[The Clumsy Photographer], France, p.c. Pathé Frères, 1906 (?), preserved Československý Filmový Ústav, Prague, as **Nesikovny Fotograf** (pp.67, 69, 95, 160 n.6)

Contactos ('Contacts'), Spain, p.c. FR Debut IA, d. Paulino Viota Cabrera, 1970 (p.265 n.7)

Correction Please, or, How We Got into Pictures, UK, p.c. Arts Council of Great Britain, d. Noël Burch, 1979, 52 minutes (p.230 n.5)

Le Coucher de la mariée (UK: 'The Bride's First Night': USA: 'Bride Retiring'), France, p.c. Cinématographe E. Pirou, ph. Lear, 1896, 200 feet (cf. **Le Coucher de la mariée, ou triste nuit de noces**, France, p.c. Star Film, 1899, 130 feet; **Le Coucher de la mariée**, France, p.c. Pathé Frères, 1904, 132 feet, et. al.) (pp.191, 200 n.13, 213-14, 215 Fig.29, 222, 224, 232 n.16)

Le Coup de vent [A Gust of Wind], France, p.c. Léon Gaumont

& Compagnie, d. Etienne Arnaud, 1906 (?), 150 feet (p.160 n.6)

Un Coup d'œil par étage ('Scenes at Every Floor'), France, p.c. Pathé Frères, r.d. February 1904, 393 feet (p.233 n.24)

Crainquebille, France/Austria, p.c. Travieux & Legrand/Vita Films (Vienna), d. Jacques Feyder, r.d. March 2nd 1923, 5,900 feet (p.76 n.2)

The Cripple and the Cyclists, France, 1906 (?), 354 feet (National Film Archive print) (pp.78 n.20, 158)

La Danse du diable [Devil's Dance], France, p.c. Pathé Frères, d. Ferdinand Zecca (?), 1904 (?) (p.228)

A Daring Daylight Burglary, UK, p.c. Sheffield Photo Company, d. Frank Mottershaw, r.d. April 1903, 275 feet (pp.103, 107 n.8, 197)

A Dash for Liberty; or, The Convict's Escape and Capture, UK, p.c. Haggar & Sons, d. William Haggar, r.d. November 1903, 300 feet (p.102)

The Dear Boys Home for the Holidays, UK, p.c. Williamson's Kinematographic Company, d. James Williamson, r.d. December 1903, 290 feet (pp.92, 94 Fig.10)

The Deserter, UK, p.c. Williamson's Kinematographic Company, d. James Williamson, r.d. October 1903, 520 feet (p.95)

Desperate Poaching Affray, UK, p.c. Haggar & Sons, d. William Haggar, r.d. July 1903, 220 feet (pp.102, 107 n.8, 185 n.7, 226)

Dévaliseurs nocturnes (UK: 'Burglary by Night'; US: 'Burglars at Work'), France, p.c. Pathé Frères, d. Gaston Velle, 1904, 246 feet (pp.67, 68 Fig.5, 78 n.20)

[The Dialogue of Legs], France, 1902 (?), preserved Filmoteka Polska, Warsaw (p.199 n.1)

La Dixième Symphonie ('The Tenth Symphony'), France, p.c. Le Film d'Art, d. Abel Gance, r.d. November 1st 1918, 6,545 feet (pp.75, 114)

The Dog and His Various Merits, France, p.c. Pathé Frères, 1906 (?), 300 feet (Library of Congress print) (p.67)

Doktor Mabuse der Spieler ('Doctor Mabuse the Gambler'), Germany, p.c. Ullstein/Uco Film/Dekla-Bioscop/Ufa, d. Fritz Lang, Part 1: r.d. April 27th 1922, 11,500 feet; Part 2: r.d. May 26th 1922, 8,400 feet (pp.184 n.5, 232 n.23)

Double Indemnity, USA, p.c. Paramount Pictures, d. Billy Wilder, r.d. July 12th 1944, 103 minutes (p.272)

Un Drame à l'usine [Tragedy in the Factory], France, p.c. Léon Gaumont & Compagnie, 1909 (p.66)

Un Drame au pays basque [Tragedy in the Basque Country], France, p.c. Léon Gaumont & Compagnie, d. Louis Feuillade, r.d. November 1913, 3,000 feet (p.65)

Un Drame en mer ('Tragedy at Sea'), France, p.c. Pathé Frères, d. Gaston Velle, 1905, 393 feet (pp.140 n.10, 184 n.3)

Dream of a Rarebit Fiend, USA, p.c. Thomas A. Edison, ph. Edwin S. Porter, US copyright February 24th 1906, 470 feet (pp.114, 200 n.13)

[The Dreams], France (?), 1906 (?), preserved Deutsches Institut für Filmkunde, Wiesbaden (p.71)

Drink and Repentance—A Convict Story, UK, p.c. Cricks & Sharp, d. Tom Green (?), July 1905, 570 feet (p.107 n.11)

[Drunkard Against His Will], France, p.c. Pathé Frères, 1902 (?), preserved Universidad Nacional Autónoma de Mexico, Mexico City, as **Borracho contra su volundad** (pp.63-4)

A Drunkard's Reformation, USA, p.c. American Mutoscope & Biograph Company, d. D.W. Griffith, r.d. April 1st 1909, 983 feet (pp.136, 178, 218, 219 Fig.30, 220)

D.T.s; or, The Effects of Drink, UK, p.c. Haggar & Sons, d. William Haggar, r.d. October 1905, 220 feet (p.102)

Un Duel abracadabrant [A Mumbo-Jumbo Duel], France, p.c. Pathé Frères, d. Ferdinand Zecca, 1902 (p.168)

The Dukes of Hazzard (TV series), USA, network CBS, first broadcast January 26th 1979, weekly 50-minute shows (pp.261-2)

An Eccentric Burglary, UK, p.c. The Sheffield Photo Company, d. Frank Mottershaw, r.d. March 1905, 400 feet (p.103)

The Eccentric Thief, UK, p.c. The Sheffield Photo Company, d. Frank Mottershaw, r.d. June 1906, 340 feet (p.103)

The Edison Kinetophone, USA, p.c. Edison Kinetophone, 1913, 331 feet (Library of Congress print) (p.237)

Les Effets du melon [Effects of a Melon], France, p.c. Pathé Frères, d. Lucien Lépine, 1906, 115 feet (p.71)

L'Enfant de Paris ('In the Clutch of the Apaches'), France, p.c. Léon Gaumont & Compagnie, d. Léonce Perret, 1913, 7,875 feet (pp.74, 173)

Entr'acte, France, p.c. Ballets Suédois de Rolf de Maré, d. René

Clair, first version: première December 4th 1924; second version: première January 26th 1926, 1,390 feet (p.241 n.1)

Entuziazm ('Enthusiasm' or 'Donbass Symphony'), USSR, p.c. Ukrainfilm, d. Dziga Vertov, r.d. April 2nd 1931, 95 minutes (p.241 n.1)

L'Envers du théâtre ('Behind the Stage'), France, p.c. Pathé Frères, d. Georges Hatot, 1905, 106 feet (pp.198-9, 201 n.16)

Erreur de porte ('The Wrong Door'), France, p.c. Pathé Frères, d. Ferdinand Zecca, 1904, 115 feet (p.71)

The Eviction, UK, p.c. Gaumont & Company, d. Alf Collins, r.d. May 1904, 225 feet (pp.103, 185 n.7)

Execution of Czolgosz, with Panorama of Auburn Prison, USA, p.c. Thomas A. Edison, ph. Edwin S. Porter, US copyright November 9th 1901, 200 feet (pp.120, 201 n.14)

Falsely Accused, UK, p.c. Hepworth Manufacturing Company, d. Lewin Fitzhamon, r.d. May 1905, 850 feet (p.177)

Fantômas, France, p.c. Léon Gaumont & Compagnie, d. Louis Feuillade, Part 1: r.d. May 1913, 3,760 feet; Part 2: r.d. September 1913, 4,225 feet; Part 3: r.d. November 1913, 6,380 feet; Part 4: r.d. February 1914, 4,180 feet; Part 5: r.d. May 1914, 6,170 feet (pp.66, 100, 139 n.5, 154, 186)

Fate's Turning, USA, p.c. The Biograph Company, d. D.W. Griffith, r.d. January 23rd 1911, 998 feet (p.108 n.13)

Faust (Phonoscène), France, p.c. Léon Gaumont & Compagnie, d. Alice Guy, r.d. August 1906, 22 parts, 4,180 feet (p.242 n.2)

La Fête à Joséphine [Josephine's Name Day], France, p.c. Pathé Frères, 1906, 312 feet (p.63)

Fêtes du jubilé de la Reine d'Angleterre, 1897 [Queen Victoria's Diamond Jubilee Celebrations], France, p.c. Société Lumière, 1897, 9 parts, 523 feet (p.53)

Les Fêtes Franco-Russes [The Tsar's Visit to France], France, p.c. Société Lumière, October 1896, 7 parts, 390 feet (p.53)

Feu Mathias Pascal ('The Late Matthew Pascal'), France, p.c. Cinégraphic/Albatros, d. Marcel L'Herbier, r.d. February 1926, 10,825 feet (p.184 n.5)

La Fille de bain indiscrète ('The Indiscreet Bathroom Maid'), France, p.c. Pathé Frères, 1902, 165 feet, preserved Stiftung Deutsche Kinemathek, Berlin (p.222)

The Finish of Bridget McKeen, USA, p.c. Thomas A. Edison, ph.

Edwin S. Porter, US copyright March 1st 1901, 75 feet (pp.113, 139 n.6, 144)

Finis Terræ, France, p.c. Société Générale de Films, d. Jean Epstein, r.d. April 19th 1929, 5,970 feet (p.78 n.19)

Fire!, UK, p.c. Williamson's Kinematographic Company, d. James Williamson, r.d. October 1901, 280 feet (p.197)

Firemen to the Rescue, UK, p.c. Hepworth Manufacturing Company, d. Cecil M. Hepworth, r.d. November 1903, 321 feet (p.107 n.8)

Foolish Wives, USA, p.c. Universal Pictures Corporation, d. Erich Von Stroheim, r.d. January 11th 1922, 14,120 feet (p.114)

Francesca da Rimini; or, The Two Brothers, USA, p.c. Vitagraph Company of America, r.d. February 1908, 990 feet (pp.129, 131, 189)

Fred Ott's Sneeze, USA, p.c. Thomas A. Edison, photographed January 1894, 50 feet (p.41 n.3)

A Friendly Marriage, USA, p.c. Vitagraph Company of America, d. Van Dyke Brooke (?), r.d. September 5th 1911, 1,000 feet (pp.131, 177)

The Gay Shoe Clerk, USA, p.c. Thomas A. Edison, ph. Edwin S. Porter, US copyright August 12th 1903, 75 feet (pp.107 n.10, 186, 191, 192 Fig.24, 201 n.15)

Gertrud, Denmark, p.c. Palladium Film, d. Carl-Theodor Dreyer, première Paris December 19th 1964, 115 minutes (pp.184, 254)

A Girl's Folly, USA, p.c. Paragon Films for World Pictures, d. Maurice Tourneur, r.d. February 26th 1917, 5 reels (c. 5,000 feet) (pp.217, 264 n.2)

Gloria, USA, p.c. Columbia Pictures Corporation, d. John Cassavetes, r.d. October 1st 1980, 121 minutes (p.266 n.14)

Goaded to Anarchy, UK, p.c. Paul's Animatograph Works, d. R.W. Paul, r.d. September 1905, 480 feet (p.95)

Gold is not All, USA, p.c. Biograph Company, d. D.W. Griffith, r.d. March 28th 1910, 988 feet (pp.248, 249 Fig.35, 250, 252)

Grandma's Reading Glass, UK, p.c. GAS Films, d. George Albert Smith, r.d. September 1900, 100 feet (pp.89, 90 Fig.8, 144)

The Great Train Robbery, USA, p.c. Edison Manufacturing Company, d. Edwin S. Porter, US copyright December 1st 1903, 740 feet (pp.35, 104, 172, 186, 193, 194 Fig.25, 197, 204, 208, 242 n.6)

La **Grève** ('The Strike'), France, p.c. Pathé Frères, d. Ferdinand Zecca, 1903, 450 feet (p.65)

La **Grève des bonnes** [The Maids' Strike], France, p.c. Pathé Frères, d. Lucien Lépine, 1906, 459 feet (pp.65-6)

The Heathen Chinese and the Sunday School Teachers, USA, p.c. American Mutoscope & Biograph Company, ph. A.E. Weed, US copyright January 8th 1904, 260 feet (p.119)

Hintertreppe [Back Stairs], Germany, p.c. Henny Porten-Film for Gloria Film, d. Leopold Jessner/Paul Leni, première December 22nd 1921, 4,590 feet (p.265 n.8)

His Only Pair, UK, p.c. Paul's Animatograph Works, d. R.W. Paul, r.d. July 1902, 75 feet (p.95)

Histoire d'un crime ('Story of a Crime'), France, p.c. Pathé Frères, d. Ferdinand Zecca, 1901, 360 feet (pp.113, 168, 169 Fig.19, 186, 187 Fig.22, 230 n.2)

L'Homme à la tête en caoutchouc (UK: 'A Swelled Head'; USA: 'The Man with the Rubber Head'), France, p.c. Star Film, d. Georges Méliès, Winter 1901-2, 165 feet (pp.165, 166 Fig.18)

The Horitz Passion Play, USA, ph. William Freeman, première February 24th 1898 (pp.144, 159 n.2)

Hot Mutton Pies, USA, p.c. American Mutoscope & Biograph Company, ph. Frank Armitage, r.d. Spring 1902, 50 feet (p.119)

How a British Bulldog Saved the Union Jack, UK, p.c. Walturdaw Company, d. David Aylott (?), r.d. September 1906, 575 feet (pp.107 n.11, 193)

How It Feels to be Run Over, UK, p.c. Hepworth Manufacturing Company, d. Cecil M. Hepworth, r.d. July 1900, 50 feet (pp.96, 202, 203 Fig.27, 226)

How They Do Things on the Bowery, USA, p.c. Thomas A. Edison, US copyright October 31st 1902, 140 feet (pp.117, 207)

Il ne faut pas d'enfants [No Children!], France, p.c. Pathé Frères, 1906 (?) (p.67)

L'Incendiaire [The Incendiary], France, p.c. Pathé Frères, d. Ferdinand Zecca (?), 1905 (?), 520 feet (p.64-5)

The Ingenious Soubrette (UK: 'Magic Picture Hanging'), France, p.c. Pathé Frères, d. Ferdinand Zecca, 1902, 131 feet (pp.191, 228, 229 Fig.34, 233 n.28, 233 n.29)

L'Inhumaine, France, p.c. Films Marcel L'Herbier/Cinégraphic, d.

Marcel L'Herbier, r.d. December 12th 1924, 8,200 feet (p.241 n.1)

In Our Alley, UK, p.c. Gaumont & Company, d. Alf Collins, r.d. March 1906, 88 feet (p.103)

Intolerance, USA, p.c. Wark Producing Company, d. D.W. Griffith, r.d. September 5th 1916, 14 reels (c. 14,000 feet) (pp.158, 177-8, 189)

The Iron Horse, USA, p.c. Fox Film Company, d. John Ford, r.d. August 28th 1924, 11,335 feet (pp.35, 208)

The Italian, USA, p.c. New York Motion Picture Company, d. Reginald Barker, r.d. January 7th 1915, 5 reels (c. 5,000 feet) (pp.140 n.11, 264 n.2)

Jalousie et folie [Jealousy and Madness], France, p.c. Pathé Frères, d. Ferdinand Zecca (?), 1906 (?) (p.65)

The Jazz Singer, USA, p.c. Warner Brothers, d. Alan Crosland, r.d. October 6th 1927, 90 minutes (pp.12, 247)

Jeanne Dielman, 23 Quai du Commerce—1080 Bruxelles, France/Belgium, p.c. Paradise Films/Unité Trois, d. Chantal Akerman, 1975, 225 minutes (pp. 163, 254)

La Jetée, France, p.c. Argos Films/RFT, d. Chris Marker, 1963, 29 minutes (p.255)

Je vais chercher du pain [I'll Fetch the Bread], France, p.c. Pathé Frères, 1905 or 1906 (p.63)

The Jilt, USA, p.c. American Mutoscope & Biograph Company, d. D.W. Griffith, r.d. May 17th 1909, 997 feet (p.135)

Judith of Bethulia, USA, p.c. Biograph Company, d. D.W. Griffith, r.d. March 8th 1914, 4 reels (c. 4,000 feet) (p.154)

The Kentucky Feud, USA, p.c. American Mutoscope & Biograph Company, ph. G.W. Bitzer, r.d. November 13th 1905, 675 feet (pp.128, 136, 153, 189, 190 Fig.23, 198)

The Kiss (also known as 'The Irwin-Rice Kiss'), USA, p.c. Thomas A. Edison, ph. Heise, photographed April 1896, 50 feet (p.29)

[Ladies' Skirts Nailed to a Fence] (National Film Archive descriptive title), p.c. Riley Brothers/Bamforth & Company (?), 1900 (?), 68 feet (National Film Archive print) (pp.96, 225-6)

Lady in the Lake, USA, p.c. Metro-Goldwyn-Mayer, d. Robert Montgomery, r.d. January 23rd 1947, 103 minutes (pp.250-2, 254, 260, 265 n.6)

Letter from an Unknown Woman, USA, p.c. Rampart Productions for Universal, d. Max Ophüls, r.d. April 28th 1948, 86 minutes (p.270)

Der letzte Mann ('The Last Laugh'), Germany, p.c. UFA, d. Friedrich Murnau, r.d. December 23rd 1924, 6,680 feet (p.265 n.8)

Levi and Cohen, the Irish Comedians, USA, p.c. American Mutoscope & Biograph Company, ph. G.W. Bitzer, r.d. August 1903, 61 feet (pp.120, 140 n.9)

Life of a Cowboy, USA, p.c. Thomas A. Edison, r.d. July 1906, 970 feet (p.152)

Life of an American Fireman, USA, p.c. Thomas A. Edison, ph. Edwin S. Porter, r.d. February 1903, 425 feet (pp.117, 186, 199 n.1, 204-7, 218, 228, 230 n.2, 230 n.3, 230 n.4, 230 n.6, 233 n.26)

Life of an American Policeman, USA, p.c. Thomas A. Edison, ph. Edwin S. Porter, US copyright December 6th 1905, 1,000 feet (p.117)

The Life of Charles Peace, UK, p.c. Sheffield Photo Company, d. Frank Mottershaw, r.d. November 1905, 870 feet (p.104)

The Light that Didn't Fail, USA, p.c. American Mutoscope & Biograph Company, ph. R.K. Bonine, US copyright December 9th 1902, 169 feet (p.116)

Little Cæsar, USA, p.c. First National, d. Mervyn Leroy, r.d. January 9th 1931, 77 minutes (p.196)

A Lodging House Comedy, UK, p.c. Gaumont & Company, d. Alf Collins, r.d. July 1906, 310 feet (p.103)

The Lonedale Operator, USA, p.c. Biograph Company, d. D.W. Griffith, r.d. March 23rd 1911, 998 feet (pp.128, 211-12)

The Lonely Villa, USA, p.c. Biograph Company, d. D.W. Griffith, r.d. June 10th 1909, 750 feet (pp.156, 211)

Madame a des envies ([Madame's Cravings]), France, p.c. Léon Gaumont & Compagnie, 1907 (pp.69, 70 Fig.6, 71)

Mary Jane's Mishap; or, Don't Fool with the Paraffin, UK, p.c. GAS Films, d. George Albert Smith, February 1903, 250 feet (p.139 n.6)

Masques and Grimaces, UK, p.c. GAS Films (?), d. George Albert Smith (?), 1901 (?), 82 feet (National Film Archive print) (p.96)

Mat' ('Mother'), USSR, p.c. Mezhrabpom-Russ, d. Vsevolod Pudovkin, r.d. October 11th 1926, 5,900 feet (p.24)

Ménilmontant, France, d. Dmitri Kirsanoff, r.d. January 1926, 4,500 feet (p.265 n.8)

Metropolis, Germany, p.c. Ufa, d. Fritz Lang, r.d. January 10th 1927, 13,750 feet (distribution print 10,400 feet) (pp.196, 206)

The Miller and the Sweep, UK, p.c. GAS Films, d. George Albert Smith, r.d. July 1897, 50 feet (pp.147-9)

Mimi Pinson, France, p.c. Pathé Frères (Part 1)/SCAGL (Parts 2 & 3), d. Georges Monca; Part 1: **Mimi Pinson aime les roses blanches**, 1909; Part 2: **Mimi Pinson aime les roses rouges**, 1910; Part 3: **Les Chagrins de Mimi Pinson**, 1910 (p.58)

Le Miracle des loups, France, p.c. Société des Films Historiques, d. Raymond Bernard, r.d. November 13th 1924, 9,850 feet (p.74)

Les Misérables, France, p.c. SCAGL, d. Albert Capellani, 1912-13, 2 parts, c. 15,750 feet (p.58)

Modern Pirates, UK, p.c. Alpha Trading Company, d. Arthur Melbourne-Cooper, r.d. October 1906, 500 feet (p.100)

Murder, My Sweet, USA, p.c. Radio-Keith-Orpheum, d. Edward Dmytryk, r.d. March 8th 1945, 93 minutes (p.251)

Napoléon, France, p.c. Films Abel Gance/Société Générale de Films, d. Abel Gance, première April 7th 1927, r.d. November 1927, release length 12,000 feet (p.75)

Next!, USA, p.c. American Mutoscope & Biograph Company, ph. A.E. Weed, r.d. November 27th 1905, 93 feet (pp.107 n.10, 207, 233 n.26)

Nick Carter series, France, p.c. Eclair Film, d. Victorin-Hyppolite Jasset; Series 1: **Nick Carter, roi des détectives**, 1908, six episodes, c. 2,000 feet each; Series 2: **Les Nouveaux exploits de Nick Carter**, 1909, nine episodes, c. 2,000 feet each; Series 3: **Nick Carter contre Paulin Broquet**, 1911, six episodes, c. 3,000 feet each (p.56)

Nieuwe Gronden ('New Earth'), Holland, p.c. CAPI, d. Joris Ivens, 1934, 33 minutes (p.241 n.1)

Le Nihiliste ('Socialism and Nihilism'), France, p.c. Pathé Frères, 1906, 557 feet (pp.65, 95)

The Nihilists, USA, p.c. American Mutoscope & Biograph Company, ph. Frank Armitage, r.d. March 27th 1905, 840 feet

(p.95)

Nouvelles luttes extravagantes (UK: 'The Wrestling Sextet'; USA: 'Fat and Lean Wrestling Match'), France, p.c. Star Film, d. Georges Méliès, Autumn 1900, 165 feet (p.269)

Off His Beat, USA, p.c. American Mutoscope & Biograph Company, ph. A.E. Weed, US copyright November 12th 1903, 62 feet (pp.107 n.10, 207, 233 n.26)

The Other Side of the Hedge (USA: 'Over the Hedge'), UK, p.c. Hepworth Manufacturing Company, d. Lewin Fitzhamon, r.d. January 1905, 100 feet (pp.96, 226)

Panorama de la place Saint-Marc pris d'un bateau [Panorama of the Piazza San Marco taken from a Gondola], France, p.c. Société Lumière, ph. Promio (?), 1896, 56 feet (p.36)

Panorama du Grand-Canal pris d'un bateau ('On the Grand Canal (Venice)'), France, p.c. Société Lumière, ph. Promio (?), 1896, 56 feet (p.36)

La Passion de Jeanne d'Arc, France, p.c. Société Générale de Films, d. Carl-Theodor Dreyer, r.d. April 21st 1928, 7,200 feet (p.272)

La Passion du Christ [Christ's Passion], France, p.c. Société Lear, Anthelm et Pacon, ph. Lear, 1897 (p.144)

Passion Play, USA, produced Rich Hollaman, d. Frank Russell/William C. Paley, première January 30th 1898, 2,200 feet (p.144)

Pauvre frac [Poor Tailcoat], France (pp.64, 69)

The Perils of Pauline, USA, p.c. Eclectic Film Company (Pathé), d. Donald Mackenzie/Louis Gasnier, 20 episodes, r.d. April 25th 1914 to December 26th 1914, each episode 2 reels (c. 2,000 feet) (p.73)

Pippa Passes, USA, p.c. Biograph Company, d. D.W. Griffith, r.d. October 4th 1909, 983 feet (pp.129, 177)

Place des Cordeliers (Lyon), France, p.c. Société Lumière, ph. Louis Lumière, première June 10th 1895, 56 feet (p.17)

Place of Work, UK, p.c. Ancona Films, d. Margaret Tait, 1976, 31 minutes (pp.259-60)

Playtime, France, p.c. Specta Films, d. Jacques Tati, 1967, 140 minutes (p.155)

The Politician, USA, p.c. Edison Kinetophone, 1913, 377 feet (Library of Congress print) (p.237)

Poruchik Kizhe ('Lieutenant Kizhé'), USSR, p.c. Belgoskino, d. Aleksandr Faintsimmer, r.d. March 7th 1934, 86 minutes (p.241 n.1)

A Practical Joke (also known as 'A Joke on the Gardener'), UK, p.c. GAS Films, d. George Albert Smith, r.d. March 1898, 50 feet (p.149)

Präsidenten ('The President'), Denmark, p.c. Nordisk Films Kompagni, d. Carl-Theodor Dreyer, r.d. February 1st 1919, 5,575 feet (p.184 n.5)

The Price is Right (TV series), USA, network NBC, first broadcast September 23rd 1957, weekly 30-minute shows (p.263)

La Probité recompensée ('Honest Peggy'), France, p.c. Pathé Frères, 1905 (?), 131 feet (p.63)

Quatre-Vingt-Treize [Seventeen Ninety-Three], France, p.c. SCAGL, d. Albert Capellani (completed by André Antoine), r.d. June 1921 (filmed Spring 1914, banned by censors for the duration of the War), c. 11,500 feet (Cinémathèque Française print, reconstructed 1985) (p.77 n.9)

Queen Elizabeth, UK, p.c. Histrionic Film, d. Henri Desfontaines/Louis Mercanton, r.d. August 16th 1912, 3,600 feet (pp.123, 126)

Ramona, USA, p.c. Biograph Company, d. D.W. Griffith, r.d. May 23rd 1910, 995 feet (p.127)

Regen ('Rain'), Holland, p.c. CAPI, d. Joris Ivens, r.d. December 14th 1929, 1,000 feet (p.241 n.1)

La Région Centrale, Canada, Michael Snow, 1971, 190 minutes (pp.255-6)

Repas de bébé ('Baby's Dinner'), France, p.c. Société Lumière, ph. Louis Lumière, première June 10th 1895, 56 feet (pp.16, 22 n.8, 24, 91)

Rescued by Rover, UK, p.c. Hepworth Manufacturing Company, d. Lewin Fitzhamon, r.d. July 1905, 425 feet (pp.87, 88 Fig.7, 89, 107 n.9, 150, 158, 160 n.14, 172, 193, 195 Fig.26, 209, 210 Fig.28, 211)

Rescued from an Eagle's Nest, USA, p.c. Edison Manufacturing Company, d. J. Searle Dawley, US copyright January 16th 1908, 515 feet (pp.113, 131)

A Reservist before and after the War, UK, p.c. Williamson's Kinematographic Company, d. James Williamson, r.d.

December 1902, 290 feet (p.95)

Rêve à la lune (UK: 'Drunkard's Dream; or, Why You Should Sign the Pledge'; USA: 'Moon Lover'), France, p.c. Pathé Frères, d. Gaston Velle, 1905, 470 feet (p.200 n.13)

Rêve d'un marmiton ('A Scullion's Dream'), France, p.c. Pathé Frères, d. Ferdinand Zecca, 1906 (?), 541 feet (p.71)

Le Révélateur, France, p.c. Zanzibar, d. Philippe Garrel, 1968, 68 minutes (pp.265 n.8, 265 n.10)

La Révolution en Russie: Les Evènements d'Odessa ('Revolution in Odessa'), France, p.c. Pathé Frères, d. Lucien Nonguet, 1905, 262 feet (p.65)

Richelieu; or, The Conspiracy, USA, p.c. Vitagraph Company of America, d. J. Stuart Blackton, r.d. January 8th 1910, 992 feet (p.189)

Robbery of the Mail Coach, UK, p.c. Sheffield Photo Company, d. Frank Mottershaw, r.d. September 1903, 375 feet (p.104)

Robinson Crusoe, UK, p.c. GAS Films (?), d. George Albert Smith (?), 1900 (?), 53 feet (National Film Archive print) (p.92)

The Rocky Horror Picture Show, USA, p.c. Twentieth-Century-Fox, d. Jim Sharman, r.d. September 20th 1975, 101 minutes (p.264 n.1)

Le Roi Léar du village ('A Village King Lear'), France, p.c. Léon Gaumont & Compagnie, d. Louis Feuillade, r.d. May 1911, 1,180 feet (p.65)

The Romance of an Umbrella, USA, p.c. Vitagraph Company of America, r.d. September 29th 1909, 450 feet (pp.131, 132 Fig.16)

Le Roman d'un mousse ('The Curse of Greed'), France, p.c. Léon Gaumont & Compagnie, d. Léonce Perret, 1913, 7,875 feet (pp.74, 173)

Rope, USA, p.c. Transatlantic Pictures for Warner Brothers, d. Alfred Hitchcock, r.d. August 26th 1948, 80 minutes (pp.252-4, 265 n.6)

Rosalie et Léontine vont au théâtre [Rosalie and Léontine go to the Theatre], France, p.c. Pathé Frères, d. Roméo Bosetti, 1911, preserved Stiftung Deutsche Kinemathek, Berlin, as 'Zwillinge im Theater' (p.220)

La Roue ('The Wheel'), France, p.c. Films Abel Gance/Charles Pathé, d. Abel Gance, r.d. February 17th 1923, 35,200 feet (distribution print 30,200 feet) (pp.35, 241 n.1)

Le Royaume des Fées (UK: 'Wonders of the Deep; or, Kingdom of the Fairies'; USA: 'Fairyland; or, The Kingdom of the Fairies'), France, p.c. Star Film, d. Georges Méliès, Summer 1903, 1,080 feet (pp.171, 198)

A Rube in the Subway, USA, p.c. American Mutoscope & Biograph Company, ph. G.W. Bitzer, US copyright June 15th 1905, 215 feet (pp.123, 152)

Le Sacre d'Edouard VII ('Special Coronation Film'), UK, p.c. Warwick Trading Company, d. Georges Méliès, Spring 1902, 350 feet (p.167)

The Sales Lady's Matinée Idol, USA, p.c. Edison Manufacturing Company, r.d. February 12th 1909, 900 feet (p.135)

The Salmon Poachers—A Midnight Melée, UK, p.c. Haggar & Sons, d. Willam Haggar, r.d. October 1905, 274 feet (pp.100, 102-3)

A Search for Evidence, USA, p.c. American Mutoscope & Biograph Company, ph. G.W. Bitzer, US copyright August 3rd 1903, 217 feet (p.222)

Skyscrapers, USA, p.c. American Mutoscope & Biograph, ph. Frank Dobson, r.d. December 8th 1906, 613 feet (pp.120, 140 n.10)

Sortie d'usine ('Employees Leaving the Lumière Factory'), France, p.c. Société Lumière; version 1: ph. Louis Lumière, photographed March 22nd 1895, 56 feet; version 2: ph. Louis Lumière, photographed July 1895, 56 feet (pp.15, 17-19, 23-4, 39, 232 n.17)

Sperduti nel buio [Sunk in the Mire], Italy, p.c. Morgana Film, d. Nino Martoglio, 1914 (p.179)

Das Stahltier [The Iron Horse], Germany, d. Willy Zielke, 1935, 72 minutes (p.35)

Stop Thief!, UK, p.c. Williamson's Kinematographic Company, d. James Williamson, r.d. October 1901, 115 feet (pp.148-9)

The Story the Biograph Told (also known as 'Caught by Moving Pictures'), USA, p.c. American Mutoscope & Biograph Company, ph. A.E. Weed, r.d. February 1904, 288 feet (pp.106 n.6, 161 n.15, 226, 227 Fig.33, 228, 233 n.27)

The Streets of New York, USA, p.c. American Mutoscope & Biograph Company, ph. Frank Dobson, r.d. January 27th 1906,

337 feet (p.123)

Der Student von Prag ('The Student of Prague'), Germany, p.c. Deutsche Bioscop, d. Stellan Rye, première August 22nd 1913, 5,045 feet (p.156)

A Subject for the Rogues Gallery, USA, p.c. American Mutoscope & Biograph Company, ph. A.E. Weed, US copyright February 2nd 1904, 54 feet (pp.107 n.10, 186, 201 n.15, 226, 271 Fig.36)

Sur la barricade [On the Barricade] (also known as 'L'Enfant de la barricade'), France, p.c. Léon Gaumont & Compagnie, d. Alice Guy, 1907, 290 feet (p.66)

Suspicion, USA, p.c. Radio-Keith-Orpheum, d. Alfred Hitchcock, r.d. November 20th 1941, 102 minutes (p.270)

The Switchtower, USA, p.c. Biograph Company, d. Anthony O'Sullivan, r.d. June 16th 1913, 998 feet (p.231 n.13)

Tempête dans une chambre à coucher ('A Bewildered Traveller'), France, p.c. Pathé Frères, d. Ferdinand Zecca, 1901, 100 feet (pp.168, 170)

Ten Nights in a Bar-Room, USA, p.c. American Mutoscope & Biograph Company, ph. Frank Armitage, produced June 1901, 166 feet (p.113)

Terrible Teddy, the Grizzly King, USA, p.c. Thomas A. Edison, ph. Edwin S. Porter, US copyright February 23rd 1901, 75 feet (pp.113, 200 n.6)

That's Incredible! (TV series), USA, network ABC, first broadcast March 3rd 1980, weekly 50-minute shows (p.263)

They Found the Leak, USA, p.c. American Mutoscope & Biograph Company, ph. Arthur Marvin, US copyright December 9th 1902, 202 feet (p.116)

The Thief, USA, p.c. Clarence Greene for United Artists, d. Russell Rouse, r.d. October 15th 1952, 85 minutes (pp.253-4, 265 n.6)

THX1138, USA, p.c. American Zoetrope, d. George Lucas, r.d. March 11th 1971, 95 minutes (p.272)

Tom, Tom, the Piper's Son, USA, p.c. American Mutoscope & Biograph Company, ph. G.W. Bitzer, r.d. March 15th 1905, 508 feet (pp.150, 152-3, 160 n.8, 158, 184 n.4, 198)

Tom, Tom, the Piper's Son, USA, Ken Jacobs, première March 1969, 86 minutes (pp.152-3, 160 n.8)

Tour du monde d'un policier ('A Detective's Tour of the World'),

France, p.c. Pathé Frères, d. Lucien Lépine, 1906, 1,148 feet (p.200 n.9)

[The Trusting Cabman], France, 1903 (?), preserved Universidad Nacional Autónoma de Mexico, Mexico City, as **Cochero confiado** (pp.78 n.21, 160 n.6)

The Tunnel Workers, USA, p.c. American Mutoscope & Biograph Company, ph. Frank Dobson, r.d. November 15th 1906, 813 feet (p.120)

Turksib, USSR, p.c. Vostok-kino, d. Viktor Turin, r.d. October 15th 1929, 5,465 feet (p.35)

Uncle Josh at the Moving Picture Show, USA, p.c. Thomas A. Edison, ph. Edwin S. Porter, US copyright January 27th 1902, 125 feet (p.116)

Uncle Tom's Cabin, USA, p.c. Vitagraph Company of America, d. J. Stuart Blackton (?), Part 1: r.d. July 26th 1910, 935 feet; Part 2: r.d. July 29th 1910, 1,000 feet; Part 3: r.d. July 30th 1910, c. 1,000 feet (p.189)

Uncle Tom's Cabin; or, Slavery Days, USA, p.c. Thomas A. Edison, ph. Edwin S. Porter, US copyright July 30th 1903, 1,100 feet (pp.188-9)

The Unfaithful Wife, USA, p.c. American Mutoscope & Biograph Co., ph. G.W. Bitzer, r.d. August 29th 1903, 168 feet (p.117)

Les Vampires [The Vampires], France, p.c. Léon Gaumont & Compagnie, d. Louis Feuillade, serial in 10 parts, r.d. November 13th 1915 to June 13th 1916, each part 4 reels (c. 4,000 feet) (pp.67, 74, 214, 232 n.18)

Vendémiaire, France, p.c. Léon Gaumont & Compagnie, d. Louis Feuillade, Part 1: r.d. January 17th 1919, 5,500 feet; Part 2: January 24th 1919, 4,500 feet (p.78 n.19)

Les Victimes de l'alcoolisme ('Alcohol and its Victims'), France, p.c. Pathé Frères, d. Ferdinand Zecca, r.d. May 1902, 460 feet (p.63)

La Vie du Christ (UK: 'Christ Among Men'), France, p.c. Léon Gaumont & Compagnie, d. Alice Guy/Georges Hatot/Victorin-Hyppolite Jasset, r.d. March 1906, 2,000 feet (p.159 n.3)

La Vie et la Passion de Jésus Christ ('The Life and the Passion of Jesus Christ'), France, p.c. Société Lumière, d. Georges Hatot, 1897, 13 parts, 800 feet (pp.144-6)

Vie et Passion de Notre Seigneur Jésus Christ ('Life and Passion of Our Lord Jesus Christ'), France, p.c. Pathé Frères, d. André Maitre, 1907 (?), 3,100 feet (p.122)

Le Vieux pays où Rimbaud est mort, Canada, p.c. Cinak-Filmoblic-INA, d. Jean-Pierre Lefebvre, première Cannes May 19th 1977, 113 minutes (p.255)

Les Vipères ('Village Gossip'), France, p.c. Léon Gaumont & Compagnie, d. Louis Feuillade, r.d. April 1911, 1,180 feet (p.65)

Visages d'enfants, France, p.c. Les Grands Films Indépendants, d. Jacques Feyder, r.d. March 27th 1925, 8,200 feet (p.76 n.2)

Vormittagsspuk ('Ghosts before Breakfast'), Germany, p.c. Tobis, d. Hans Richter, 1928, c. 600 feet (p.241 n.1)

Le Voyage à travers l'impossible (UK: 'Whirling the Worlds'; USA: 'An Impossible Voyage'), France, p.c. Star Film, d. Georges Méliès, Autumn 1904, 1,414 feet (pp.198, 206-7, 231 n.7)

Voyage dans la lune ('A Trip to the Moon'), France, p.c. Star Film, d. Georges Méliès, Autumn 1902, 845 feet (pp.113, 168, 186, 198)

Le Voyage de Monsieur le Président de la République (Félix Faure) en Russie [Tour of the President of the French Republic through Russia], France, p.c. Société Lumière, ph. Promio, August 1897, 14 parts, 780 feet (p.53)

Le Voyage de Monsieur le Président de la République (Félix Faure) en Vendée ('Tour of the President of the French Republic through Vendée'), France, p.c. Société Lumière, 1897, 19 parts, 1,050 feet (p.53)

Wait till Jack Comes Home, UK, p.c. Williamson's Kinematographic Company, d. James Williamson, r.d. September 1903, 430 feet (p.95)

Wavelength, USA, Michael Snow, première May 1967, 45 minutes (pp.256-8, 265 n.9)

What Happened on 23rd Street, New York City, USA, p.c. Thomas A. Edison, ph. Edwin S. Porter, US copyright August 21st 1901, 50 feet (pp.202, 230 n.1)

What the Curate Really Did, UK, p.c. Hepworth Manufacturing Company, d. Lewin Fitzhamon, r.d. September 1905, 250 feet (pp.187, 230 n.2)

When Extremes Meet, UK, p.c. Gaumont & Company, d. Alf Collins, r.d. September 1905, 150 feet (pp.87, 104, 226)

The White Caps, USA, p.c. Thomas A. Edison, d. Wallace McCutcheon/Edwin S. Porter, US copyright September 14th 1905, 835 feet (p.128)

The Wind, USA, p.c. Metro-Goldwyn-Mayer, d. Viktor Sjöström, r.d. November 23rd 1928, 6,721 feet (p.265 n.8)

Z, Algeria/France, p.c. ONCIC/Reggane Film, d. Costa-Gavras, 1968, 125 minutes (p.160 n.7)

Zigomar, France, p.c. Eclair Films, d. Victorin-Hyppolite Jasset, Series 1: **Zigomar roi des voleurs** ([Zigomar, King of the Thieves]), 1911, 3,000 feet; Series 2: **Zigomar contre Nick Carter** ([Zigomar versus Nick Carter]), 1911, 3,500 feet; Series 3: **Zigomar Peau d'anguille** ('Zigomar Eelskin'), 1913, 3,250 feet (pp.100, 139 n.5, 173)

↔ ('Back and Forth'), USA, Michael Snow, 1969, 52 minutes (pp.256, 258)

Index

For references to film titles, see the *Filmography*.

Cricks and Sharp, 107 n.11
cutaway, 218
cut-in, see 'match, axial'
Cyclorama, 42 n.11
Czolgosz, Leon, 120

Daguerre, Louis-Jacques-Mandé, 6, 14, 37, 86, 170, 248
Daguerrotype, 7
Dana, Jorge, 4, 232 n.23
Dawley, J. Searle, 113
Dean, James, 268
deconstruction, 3, 230 n.6, 272
deep staging, 15, 35, 74, 131, 170, 172-3, 176, 180, 183-4, 184 n.5, 185 n.6, 200 n.11
DeForest, Lee, 36, 41 n.2
Degas, Hilaire-Germain-Edgar, 22 n.4, 22 n.7
Delluc, Louis, 59, 77 n.10
Demenÿ, Georges, 18, 26-8, 155, 237
DeMille, Cecil Blount, 85, 179, 212, 217, 231 n.15, 238, 264 n.2
depressive position, 270
depth of field, 185 n.6
depth versus surface, 41
Deslandes, Jacques, 54, 76 n.4, 76 n.6
Dickens, Charles, 91
Dickson, William Kennedy Laurie, 14, 27-9, 30 Fig.2, 32-3, 41 n.5, 113, 145, 152, 155, 234
diegesis (diegetic effect, production and process), 39, 134, 140 n.10, 151-2, 154-5, 188, 193, 196, 198, 206, 208, 228, 244-7, 250-60, 262-3, 265 n.8, 265 n.9, 265 n.11, 267
Diorama, 6, 20, 54, 86, 170, 248
directing, film, 19-20, 46, 126-7, 141 n.19
distance, camera-subject, 15-16, 24, 39, 74, 133, 141 n.19, 153, 160 n.10, 164, 171, 188, 197, 199 n.1, 207, 216, 242 n.6, 265 n.7, 270
distantiation, 142 n.22, 154-5, 189, 255, 262
Doane, Mary Ann, 232 n.20, 272

Dobson, Frank, 120
documentary, ideology of, 15-17, 19, 34, 51-2, 55, 86, 140 n.10, 143, 241 n.1
Doublier, François, 15
Dreyer, Carl Theodor, 184, 184 n.5, 254, 272
Dubosq, Jules, 14, 21 n.1
Ducos du Hauron, Louis, 21 n.9
Dufy, Raoul, 171
Dulac, Germaine, 13, 241
Durand, Jean, 69, 114
Duvivier, Julien, 74, 206

Eastwood, Clint, 262
Eclair Film, 56, 58, 73, 172
edification,
    rarity in French films, 62, 76 n.6
    typicality in American films, 116, 123, 129
Edison, Thomas Alva, 6-7, 14, 18, 27-9, 32-3, 40, 41 n.5, 41 n.7, 118, 234, 237-8, 240
    in L'Eve future, 29, 31-2
Edison studios (Thomas A. Edison, Inc., Edison Film Manufacturing Company, etc.), 29, 32, 35, 104, 114, 116, 128, 152, 177, 197, 204-6, 224, 230 n.4
    see also 'Black Maria'
Edison Trust (Motion Picture Patents Company), 126
editing, 19, 24, 55, 135, 143, 151, 172, 180, 183, 199 n.1, 204-7, 224-5, 231 n.14, 238, 253, 269
    alternating, 39, 78 n.20, 131, 135, 157-8, 205-6, 230 n.4, 231 n.15
    fragmentatory or dissecting, 269-70
    frequentative or durational, 149, 159 n.5
    primitive experiments in, 29, 67, 74, 78 n.20, 87, 89, 102, 107 n.8, 107 n.11, 140 n.9, 149, 186, 199 n.1, 208
Eggeling, Viking, 255
Eisenschitz, Bernard, 78 n.19

Tourneur, Maurice, 217, 264 n.2
trade press, cinematic,
  American, 126-7, 131, 132-4, 139 n.5
  British, 242 n.9
  French, 47, 49-50, 52, 58-60
Trauner, Alexandre, 71
trick film, 49-51, 61-3, 71, 76 n.5, 78
  n.16, 95, 167, 171, 191, 193, 224,
  269
Turner, Florence, 268
Turner, William, 8
Tussaud, Marie, 6
Tynyanov, Yury Nikolaevich, 241 n.1

Ubersfeld, Anne, 78 n.15
ubiquity of camera/spectator, 87, 133,
  141 n.19, 148, 181, 186, 204-5, 207,
  209, 216, 218, 225, 228, 264 n.2,
  269
Urban, Charles, 97
  see also 'Charles Urban Trading
  Company'

Valentino, Rudolph, 268
vaudeville, American, 111-14, 115
  Fig.12, 116-17, 119-21, 123, 129,
  138, 207, 232 n.16
  as site of film exhibition, 113-14,
  116-19, 139 n.4, 200 n.3, 226
  audience of, 111-14, 115 Fig.2, 116-
  17, 120, 123, 139 n.4
vaudeville, European, 148
Vecchiali, Paul, 76 n.2
Velle, Gaston, 78 n.16, 140 n.10
Verleugnung, 183, 252
Verne, Jules, 41 n.6
vertical shots, 228, 229 Fig.34, 231
  n.11, 233 n.28, 233 n.29
Vertov, Dziga, 1, 3, 13, 189, 241 n.1
La Vie telle qu'elle est (film series), 65
vignette, 151, 178-9
Villiers de l'Isle-Adam, Philippe

Auguste, comte de, 29, 31-3, 240
Viota Cabrera, Paulino, 265 n.7
Vitagraph Company of America, 129,
  130 Fig.15, 131, 132 Fig.16, 177,
  179, 189
Vitagraph Girl, see 'Turner, Florence'
Vitascope, 29, 118
Von Stroheim, Erich, 241
Vuillermoz, Emile, 59

Wagnerianism, 28
Wakhevitch, Georges, 71
Walsh, Raoul, 136
Walturdaw, 107 n.11, 159 n.4
Ward, Fannie, 212, 217-18
Warwick Trading Company, 35
Watteau, Jean-Antoine, 153
Weber, Max, 21 n.2
Welles, Orson, 173
Wesley, John, 91
Western film, 114, 272
Williamson, James, 37, 92, 93 Fig.9,
  94 Fig.10, 95, 100, 103-4, 107 n.8,
  148-50, 157, 197, 220, 221 Fig.31
Wollen, Peter, 231 n.10
Woods, Frank ('The Spectator'), 133-
  6, 216-17
working men's clubs, 83
Wright, Willard Huntington, 185 n.13
Wyler, William, 173

X-rays, 32

Zecca, Ferdinand, 17, 41, 64-5, 71-2,
  76 n.2, 78 n.16, 80, 96, 102, 114,
  168, 169 Fig.19, 170, 186, 191,
  197-8, 222, 229 Fig.34
Zoetrope, 10
Zola, Emile, 41 n.1, 65
Zoogyroscope, 11
Zoopraxinoscope, 11
Zukor, Adolph, 121-3, 126, 140 n.12